Pharmaceutical Process Design and Management

Pharmaceutical Process Design and Management

KATE MCCORMICK
and
D. WYLIE MCVAY JR

Routledge
Taylor & Francis Group

LONDON AND NEW YORK

First published 2012 by Gower Publishing

Published 2016 by Routledge
2 Park Square, Milton Park, Abingdon, Oxfordshire OX14 4RN
711 Third Avenue, New York, NY 10017, USA

First issued in paperback 2016

Routledge is an imprint of the Taylor & Francis Group, an informa business

British Library Cataloguing in Publication Data
    McCormick, Kate.
    Pharmaceutical process design and management.
    1. Pharmaceutical industry--Quality control.
    2. Pharmaceutical industry--Production control.
    3. Manufacturing processes--Human factors.
    I. Title II. McVay, D. Wylie.
    338.4'561519-dc23

Library of Congress Cataloging-in-Publication Data
McCormick, Kate.
    Pharmaceutical process design and management / by Kate McCormick and
    D. Wylie McVay Jr.
        p. ; cm.
    Includes bibliographical references and index.
    ISBN 978-1-4094-2711-7 (hbk)
    I. McVay, D. Wylie. II. Title.
    [DNLM: 1. Pharmaceutical Preparations. 2. Technology,
Pharmaceutical--methods. 3. Drug Design. 4. Drug Industry--organization &
administration. 5. Total Quality Management. QV 778]

    615.1'9--dc23

                                                                        2011052071

ISBN 13: 978-1-138-25550-0 (pbk)
ISBN 13: 978-1-4094-2711-7 (hbk)

Contents

PART III   EFFECTIVE PHARMACEUTICAL PROCESS DESIGN AND MANAGEMENT

List of Figures

List of Tables

About the Authors

Dr Kate McCormick is a writer and manufacturing consultant with extensive management experience in the pharmaceutical industry. She has worked with multinationals, small and medium-sized enterprises, non-governmental organizations (NGOs) and national regulatory authorities in more than 50 countries. She is the author of *Quality* (a textbook within the Butterworth Heinemann pharmaceutical engineering series) and *Manufacturing in the Global Pharmaceuticals Industry*. She has been editor of *gmp Review* and International Education Advisor for the International Society for Pharmaceutical Engineering (ISPE). Dr McCormick has a degree in biochemistry and a doctorate in microbiology, both from the University of London. She also has a Master's in Business Administration from Cranfield University. She is registered as a senior GMP expert for the purposes of EU-funded projects and is eligible to act as a QP under the terms of the EU Directive.

D. Wylie McVay Jr. has worked in the field of pharmaceutical quality control and assurance functions and regulatory Chemistry and Manufacturing Controls for over 30 years. He has worked for large multinational firms as well as start-up companies. His diverse experience includes supply chain management, continuous improvement of pre-existing quality systems and development of innovative, new quality systems. He is a member of the Editorial Advisory Board of AdvanStar Publications and has contributed articles to the *Journal of Validation Technology* and the *Journal of GxP Compliance*. Additionally, he has written several articles for the Regulatory Affairs Professional Society (RAPS) magazine and is a contributing columnist for *gmp Review* and *Pharmacovigilance Review*. He has also presented supplier certification training for the Parenteral Drug Association. Mr McVay holds a degree in chemistry, a Master's in Business Administration and a Master of Science in Quality Assurance and Regulatory Affairs in addition to certifications from the American Society for Quality and the Regulatory Affairs Professional Society.

Acknowledgements

Wylie and Kate

Writing a book that integrates theory and experience is a process that begins in childhood and only comes into fruition later in life. Along the way there are countless exchanges with influential persons a few of whom we wish to recognize and thank. To our many friends and colleagues, past and present, who have engaged in lively debate on the subject of pharmaceutical manufacturing, process management and quality.

Wylie

In memory of my grandfather, Guy Hyland, who gave me a pragmatic view of business. To my father, Donald McVay, a certified accountant, who was ahead of his time in applying process management. To my mother, Yula McVay, who drilled me in task organization as only a mother can. In memory of T. Wilmer Jett, my father-in-law, who provided hours of recollections of the early years of manufacturing in the US. To our children, Powell and Savannah, who taught me patience. And most importantly, to my wife of nearly 30 years, Deborah Jett McVay, who has provided constant and patient support during the writing of this text.

Kate

To Michael — as always.

List of Abbreviations

ANDA   Abbreviated New Drug Application
ANVISA   Agência National de Vigilência Sanitária (of Brazil)
APEC   Asia-Pacific Economic Co-operation
API   Active Pharmaceutical Ingredient
APR   Annual Product Review
BSE   Bovine Spongiform Encephalopathy
CAD   Computer Aided Design
CAM   Computer Aided Manufacture
CAPA   Corrective Action and Preventive Action
cGMP   Current Good Manufacturing Practice
CMC   Chemistry and Manufacturing Controls
CTD   Common Technical Document
DOE   Design of Experiment
EMA   European Medicines Agency
FDA   Food and Drug Administration (of United States)
FMEA   Failure Mode and Effects Analysis
GC   Gas Chromatograph
GHTF   Global Harmonization Task Force
GMP   Good Manufacturing Practice
HC   Health Canada
HPLC   High-Performance Liquid Chromatograph
HPLC-MS   High-Performance Liquid Chromatograph-Mass Spectrometer
HVAC   Heating, Ventilation and Air Conditioning
ICH   International Conference on Harmonisation
ISO   International Standards Organization
ISPE   International Society for Pharmaceutical Engineering
LoD   Limit of Detection
LoQ   Limit of Quantitation
NIR   Near-Infrared
OOS   Out of Specification

PAHO   Pan American Health Organization
PAT   Process Analytical Technology
PDA   Parenteral Drug Association
PIA   Process Integrated Accounting
PIC/S   Pharmaceutical Inspection Convention and Pharmaceutical
          Inspection Cooperation Scheme
PM   Preventative Maintenance
QbD   Quality by Design
QC   Quality Control
QRM   Quality Risk Management
QU   Quality Unit
R&D   Research and Development
ROI   Return on Investment
RTRT   Real-time Release Testing
SADC   Southern African Development Community
SOP   Standard Operating Procedure
SPC   Statistical Process Control
StN   Signal to Noise
TLC   Thin-layer Chromatograph
TQM   Total Quality Management
TSE   Transmittable Spongiform Encephalopathy
USP   United States Pharmacopoeia
UV   Ultraviolet
UV-Vis   Ultraviolet-Visible Spectrometer
VoP   Voice of the Process
WCM   World Class Manufacturing
WHO   World Health Organization

Introduction

Thanks for taking the time to explore our ideas about process design and process management. This text is a personal distillation of proper application and the all-too-often misapplication of process design principles. The more complex business logistics has become, the further companies have strayed from the simple approaches based on fundamentals that are universally applicable to designing, controlling and otherwise managing a pharmaceutical process.

None of the information in this book is new. However, the approach used to implement processes is novel. We propose the adoption of an Artisan Model approach to process design, management and continuous improvement. The Artisan Model involves consideration of any process as a combination of five key elements: *man, machine, materials, methods and environment*. Users of the well-known problem organization tool the Fishbone Diagram will recognize this approach. We believe the format to be ideal for organizing a pharmaceutical process proactively from step one.

Our approach to process design and management is deceptively simple and we are letting readers know upfront that this is the case. However, given the poor productivity of the pharmaceutical industry today, something different has to be undertaken to help the industry regain control of the production process.

Our book is written in three parts. Part I consists of two chapters which discuss the evolution of process design and management and introduce the Artisan Model with an overview of processes over the past four millennia. Part II consists of five chapters, one for each of the five process elements. In each case, challenges relating to modern pharmaceutical manufacturing are discussed, together with our suggestions for how these challenges can be overcome. Part III is the longest, with nine chapters looking at how pharmaceutical process design and management can be made more effective by stripping out the complexities, going back to basics and keeping it simple. It includes a chapter on common tools and techniques, a review of the 'new paradigm' thinking from the regulators and a methodology for Process Integrated Accounting.

The reader will see that Part I is theoretical in nature, of historical interest more than practical application; readers can skip to Parts II and III if they are eager to get started on improving their process design and management. However, we believe it is important to set this in its historical context and hope the reader will find time to peruse the opening chapters at some point as well.

PART I

Evolution of Process Design and Management

1

Why Process Management is Important

> We can't solve problems by using the same kind of thinking we used when we created them.
>
> (Albert Einstein, 1879–1955, German theoretical physicist)

Introduction

The past 50 years of pharmaceutical manufacturing have witnessed significant and continual change in technological speed and precision. There has been an information avalanche created by the internet and high-speed computing. The global patient population has expanded and lifestyles have changed, resulting in continuous identification of unmet medical needs. A busy pipeline has produced new drug product offerings of novel compounds. The structure of the industry has also changed, with mergers and acquisitions turning competitors into colleagues. Yet for all the changes, the basic principles for managing pharmaceutical process design and management have remained constant.

Unquestionably, the overall system has become complex and chaotic, a state that is counterproductive to product consistency and profitability. It is regrettable, but not surprising, to see an increasing number of products that fail to maintain safety and efficacy profiles throughout the life of the product. In this book, we propose the application of proven techniques to simplify and organize business resources and provide accurate information for timely management of product manufacture.

Why Process?

While on the surface this book may seem like another quality programme, we depart from past texts in that we provide a framework for designing and managing processes across the whole organization, beginning with raw material characteristics and ending with release to the marketplace. In addition, we link the process of manufacturing pharmaceuticals to financial reporting considerations.

Throughout the book, we acknowledge that any single change to one process element is likely to have an effect on one or more other process elements. Process elements are intertwined and change, such as improvement, to any single element must be considered in the context of impact on the others, otherwise it is easy to fall victim to the law of unintended consequences.

This book is a blueprint for pharmaceutical companies that wish to design and manage their processes simply and effectively. Our approach is the correct application of existing tools and techniques. The time is right to simplify the convoluted business environment. By doing so, the pharmaceutical industry will be able to make safe medicines more cost-effectively using a more consistent and predictable business model.

The accomplishment of business objectives in an efficient and effective manner is not a new topic. In our industry, as in all others, each generation of business leaders hopes to discover a combination of business strategies and operating techniques to foster economic growth of the business and personal reward for themselves as well as the company's employees. The measures of success are typically quantified in terms of net profit and safe, high-quality pharmaceuticals to meet patient needs. While these measures are certainly appropriate from a gross financial accounting and manufacturing or marketing sense, the terms 'profit' and 'quality' are far too general to foster sustained competitive advantage.

A simple, uncomplicated, resource-integrated and transparent system is the only way to assure timely process corrections when necessary. Traditional financial accounting rules mandate cost aggregation in a way that masks process cost issues at the point of occurrence through the grouping of dissimilar business activities for quarterly or annual governmental reporting. A process-synchronized managerial accounting design is necessary to overcome the effects of cost aggregation at the frontline. When a process design is no more than a group of nebulous characteristics that fluctuate to meet short-term goals and objectives on the average, the work effort is aggregated in a manner similar to financial reporting. A discretely designed process, with five defined elements, is the only way to illuminate work efforts to assure timely correction. Product consistency and profit sustainability are reserved for organizations that can accurately identify conditions outside of the planned design process and resolve the issues quickly and completely. In our experience, few organizations within the twenty-first-century pharmaceutical industry have realized this state of operations.

Designing for process excellence is a simple and straightforward task, which requires integration of three general considerations to be successful:

- proper understanding of system capacity range – often referred to as the relevant range;

- system designers with hands-on experience and theoretical understanding;

- effective controls that are consistent with a statistical model of the process.

Simplicity of process configuration cannot be stressed enough. Without this key consideration, the overall control of product quality will be lost amid the chaos of today's digital media explosion in a globally competitive world.

Consider, for example, Toyota and the numerous recent recalls. Until two or three years ago, Toyota was considered the undisputed leader of process and quality excellence in the automotive industry. However, in the last quarter of 2009 and into 2010, the company temporarily stopped sales of vehicles and conducted major recalls. During the year, the list kept on expanding. The inevitable conclusion was Toyota had quality and process problems. The underlying issue involved Toyota's single-source supply experiencing a catastrophic closure. The event forced the company to seek a second source of accelerator pedals. Unfortunately, the replacement parts were not functionally identical to the original and would sometimes cause the car to accelerate uncontrollably.

A key reason for Toyota's problems was a complex management system which obscured the problem and slowed implementation of the appropriate solution. In the context of this book, the process design had flaws in three areas: *materials*, *methods* and *environment*. The accelerator pedal assembly – *materials* – from a new second source supplier was discovered to fail during operation. *Methods* may have lacked sufficient sensitivity to identify key differences between the parts and if differences were identified, they were considered insignificant to product performance. Finally, the cultural *environment* hindered timely and accurate assessment of the accelerator problem, leaving Toyota faced with customer complaints, recalls and US Congressional inquiries into product safety.

Historically, process design has not been directly considered in the development of a pharmaceutical product. Rather, end-product quality control inspection requirements, imposed by governmental regulations, were meant to ensure high standards of the final product. Process design efforts have been historically directed towards the standardization of finished goods or the classification of defective materials and accountability; enforcement was limited to civil or criminal prosecution for poor craftsmanship (Juran 1998). In other words, the legacy of process management has centred on controlling pharmaceutical quality through inspection or other means such as governmental penalties.

Traditionally, the control of quality relied on extensive hands-on training through apprenticeship programmes. This approach developed a complete skillset related to the successful manufacture of a finished product. In the custom furniture industry, for example, the artisan – *man* – understood the impact of moisture on a particular species of wood – *material* – for construction and finishing purposes; the artisan provided designs that allowed proper tolerances for potentially destructive movement due to humidity-related changes of size – *method* – and learned of the need for razor-sharp saws or chisels – *machine* – to maximize ease of construction, minimize safety hazards and optimize the appearance of the final product. Attention to the *environment* was limited at best to personal tolerance of temperature fluctuations and a general understanding of gross toxic effects of certain types of wood. The process was an artisan with a virtually complete set of process skills contained within one individual, especially as the skills pertain to process mastery of materials, methods and machines. The experience gained during the apprenticeship period resulted in a merger of contextual understanding of the critical theoretical factors required in order to consistently meet all expectations for product performance. Further, the apprentice developed expertise through repetition.

Contextual understanding is defined as the iterative knowledge gained through the combination of theoretical understanding and direct work experience. In the modern pharmaceutical industry, it is a challenge to locate contextual understanding in the public domain, as little work experience is published. In fact, we have observed that experience is a key element missing in many of our companies today. This is particularly true where rationalization programmes have led to high numbers of redundancies among the older, more experienced employees or where technology transfer has not been recognized as a critical element of a factory closure project. In one case, we observed a complicated manufacturing process for an oral suspension being transferred from one site to another. Little or no attempt was made to capture or transfer the experience of the original workforce and, as a consequence, there were significant start-up problems in the second site.

Designing processes is not a complex activity; it is simple, straightforward and basic. Those assigned to design processes must strive for simplicity and transparency. The relevant theoretical techniques for designing and running agile commercial processes are published and well known and are not the subject of this book. From this perspective, few new concepts can be offered. Our purpose is to present process design and development from a new perspective that integrates diverse and sometimes forgotten concepts in a new and novel manner. By considering our prospective process design approach of new and old principles, a pharmaceutical manufacturing company can achieve agile process design and responsive operational management. It can move away from a rather sophisticated array of final product inspection programmes, the results of which tend to be transient in nature and short-lived.

Universal Principles of Process

Four outcomes may be expected when using the process modelling technique described within this book:

- process-related organizational chaos will be reduced;

- process deviations will become apparent and have a specific, resolvable root cause;

- process data will become more accurate when used for predictive estimations;

- actual product characteristics will closely align to the intended product characteristics.

In other words, results will be timely, accurate and authentic. It is our observation that process design is often considered to be synonymous with 'in vogue' quality programmes, such as Total Quality Management (TQM), Six-Sigma or Quality Circles. Stated differently, some organizations believe that if they implement a six-sigma programme, let us say using only certified black belts, that the final result will be the total elimination of problems. However, repetitive and continuing problems across the pharmaceutical industrial landscape in the form of recalled products would suggest that this approach is not universally successful.

Designing for process excellence should and does incorporate current quality techniques as one aspect of the methodology (one of the five elements in process design). However, it cannot be said that widespread use of current quality tools alone on an existing process will necessarily lead to product excellence. Well-conceived process designs will always produce quality product, but quality product can also be made using a poorly designed process where employees have learned to overcome systemic flaws for the most part. It is just that the cost of reject inspection and recalls associated with poorly designed processes happens to be extraordinarily large. The historical response to this fact can be observed with a simple review of the quality techniques that have been implemented since the early 1980s, such as Zero Defects, Quality Circles, Six-Sigma or Lean. Each programme was heralded as 'the one' way to fix product problems and reduce cost. Legacy techniques such as histograms, run charts and control charts were deemed less effective or boring and were subsequently put aside.

All too often, business leaders rely on academic research or the latest 'breakthrough' business article to meet short-term aims. While academic theory and industry legends may hold key insights, one important building block, pragmatic implementation of the basics, is often somewhat lacking or missing altogether. Pragmatic process management is mundane and deals with tedium, facts and countless simple effective problem resolutions. Academic research and 'breakthrough' cost containment are exciting, thrilling and make for lively discussions at business conferences. But experience shows these approaches to be transient in nature. In the past 30 years, we have watched, and even participated in, many of the programmes listed above: in each case, we have aimed at the same benefits – faster time to market, reduced wastage, lower inventories, higher productivity, etc. The presentation slides being shown today mirror exactly those we saw in the 1980s. Our industry does not appear to have advanced significantly as a result of all the different approaches.

Are the operational and financial results as suggested in this book consistently achievable as a long-term strategy? We believe so. In an era of instant digital data, when time-to-market pressures have been elevated and accelerated as the number one priority, decision information is being blurred to the extent that actual results and chaotic noise may look the same. The organization that responds to noise will be unknowingly heading towards premature failure or loss of market share.

We believe it is time to re-evaluate the implementation of simple, time-proven fundamentals that have been pushed into the background for any number of reasons. We will not research the myriad root causes for passing over the simple common-sense approaches; the reasons are not relevant other than to define the boundaries of what works and what does not work. Rather, we will dust off process basics and show them in a new light.

Lessons in principle, which were developed through careful observation and trial and error, form the basis of our model. Process knowledge troubleshooting tools most closely associated with after-the-fact problem resolution, such as the Ishkawa or Fishbone Diagram (Ishikawa 1986), will find use in the initial design of the process. In other words, our approach integrates time-proven design principles in a holistic, understandable, novel and straightforward manner.

Revolutionary Thinkers on Process

Of the significant numbers of astute observers over the centuries, we wish to focus on a group of revolutionary thinkers whose simple messages have been overlooked or even misunderstood. We chose this grouping for one reason: each individual carefully studied and observed process outcomes over a significant number of years before distilling their wisdom in published form. This is a significant departure from today's fast-paced chaos. As stated earlier, few of the ideas presented in this text are process revelations. Rather, we choose to consider and combine diverse insights for a novel way of defining process management practices. The philosophies of the thinkers presented in this text are relevent to successfully producing goods or services by proper design of a process. The concept each person provides reveals a perspective that is needed

Table 1.1   Critical thinkers of process principles

Thinker	Message
Leonardo Da Vinci	'Simplicity is the ultimate sophistication'.
Francis Bacon	Philosopher and statesman. Proponent of the modern scientific method. If you start with the presumption of knowing the end result, you will never find the solution to your problems (keep an open mind).
Adam Smith	Scottish economist; division of labour (specialization). Don't subdivide a process to the point of meaninglessness. Over-specialization causes human brains to sleep.
Albert Einstein	PhD in experimental physics. Keep it simple and use meaningful estimates for concepts beyond human comprehension ($E = mc^2$).
Gestalt Theory	The human mind is not capable of ordering or understanding or thriving in an environment of perpetual chaos.
Walter Shewhart	PhD, physicist, father of modern Quality Control. Processes must be evaluated systematically to determine economic ways to manage product quality.
W. Edwards Deming	PhD, statistician. Management is accountable for developing a system that allows workers to succeed.
Eli Goldratt	PhD, physicist. Bottlenecks, inherent to unbalanced process designs, undermine economic profitability and productivity.
Charles Kepner and Benjamin Tregoe	PhD in philosophy and researcher. Problems are related to designs of process. Problems are bounded by the universe of 'what is and what is not'.
Kaoru Ishikawa	PhD in engineering and Japanese business leader. Pictorial summarizations and logical groupings are essential to reveal counter-productive process patterns.

in our competitive, global business world – a simple process design capable of rapid deployment and prompt corrections.

The list of critical process design thinkers presented in Table 1.1 is by no means fully inclusive, but the messages and ideas of these thinkers are important in understanding the development of processes.

Two of our prominent critical thinkers, Leonardo Da Vinci and Albert Einstein, recognized the value and benefit of striving for simple solutions to seemingly complex issues. Da Vinci recognized simplicity as the greatest common denominator for success. Einstein, on the other hand, was able to take a highly complex idea and develop a meaningful summation in the famous equation for energy: $E = mc^2$.

Sir Francis Bacon contributed two significant thoughts for process management that are relevant to our discussion. He pointed out the need to deal with robust data acquired through careful study. He is credited with being the father of the scientific method as a means of differentiating between a charlatan and a scientist. In addition, he recognized the fallacy and risks of presuming full knowledge of the subject equated to comprehensive understanding and thereby overlooking or rationalizing results to suit one's needs (Bacon [1620] 2000).

Adam Smith ([1776] 1904) in the mid-eighteenth century closely examined the economics of business practice. He is probably best remembered for his discussion of the division of labour as the basis of specialties organized within a business. He foresaw problems with over-specialization or irrational process design which could have the effect of stifling human creativity. In his words:

> *The man whose whole life is spent in performing a few simple operations, of which the effects are perhaps always the same, or very nearly the same, has no occasion to exert his understanding or to exercise his invention in finding out expedients for removing difficulties which never occur. He naturally loses, therefore, the habit of such exertion, and generally becomes as stupid and ignorant as it is possible for a human creature to become.*

The Gestalt theory of the late nineteenth and early twentieth centuries focused on whole thinking and the lack of human response when predictability gives way to chaos.

Walter Shewhart, known as the father of control charts, actually contributed significantly more to understanding process control than he is credited with. He discusses at length, among other things, the economic consideration of neither over-analysing nor under-analysing process data. A significant point of this work is the fact that Western Electric endorsed and supported the five years of actual data that underlie his conclusions (Shewhart 1931).

W. Edwards Deming, while a statistician by academic training, focused on the need for consistency of purpose with respect to production of goods and services throughout an organization. He defined management as the owners of the process and the employees as the participants who followed the rules of process established by management (Deming [1993] 2000).

Eli Goldratt turned to the analysis of business issues and added the theory of constraints to the body of process management understanding. In his series of books, he discusses the effects of bottlenecks and process imbalance on workflow and the financial results (Dettmer 1997).

Kepner and Tregoe researched and wrote about effective problem resolution and investigations. The important message of their work with respect to process management can be summarized as: know what are possible and impossible, probable and improbable process outcomes, based on the process design (Kepner and Tregoe 1981).

Finally, several Japanese process masters have expanded process management from purely mathematical summarizations to encouraging the use of visual aids and logical grouping to reveal subtle changes in a process as an advance warning of unexpected events. In this book we will focus on Kaoru Ishikawa.

Effective process design and management will, in virtually all respects, result in greater consistency of the overall quality of finished pharmaceutical. A key distinction presented in this text is that quality is an inductive or average concept, whereas process management, as we describe the approach, is a discrete, actionable concept. Quality is best viewed as the total effectiveness of managing the five discrete elements of the process – *man*, *machine*, *method*, *material* and *environment*. The ability to manage these discrete building blocks of the process means timely and effective resolution of non-conforming products. Further, and more importantly, initially building a process by utilizing the discrete blocks provides a high level of confidence regarding achieving right-first-time quality results. Building a process with due consideration given to each element is much more cost-effective than learning of problems after the fact. Estimates of the cost of fixing post-manufacture problems with associated support costs ranges from 15 to 40 per cent of gross sales (Deming [1993] 2000).

When working through this book, we hope that the reader will appreciate the application of simple principles that will specifically overcome some pressing business challenges, such as reducing cost of goods sold or discovering and bringing new products to market. The simplicity and specificity of integrated process elements will ensure an agile response to problems if and when they occur.

Properly deployed process elements capture accurate histories of manufacturing activities, costs and issues, and reduce risk across the organization. The approach presented here differs from previous approaches in one key consideration: the tool of choice must simplify rather than mystify. Simplicity breeds success by aligning process output with process intent.

Rethinking simple process design often leads to common tools being used in uncommon manners to develop measures of value. Return on Investment (ROI), in principle, seeks to determine the impact of current expenditures in terms of value created. The measure is often viewed in percentages. However, the concept can be modified in form to evaluate characteristically softer business costs, such as maximizing process-related staff work time by making an expenditure that reduces job-related administrative time components. Two examples from our experience serve to make this point.

A laboratory operation analysed approximately 2,000 samples per year. The staff of 35 full-time employees spent about 75 minutes on average researching compendia to determine the current regulatory test scheme for each material sampled. In total, about 2,500 man-hours, or about 2 man-weeks per employee per year, were spent in determining what tests were currently required. At an average hourly rate of €40.50 ($54.50) in salary and benefits, the cost amounted to nearly €102,000 ($137,325) annually. The purchase of a multiple-user electronic compendia cost approximately €22,500 ($30,300) and reduced the 'research' to a manageable 15 minutes per test item or an increase in productive process-related activity time of more than 1.5 weeks per employee per year. A spend of €22,500 ($30,300) resulted in a cost saving of €79,500 ($107,100) per year while releasing resources for an increase in productive capacity.

When running a laboratory operation within a contract manufacturing facility, one of us was faced with a decision on whether or not to purchase a €18,000 ($24,250) add-on to an analytical instrument. The recently designed local managerial accounting system contained sufficient hard cost data, such as contract laboratory test costs and material release delays to establish a payback period of six to nine months, and an ROI of well over €90,000 ($121,200) or 500 per cent during the anticipated life of the instrument. The bonus was a decrease in a significant bottleneck with faster response to manufacturing and the virtual elimination of delays in material release.

Language and Boundaries

Simplicity can only exist at the intersection of theory, direct experience and clear communication. All three must coexist for optimum organizational performance. We have observed that businesses that rely solely on current peer-reviewed research articles or business periodicals inadvertently push simple, pragmatic, experiential process knowledge aside and it becomes buried in history. In the past, hands-on experiences were seldom published, although this appears to be changing in the pharmaceutical industry. The most successful conferences and seminars are those which present not theories but applications in the form of case studies.

Haskins (2006) describes a number of logical fallacies, three of which are applicable to this discussion:

- Critical thinking may be compromised by time pressures to produce significant volumes of research and business articles. This is termed positive outcome bias. The risk to the process management is to potentially introduce superficial change, extrapolations of conclusions and wrong decisions based on inductive information.

- Critical thinking can be biased through publications that fall within a narrow field and are repetitious of current business themes. The risk to running a well-managed process is expressed as the Ad Populum Fallacy (or Bandwagon Fallacy) or the Communical Reinforcement Fallacy, where process actions and strategies are taken in response to popular beliefs or extraordinary singular successes by one firm in the industrial community.

- Increasingly narrow conclusions observed from research may inadvertently be narrowing universally valid information and widening process variability through the introduction of chaos. To re-state this point, adopting any conclusion derived from a valid research study can stall a business due to increased effort to separate chaotic noise from fact. The risk to a well-managed process is described as the Regressive Fallacy, in which there is a failure to account for ever-present natural variability and inherent interactions of seemingly unrelated actions. Hence, much of what is read may exclude past understanding which could reveal the conclusion to be a normal and natural event, rather than the next breakthrough business strategy.

In all three of these scenarios it is likely that apparently logical research will have been built upon previous work that may only have unique application to limited circumstances. In other words, the research may lack relevant context due to conceptual drift.

Consider, for example, the rote learning of multiplication tables in primary school. Within the education system in many countries today, memorization is frowned upon and is seen as unnecessary on the path to critical thinking. So, of what value was this exercise that had been practised for decades in past primary school applications? For one thing, it developed the ability in children to estimate the answer to a mathematical calculation and thus to check how rational the final answer is. This is the skill, for example, that allows someone to scan a supermarket receipt rapidly and estimate the total before challenging what they believe to be an incorrect amount requested at the checkout. Being able to approximate the end result is an outdated skill which has been replaced by spreadsheets or calculators. However, the answer may be wrong, due to unnoticed errors in programming. We look to ameliorate this situation by building on past principles and framing them within the context of today's issues and challenges. Our experiences will be captured in each chapter to demonstrate the value and importance of proper context on the business process.

Process design is based on simple concepts of integrating five common elements – *man, machine, method, material* and *environment*. This concept was first introduced by Ishikawa (1986), but has been used exclusively as a problem assessment tool. We will use the Fishbone Diagram concept as a means of aligning the discrete process elements at the point of process inception.

Man generally covers the human resources aspect of employees and is covered in Chapter 3. *Machine* speaks to the equipment necessary for converting materials from a raw or intermediate in-process good to a finished pharmaceutical and is discussed in Chapter 4. *Method* includes techniques of quality control and quality assurance in addition to the coordination of a stepwise order of activities and is expanded upon in Chapter 5. *Material* speaks to the characteristics and requirements of raw materials in terms of physical and chemical properties, among other points, and is covered in Chapter 6. *Environment,* which is discussed in Chapter 7, speaks not only to the physical condition of the buildings and utilities, such as water, air and temperature, but also includes the state of attitude held by employees at all levels within the organization.

Conclusion

These five elements set the linguistic framework for properly configuring a process to meet the intended outcomes of product performance and quality.

Understanding the language of process design, the interrelation and assembly of the five elements and the need to keep the process as simple as possible are key to achieving product consistency. Ideally a process will be initially configured at the design stage with these considerations in mind. It is possible through process re-engineering to reach the same point, but it takes significantly greater effort to overcome existing history, company legacy procedures and policies, and accounting conventions.

Every process must have a goal of simplicity of design and operation to remain competitive. Simplicity ensures that the process performance will be transparent in terms of results. At the same time, companies can integrate current technological tools to remain economical.

2

Artisan Heritage

We should not look back unless it is to derive useful lessons from past errors, and for the purpose of profiting by dearly bought experience.
(George Washington, 1732–1799, American military and political leader)

Introduction

The paradigms of process design and implementation in the twenty-first-century pharmaceutical industry can gain significant insights from studying historical methods and techniques used by artisan trades in the construction of buildings and furniture. The pharmaceutical industry is only just learning to focus on robust processes, despite the fact that the science underlying drug products is technologically advanced. Skilled formulation scientists know from experience which materials can be combined in a tablet to prevent capping. However, the same scientists may not necessarily understand the potential impact on bioequivalence of slight changes in the polymorphic state of the active pharmaceutical ingredient (API). Such changes could occur, for example, by a change of supplier or by a change in practice by a current supplier.

While historical artisan approaches would not meet the regulatory requirements protecting today's patients, some aspects of process system design are as applicable today as they were in 2000 BC when the Wonders of the World were built. Evidence of early human understanding of the application and integration of five process elements – *man*, *machine*, *method*, *material* and *environment* – abound throughout history. Evidence of man's process understanding includes structures such as the Parthenon, the Pyramids, cathedrals and castles of the English countryside, Stone Age tool manufacture and period furniture.

Equally, evidence can be seen of the dilution of process principles over time. Take as an example the sourcing of raw materials. Skilled artisans were trained to identify and select the most suitable types of stone to be used in their buildings. The master artisan alone was responsible for ensuring that the proper materials were chosen. In today's pharmaceutical world, alternately-sourced APIs may be purchased with the focus on compendia specification and lowest cost. The purchasing employee may lack understanding of potential changes to bioequivalence or blending homogeneity that result from the physical properties of the API. In this chapter, we discuss the transformation of process management from the days of skilled artisans to the current situation of fragmented global manufacturers.

The five process elements are intertwined and a change to any single element must be considered in the context of its impact on all the others. This is true even when the original change is considered to be an improvement. If all impacts are not considered, an imbalance may occur which can undermine the intended consistency of the final product, whether this is an API or a finished dosage form.

Introduction of the Artisan Model

In this chapter, we summarize a generalized evolution of process management over the past 4,000 years. We consider implications of this evolution for the business enterprise, along with adaptations of technology and science. Over time, a process manager has evolved from a single artisan who knew, understood and practiced the five process elements to highly specialized employees who are experts in their own narrow field but have limited experience in the wider aspects of the pharmaceutical manufacturing process.

We have split the history into five fundamental eras in which new process requirements were introduced. The terms for the eras, and their durations, are arbitrary. Each era covers significant advances in science, mathematics and economics, all of which were influential on process management. The elapsed years between eras has shortened with each new technology or other political or religious factors influential to and present in the global economy. This phenomenon will be familiar to pharmaceutical professionals who have seen the lead times for market exclusivity fall from ten years in the 1970s to just a few months by the 1990s (McCormick 2008).

Table 2.1   Overview of the development of the Artisan Model

Time/Era Process Element	Macro 2000 BC to 1600 AD	Sub-Macro 1600 AD to 1800 AD	Globalization 1800 AD to 1920 AD	Micro 1920 AD to 2000 AD	Nano 2000 AD onwards
Elapsed time	3,600 years	200 years	120 years	80 years	< 80 years
Key events	Bronze Age to Iron Age transition. Use of lead for protection of iron. Building with limestone and marble. Ruling class. Worship of gods	Iron Age transition to production of steel. Wind-powered vessels. Scientific method, Dark Ages transition to Age of Enlightenment. Church-sponsored education	Economic and money theory. Division of labour. Water power. Global travel. Capital investment. Analogue/mechanical equipment. Community education	Rail, air, sea and vehicle transportation. Digital computing. Taxes in US global trade. Scientific developments in chemistry, physics, biology. Process management for durable goods. Public education	Scientific developments in chemistry, physics, biology. Safe and efficacious drug laws. Global standardization. Outsourcing. Broader use of statistics. Secondary education
Man	• Skilled artisan	• Skilled artisan and trade unions • Local labourer	• Skilled artisan and trade unions • Local labourer • Factory worker	• Local labourer • Factory worker • Academically qualified	• Academically qualified
Machine	• Hand tools	• Hand tools • Simple machines	• Hand tools • Simple machines driven by natural sources, i.e. water • Part-standardization	• Simple machines • Part-standardization • Analogue electronics powered by electric/gas/diesel	• Part-perfection • Powered by electric/gas/diesel • Digital electronics • Precision milling and moulding
Method	• Traditional transfer techniques	• Traditional transfer techniques • Begin scientific standards	• Traditional transfer techniques • Scientific standards and metrology standards • Government standards	• Scientific standards and metrology standards • Government standards • Testing/quality	• Predictive modelling • Government standards

Table 2.1 Continued

Time/Era Process Element	Macro 2000 BC to 1600 AD	Sub-Macro 1600 AD to 1800 AD	Globalization 1800 AD to 1920 AD	Micro 1920 AD to 2000 AD	Nano 2000 AD onwards
Material	• Stone • Stone/metal • Stone/cement	• Stone • Stone/metal • Stone/cement • Wooden structures.	• Brick/cement • Wooden structures • Metals	• Brick/cement • Wooden structures • Metals and alloys	• Brick/cement • Wooden structures • Metals and alloys
Environment	• Normal ambient outdoor conditions • Political considerations of king/servant	• Normal ambient outdoor conditions. • Political considerations of king/servant • and local officials	• Shop and factory floor • Political considerations of king/servant • and local officials	• Shop and factory floor • Political considerations • of local officials	• Shop and factory floor • Political considerations • of local officials
Pharma implications	• Herbs, natural elements, e.g. sun heat, observation	• Scientific method introduced. Alchemists and charlatans	Scientific experimentation, observation, traditional skills, governmental regulation, vaccine safety, drug purity, superficial and dangerous cures	Laboratory experimentation, observation, expanded governmental regulation, vaccine safety, drug purity and safety, drug study requirements and broad spectrum cures (antibiotics)	Laboratory experimentation, observation, expanded governmental regulation, vaccine safety, drug purity and safety, drug study requirements, individualized medicines
Business enterprise	• Primarily barter for subsistence	• Evolving merchant/ businessman environment	Mass production and standardized units Investment-driven business Reduced cost of goods	Mass production and standardized units Investment-driven business Wealth extremes resulting from wars Reduced cost of goods Domestic sourcing	Mass production and standardized units Investment-driven business Wealth extremes resulting from wars Reduced cost of goods Global outsourcing

Despite the rapid evolution and advancements of science and technology, the design of pharmaceutical industrial processes has not improved; in fact, quite the reverse. In many instances advances have been hindered by a failure to properly deploy the fundamentals of good process design before jumping into sophisticated theoretical models. As the adage goes, just because you can (use the latest model) does not mean you should (use the latest model).

Macro Era (Approximately 2000 BC to 1600 AD)

We start with the ancients, Egyptian and Greek craftsmen, and their magnificent building accomplishments. We have called this period the *macro era* to denote the use of scale plans by artisan craftsmen to create buildings and other large structures. In many respects, process results accomplished in either culture cannot be matched today for precision and durability.

Generally, the ancients' products were constructed using scale drawings and models. Few written records remain to provide insight into the extent of their experiential knowledge, so we are left to uncover the lessons through archaeological discovery. The concept of process during this era can be characterized as slow but accurate transfer of dimensional and proportional requirements by highly skilled artisans using devices called story sticks or pointers. Mass production did not exist and there is evidence that dedicated, unique building part specifications were used (Hadingham 2008). Change was incorporated during the process to accommodate inherent minor variation of finished parts. The artisans selected the materials, the tools and the techniques to be used in the construction. Human and animal power allowed the heavy materials to be moved into place. Proportions were determined by mathematical study and experience. Structures were often tributes to gods or rulers and therefore cost was a secondary factor.

As for pharmaceutical processes and products, these consisted primarily of local remedies discovered by chance. In other words, it was 'kill or cure' by non-scientific techniques, ancestral observation and folk medicines.

MAN

Skilled artisans developed their craft over years of apprenticeship under the watchful eyes of a master. They learned all aspects of process within their immediate control: materials, methods and machines. Their use of the senses – smell, touch, sight and hearing – was highly developed.

MACHINE

Hand tools were durable and able to accomplish the job of cutting and shaping hard materials to exacting fit. Man provided the power to drive the machine.

MATERIAL

Selection of minimally flawed or unflawed materials was done by the artisan craftsman. For example, Native Americans selected flint stone for tools and weapons from the characteristic bell-like ringing sound made when two pieces of flint were struck together.

METHOD

Methods included accurate and reproducible duplication of size requirements by manual 'touch sensitive' transfer techniques, such as story sticks or pointers. The techniques relied on the natural sensitivity of human fingers and eyes to sense design requirements. A book for machinist apprentices published in 1925 reports 'Using suitable tools … the skilled mechanic can readily "feel" the difference (lathe turning) in contact made by changes of dimensions as small as 0.00025 inches' (Fairfield et al. 1917). An article in the *Smithsonian* magazine (Hadingham 2008) reported that full-size drawings, a 'single copy blueprint', were observed on building floors. This served as a single reference, ensuring accurate size replication. Arithmetic and geometric proportions of structures were understood.

ENVIRONMENT

Materials were perhaps selected to take advantage of natural weathering properties, such as the ability of limestone to weather and deposit trace amounts of minerals in cracks and fractures. The Greeks used molten lead to encase iron pins used to hold marble column blocks in place and prevent failure by rust (Hadingham 2008).

LESSONS FOR THE PHARMACEUTICAL INDUSTRY

In the macro era, process understanding was held by single, skilled masters. Work processes were slow but enduring. The lessons applicable to today's pharmaceutical industry are:

- process designers must be knowledgeable in all process elements;

- single standards lead to consistent results;

- all process elements must work in concert for optimum performance.

Sub-macro Era (Approximately 1600 AD to 1800 AD)

During the *sub-macro era* significant advancements in many fields of science, mathematics and economics were utilized in commercial enterprise. Research and study efforts led to discovery of natural laws to facilitate predictive understanding. Sir Francis Bacon ([1620] 2000) postulated the need to study phenomena with greater scientific rigour and eliminate the chaos of inductive thinking. The mathematics of calculus and integrals were refined. Adam Smith introduced the division of labour as a tool for increasing productivity ([1776] 1904). Process design was changing out of a need to better control production. Trade was facilitated by standardization of the 'purity of currency', the pound sterling.

MAN

Work tasks were becoming subdivided to accomplish greater output, but with the risk of making the job scope too narrow. As discussed earlier, Smith pointed out that 'too much specialization causes workers to become stupid'. Process understanding for the employee now included concepts of exchange and government regulations.

MACHINE

Greater emphasis was given to replacing human power with natural sources of power, such as wind and water, to service centralized manufacturing facilities.

METHOD

Manufacturing was becoming more standardized. Interchangeable parts, especially for military weapons, were developed by Eli Whitney in the USA and Jean Baptiste Vaquette de Gibeauval in France. The concept of uniquely sized individual parts was starting to be replaced by the Industrial Revolution model. From a process perspective, the need to control dimension variables had been introduced. According to Juran (1998), control of the quality of product was accomplished by 100 per cent inspection to meet the requirements of national governments or trade unions. The division of labour within the process needed to be rational and related to the business type. For example, a farmer would be unlikely to benefit from specialization, whereas a factory owner would benefit (Smith [1776] 1904).

MATERIALS

Raw materials were becoming commercially available. Artisan selection of raw materials was changing as it was becoming more economical to purchase from regions of specialized production and hence to purchase in bulk.

ENVIRONMENT

The business environment was shifting the economy from agrarian and skilled artisan to factory worker. The factory environment undermined the process understanding of the skilled artisan.

LESSONS FOR THE PHARMACEUTICAL INDUSTRY

The changes in the fields of science, mathematics, economics and engineering were starting to replace individual artisans with more narrowly configured job responsibilities within corporate enterprise. The pride in workmanship of the individual artisan was changing to accommodate the evolving corporate business model. Implications for the pharmaceutical company included:

- control and management of globally procured starting materials;

- rational design of process roles to maintain peak skill contributions;

- the need to educate workers in all aspects of the process.

Globalization Era (Approximately 1800 AD to 1920 AD)

The *globalization era* introduced changes to the process elements at an even faster pace. Economic booms and global wars provided impetus to large-scale manufacture. Statistical theory was refined, and chemistry and physics evolved into more robust scientific fields, as did economics and academic business training. Companies such as L.C. Starrett developed measuring tools capable of accurately and consistently measuring 0.001 inches. Western Electric Company provided a learning workshop for physicist Dr Walter Shewhart to study and understand economic production controls. When the results of years of research into process understanding were published (Shewhart 1931), the text was a nightmare for the non-process-oriented, statistically challenged person. On the other hand, if the reader could get past the integrals and derivative calculations, Shewhart captured all the salient points of how to design for quality, how to configure controls and, in the end, how to produce products economically.

During this time, the concept of quality was used as a term to reflect the final characteristic of the product. This definition inadvertently ignored the discrete elements of process necessary to assure control and problem solving sensitivity. Process management changed to integrate and accommodate new scientific and technical understanding.

MAN

Unskilled workers could be employed in manufacturing with proper supervision. Skilled craftsmen, such as mechanics and electricians, still followed an artisan model of apprenticeship to master tools and techniques. The value of labour and raw materials was minor in comparison to machine costs, so labour in a sense became expendable. Statistical concepts, such as random sampling, replaced 100 per cent inspection to reduce costs.

The workplace requirements for labour changed and included fundamental mathematical concepts. Business disciplines were segregated into departments of related activities, such as accounting, purchasing, manufacturing and quality control. Governmental regulations defined financial reporting standards based on the existing cost models in the early twentieth century (which are still in use for the most part today).

MACHINE

Equipment constituted the major cost of doing business as simple machines were replaced by more precise and complex designs. Machines could be made of new, more durable materials and could be powered by electricity. The machine operators did not necessarily learn the 'touch and feel' of the machine.

METHOD

New, faster and less destructive methods of inspection and control were developed. The new techniques relied on statistical modelling to achieve economic production. Wet chemistry analytical methods were sufficiently developed to assure the purity of the products sold. Job scope within manufacturing continued to narrow and become less challenging to an experienced worker.

MATERIAL

New materials were being introduced as a replacement for naturally occurring ones. Plastics such as plasticized polyvinylchloride (PVC) and low density polyethylene were developed, each with unique and unknown properties. The behaviour of plastics was new and different from naturally occurring materials.

ENVIRONMENT

The US government enacted weak consumer protections in the early 1900s, but this represented the beginning of modern regulation of the pharmaceutical industry. Academic and industrial research focused on the improvement of productivity as a function of the physical environment. Studies of hygiene factors by Hertzberg, Mausner and Snyderman (1959) and the Hawthorne Studies by Western Electric (Mayo 1949) attempted to discover predictable factors, controllable by business managers, which promoted optimum output. Governmental regulation of working conditions and product safety was introduced.

LESSONS FOR THE PHARMACEUTICAL INDUSTRY

The speed of change was limited only by the prevailing technology, primarily analogue controls and manual paper systems. Pharmaceutical products were not developed by rigorous scientific methods and were often unsafe. Governmental controls started to increase. Systems tended to be less complex and common sense was a valued asset. The cost of attaining a 'perfect result' was balanced by business pragmatism and less than perfect content could be tolerated. The single most important lesson for today's pharmaceutical industry is that jobs with narrow and repetitive duties are to be avoided in the process design.

Micro Era (approximately 1920 AD to 2000 AD)

Starting in the early twentieth century we reach the *micro era* of process management. This was the point where large-scale analogue technology started to be successfully replaced by miniaturized digital devices. Theoretical possibilities accelerated faster than they could be economically deployed in a modern factory. The issues of process management involved deploying effective controls in a way to ensure economic success, product safety and customer satisfaction.

MAN

Human resources spanning two eras coexisted in the business environment. Older workers tended to embrace lifetime employment with loyalty both to and from the company. On the other hand, younger workers tended to have more short-term employers. Corporate downsizing depleted experienced resources that had historically been used in a mentoring capacity to supplement academic training. Personnel costs started to eclipse machine costs. However, the century-old costing model was often still used.

MACHINE

Manual techniques were replaced as Computer Aided Design (CAD) and Computer Aided Manufacture (CAM) were used to develop equipment with exacting tolerances. Mechanic and operator 'touch feel' gave way to embedded automated controllers which could sense pending problems, react to perceived shifts in the manufacturing acceptance targets and keep real-time track of machine performance.

METHOD

Computerized machine processing was extraordinarily successful in reducing cycle times on a global scale. However, with these new methods came challenges. To start with, the process designer must ask 'what level of accuracy should a method possess so as to ensure the integrity and reliability of process data?'. New techniques, such as in-line laser micrometers and near-infrared chromatography, are key components of Process Analytical Technology (PAT), but their use should be carefully considered against the true needs of the process. Too much precision applied in a universal manner is not necessarily a prerequisite for a good method.

Another challenge to method validity is expressed in the logical Fallacy of Large Numbers (Haskins 2006), which states 'when the sample size approaches the population size, what appears to be impossible is actually possible'. In other words, large data-driven methods such as Six-Sigma might be detrimental to process management and control of quality because too much data is generated. Methods were increasingly being driven towards statistical modelling and the prediction of future states. However, the key point of process management is identifying and making effective and accurate decisions in real time at the quality control point, based on historical knowledge of the process. For example, Military Standard 105A (1950) was introduced for acceptance of products by attributes, representing a significant shift in technique from the direct inspection of every piece to the probability of acceptance of randomly sampled units.

Finally, new programmes and techniques were introduced in such a volume that the result was often chaos rather than improvement. Programmes such as Zero Defects (Crosby 1979), Quality Circles (Ishikawa 1980), Process Re-engineering (Hammer and Champy 1993) and, most recently, PAT and Quality by Design (QbD) were introduced so quickly that organizations often wasted large amounts of time redirecting the organizational inertia to meet the pro-forma requirements. An unintended consequence of rapid introduction of such programmes is best expressed by the Gestalt theory, which postulates humans seek to organize and achieve predictable environments. If workers are placed into continual chaos, they may become ambivalent and non-participative.

MATERIAL

Low-cost purchasing on a global scale characterized materials used in processes. This practice led to unsettling consequences in several industries such as pharmaceuticals, children's toys and food ingredients. Sometimes, key knowledge about in-process materials, such as the quality of print on a gelatin capsule, can best be gained visually. Acceptance sampling and testing, physical and chemical consistency, or controls used by the supplier can only be assessed for relevance by knowledgeable and experienced workers.

ENVIRONMENT

Greater emphasis was being placed on 'green' operations as contamination and new scientific evidence pointed to significant health risks today as well as for future generations. Issues have become global, with key industrialized countries leading for better control of manufacturing byproducts.

LESSONS FOR THE PHARMACEUTICAL INDUSTRY

To summarize, the implications for pharmaceutical operations were:

- careful consideration of the volumes of data from new process techniques; and

- increased control of global sources of raw materials.

Nano Era (Approximately 2000 AD Onwards)

The *nano era* is evolving presently and will drive process management integration issues of the future. Within the pharmaceutical industry, the current technologies that need to apply process management techniques include biotechnology products, monoclonal antibodies, carbon nanotube devices or drugs and genetically modified organisms. The principles of process management discussed in this book will provide the framework for achieving the highest level of product consistency.

The challenges to process management adoption at this time are fivefold:

- the fundamental wisdom of past research must be distilled and applied as appropriate in today's process management;

- the relevant range of the process must be clearly understood and pragmatically bounded;

- process management programmes must include 'what works' in greater balance with conceptual possibilities;

- business must simplify and align process management to the safest and most economically profitable point; and

- processes must be aligned with managerial accounting principles and measures with proper elevation into the financial reporting system.

Efficiency, effectiveness and the profitability of business enterprises are at stake. The cost of operating in chaos or failing to identify and resolve problems when they occur is high. Even the best companies lose between 15 and 40 per cent of gross sales on 'poor quality' (Deming [1993] 2000). It is clear that Deming intended his comment to reflect on the final output of a process. The term 'quality' is non-specific and ever-changing – quality is in the eye of the beholder – but process management is the only way to consistently meet the customers' demands. Companies must recognize and define the five discrete process elements – *man, machine, method, material* and *environment* – in order to develop deductive measures of true process performance which drive and promote operational stability and robust business strategy.

Conclusion

Process management must consider all five elements in concert or run the risk of imbalance and the loss of problem-solving discrimination. Any change, great or small, to one element will have either an immediate or long-term impact on the other elements.

Process management has evolved from a single artisan, who was knowledgeable in all elements of a process, through extensive apprenticeship and practice to collective groups of individuals, each accountable for small, narrow segments of product or service creation.

The challenge of process design today is the simplification and clarification of the boundaries and the range of outcomes for each of the five elements.

The study of past practices can reveal insights lost over time as the speed of technology has accelerated and business departments and groups have inadvertently over-specialized the business.

Process management is not about predicting the future, but rather making proper decisions about the consistency between intended and actual product characteristics.

Process management relies both on theory and experience in proper combination to achieve product excellence. Relying on theory alone can result in logical fallacies that undermine the effectiveness of production controls.

The goal of process management is to integrate business resources in a systematic manner to create predictable outcomes. Process management can be summarized by the equation:

man + machine + method + material + environment = predictable process outcome

All process design work must be documented. Why go to the trouble of prospectively anticipating elements of the process groups only to struggle with change management issues?

There are a number of reasons why recording the process design analysis is critical in the pharmaceutical industry:

- the spirit of Good Manufacturing Practice (GMP) presumes that all pharmaceutical products have been developed under rigorous scientific and technical thinking. The only evidence is the written word;

- process design history is good business practice in today's competitive environment, since it can lead to broader organizational knowledge;

- written plans serve as a starting point for future projects by providing valuable history;

- a written design plan can be reviewed and modified in light of inevitable changes during a project;

- most importantly for regulatory professionals, process design history will streamline compilation of the Chemistry and Manufacturing Controls (CMC) section of product approval submission dossiers.

Additional information regarding the basics of process design and problem resolution can be found in Ishikawa's writing on quality control (1986). While Dr Ishikawa's work originates in the automotive industry and focuses on the cause and effect of problems, reverse extension of his problem-solving approach leads to an effective model for process design and is the premise of this book. What we present here is not novel in the sense of first discovery, but rather novel from the proper application of existing techniques.

PART II
Five Process Elements

3

Man: The Mind of the Process

An investment in knowledge pays the best interest.
(Benjamin Franklin, 1706–1790, American Founding Father)

Introduction

Knowledgeable and skilled employees, capable of effective process management, are critical for successful pharmaceutical manufacturing. Previously, such job knowledge was acquired via apprenticeships to experienced employees and would be broad-based. Today, employees tend to have more academic qualifications in narrower fields, but less practical training and knowledge. This move towards highly educated specialists has been accompanied by greater emphasis on planning and scheduling rather than efficient execution of the process.

The pharmaceutical industry has evolved rapidly in the past few decades. It is a highly regulated environment. In the current economic climate, companies are also under huge pressure to reduce costs and improve productivity. At the same time, jobs have evolved from routine, fairly simple tasks to complex coordinated activities. Operators have moved away from sensory process monitoring and documentation and now rely on micro- and nano-instrumentation, with the resulting output of numbers, lines, graphs and charts. There may be frequent changes in corporate strategy, which can be confusing for employees. If companies downsize after a merger or an acquisition, experience and product knowledge can be lost. Job descriptions are often unrelated to process management.

As a result of the above environmental issues, an employee's responsibility for identifying and addressing the sources of process shift and drift become secondary considerations to meeting immediate short-term performance goals.

For example, a standard job description of a pharmaceutical supervisor is often limited to review and approval of current test results against a specification range, assurance that the operator followed all current procedures, etc. There is frequently no requirement to look for evidence of trends or shifts that signal the beginning of process drift. This exact situation was observed in a laboratory, where dissolution results fell over a three-month period but a root cause investigation was not initiated until the average result had fallen by about 22 per cent to fail the specification of 'greater than 80% release at the final test'.

Process Elements Interwoven

The five process elements – *man, machine, method, material* and *environment* – are tightly interwoven. A change to one element directly or indirectly impacts one or more of the others. Table 3.1 lists changes in the other four elements of the process within the pharmaceutical industry which can impact on *man* (the workforce) and the way in which it manages the process.

In order to ensure successful process design, it is important to create knowledge and understanding across the entire workforce. Looking at the changes to the other four elements listed in Table 3.1, it can be seen that the training needs are broad and diverse.

Table 3.1   **Changes in pharmaceutical processes that impact on employees**

Process element	Changes
MACHINE	- Robotics - Servo feedback controllers
METHOD	- QbD, PAT - x-ray diffraction - HPLC, GC, mass spectrometry
MATERIAL	- Polymorphism - Chirality - Brittle fracture/elastic deformation - Impurities
ENVIRONMENT	- Hygroscopicity - Photo reactivity - Thermal degradation - Oxidation - Microbial contamination - Mergers and downsizing - Highly litigious environment

Employees must be considered as a renewable and dynamic resource, capable of adapting to change in the other process elements. If human resources are considered merely as an asset or a discretionary direct expense, this will create barriers between the various layers of the organization and will undermine process performance.

Of the five elements, *man* has been the single catalyst of success in the application of innovative technology or scientific discovery to the process. However, technology is rapidly making human labour obsolete with the goal of reducing cost and improving process consistency. If technology replaces the person who is performing a mindless and repetitive task, this is appropriate. However, if technology is applied as a wholesale replacement for human intellect, the process will suffer. If the process does not work properly, there needs to be human intervention and human creativity to identify and eliminate problems, thus minimizing the business losses.

Continuous Learning

In order to ensure that the workforce can manage the process effectively, it is important to provide suitable training. In particular, companies need to learn from previous experience in order to develop a continuous learning environment. Figure 3.1 on the following page shows the impact of failure to create such a continuous learning environment. The first figure demonstrates a company on a constant but discontinuous learning curve. The second figure demonstrates a company that has been able to integrate incremental continuous learning as a knowledge platform.

The first situation might occur when a company, for cost containment reasons, keeps employment levels at a minimum, topped up with temporary employees when necessary. It would also occur in a company with a high turnover of staff. The second situation would occur when all employees are on full-time contracts and the training system is well integrated with process design. Cumulative knowledge becomes an additive asset.

The starting point for better process performance is a well-conceived, process-oriented job description and supporting training programme. Consistency of product, the hallmark of process excellence, is the reward for effective training. In order to renew the human resource in the pharmaceutical

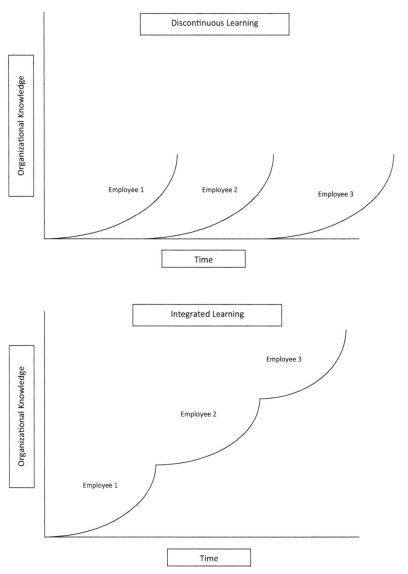

Figure 3.1   Integrated versus discontinuous learning environments

industry, we propose five dimensions of the employee skill development that must be fully recognized and thoughtfully integrated into the process:

- training in technical skills, including sciences, mathematics and pharmacology;

- training in recognition of meaningful deviation from process design;

- training in effective process problem resolution skills;

- training in system maintenance skills;

- training in documentation skills.

Each of these propositions is dealt with in more detail later in this chapter. Generally, the job description should contain sufficient responsibility and breadth to foster human creativity and intellectual participation in the work process. The employee should have experience of analysing the input, monitoring the conversion process and analysing the output to ensure that the product has been made under statistically stable conditions. A stable process is a prerequisite for meeting all specification requirements. The process aim should be consistent with the historical characteristics of input materials, processing conditions and output stability.

For example, the job description for a tablet press operator may describe three distinct responsibilities of the employee's role within the process:

- to assess the consistency of input materials from the granulation or compounding step;

- to monitor the immediate process conversions using documented historic performance and target values described in the specification to judge product consistency. The boundaries of routine and normal troubleshooting situations in which the equipment is shifting or drifting should be clearly understood;

- to be aware of next steps in the process and how decisions and actions at this step affect the ability of the next step to be performed.

We suggest a new approach to express individual process responsibility of all job descriptions: the aim or main purpose of all employees is to identify and resolve *meaningful* process design inconsistencies within the scope of responsibility.

Job descriptions frequently fail to articulate an employee's need to proactively identify and resolve process inconsistencies regardless of whether or not the product meets specification ranges.

For example, a chemist's job description often focuses on academic qualifications, instrument familiarity and the ability to complete testing assignments and process samples quickly. Suppose the job description was altered to focus on performance consistency between current sample data and historic product performance. Further, the chemist would have the responsibility to investigate process-related deviations even when the product meets specification. The job requirements would create active engagement for the employee to assess the validity of the data generated. The quality of the data would be subject to design expectations rather than blindly being accepted when within regulatory or compendial specification ranges.

In an operating environment where priority is given to process management, a tablet press operator's job description would not be to 'operate the tablet press to meet the production schedule as a first priority' and a chemist's job description would not include concepts such as 'run the HPLC to release the lot by tomorrow morning'. These statements would be too general to describe the care necessary for effective process management. Additionally, they imply that keeping to schedule is a more valuable goal than stable systems and consistent products.

Instead, the job description for a tablet press operator in such an operation should include the sort of responsibilities shown below:

- use the rotary tablet compaction equipment to convert powder granules into tablets with specified characteristics;

- assess the granulation characteristics for consistency of flow and particle shape;

- optimize tablet compaction by the proper choice of machine settings which lie within the validated range;

- monitor finished tablets for physical characteristics to minimize product-handling damage to promote successful packaging;

- ensure that input, processing and output do not drift during use.

Meeting the production schedule should be a second-tier priority in the production of pharmaceutical products. Production schedules are more likely to be met when the process is stable. Companies that focus on forcing the process to meet the schedule are building in a significant quantity of hidden risk from process design problems that become submerged and are not identified until too late. If a schedule is missed, there is a meaningful root cause to be investigated because the process did not run as designed. A key point is to hone the ability of the *man* process element to recognize differences from the intended design and to be able to effectively implement corrective actions according to governmental requirements.

Training for Technical Skills

A job description should be more than a list of required knowledge, skills and abilities used for comparison between companies and industries to establish salary ranges. Training should not be limited to knowledge of the complete index of standard operating procedures.

Broad-based training is the foundation for all other aspects of human resource effectiveness. Job descriptions must include appropriate considerations of process roles, problem-solving responsibilities, process maintenance and documentation practices. Many job descriptions used in the modern pharmaceutical industry have an overly specialized and narrow scope. They compromise the employee's clear understanding of the process role and outcome. Such job descriptions are more directed towards establishing a legally robust document rather than providing clear boundaries to create successful job performance.

That the current approach to job descriptions is out of date is evidenced by increasing numbers of recalls and regulatory product problems even in the face of process excellence models such as QbD and PAT.

It is necessary to establish a broad-based training programme beyond a compliance focus on GMP. The training must connect the employee with a number of issues, including technical considerations of the materials and manufacturing process and business concerns directed towards the creation of value (rather than solely cost containment). Employees also need an understanding of both disease progression and patient risks introduced by process excursions or deviations. For example, if the disease state reduces a patient's resistance to normal bacteria, then tablet processing would need to include more stringent microbiological controls for excipients and processing solutions. The outcome of a robust, broad-based training programme is full company engagement in the process of maximizing patient benefit.

When we first joined the pharmaceutical industry, it was not uncommon for the granulation operator to also have tablet press responsibility. Since that time, these would be seen as distinct jobs, each with their own responsibilities and training requirements. Distinct jobs have led to a myopic understanding of the interrelations that exist within the company. Table 3.1 points to the need for solid understanding of basic sciences to appreciate the state of patient health and the associated drug product risks.

All employees should have three process accountabilities in a pharmaceutical enterprise: being an astute observer, a change assessor and an empowered problem solver. Adam Smith ([1776] 1904) made the argument for adopting the division of labour as a means of improving the economy of a country. Certainly, an appropriate division of labour benefits productivity and profitability. However, Smith's proposal has been misconstrued to mean job specialization rather than rational process optimization through proper subgroup design. As shown in Chapter 1, Smith also argues against over-specialization of a specific job or task.

In order to remedy over-specialization and narrow job responsibility, the employee must be considered as a flexible and dynamic resource. This approach will increase the opportunities for invention and creative process improvement thinking. Experienced technical understanding, which can only be gained and mastered over time, must be captured as examples of the practical and correct application of the theory.

Training in Recognition of Meaningful Deviations

Only statistical stability of the process within the required range can ensure that drug products will meet all specifications and be fit for intended use. Skill in problem recognition begins with a basic understanding of the random nature of a process and how it relates to expected and unexpected change. Adding process stability concepts to the job description will promote a clear understanding of what constitutes meaningful process deviations and non-conforming materials during processing.

In terms of deviation recognition, the job description would need to identify the process starting point. Firstly, our tablet press operator would consider input stability: powder flow; granule characteristics such as size and texture; colour consistency; and the amount of start-up or stabilization time necessary for the tablet press to produce acceptable tablets. Any deviations, based on experience, would be communicated to appropriate technical support staff, as differences are a signal of instability, subtle differences of materials or unexpected/undetected variation at earlier steps in the process.

Next, the operator would consider the stability characteristics of the tablet press during operation. Does the machine work smoothly or is there a slight vibration? Do the finished tablets have the same 'pharmaceutical elegance' or are they dusty and pitted? Deviations from past experience are signals of process instability, subtle differences of materials at compression forces, 5 tons for example, and a need to investigate a root cause, even if the tablets meet all specification requirements.

Finally, the tablet press operator should consider the production period from start to finish, determining consistency across the running time as a means of ensuring that the packaging of the lot will proceed without problems.

Training in Problem Resolution

Currently, problem resolution responsibilities and boundaries are not clearly stated in job descriptions with respect to the process design. In the pharmaceutical industry, this important concept plays out as corrective action and preventive action (CAPA). Without a well-configured responsibility boundary in the job description, the final CAPA actions are often inconsistent with process data, scientific understanding and patient risks.

Often, the problem solution is not developed by the employee responsible for the process, but by a third party from quality assurance (QA) who is assigned the task of investigating a non-conformance. In effect, this removes the 'process expert' from direct responsibility for the solution to the process deviation. It also introduces an element of interpretation by the third party, since they were not present and did not observe the subtle conditions existing during the non-conformance.

Such 'employee disempowerment' gives the impression that the process controls may not be sufficient, since an external third party was required to perform the investigation. It also suggests that the process continues to run during the investigation period in order to meet production schedules.

Process facts, scientific principle and patient health must all be considered as relevant to CAPA when the process deviates from the stable state. For example, endotoxin in an injection would generally not be problematic when it conforms to compendial limits. If, however, the drug product is given to both neonates and mature adults, then an atypical increase in endotoxin may pose health risks to the neonate patient. Dr Deming ([1993] 2000) provides insights into the importance of consistency of aim to the final result. All levels of employees must understand their process role in addition to understanding the intended use of the product. Covey (2004) states a similar contention of 'begin with the end in mind'. These are key points in effective problem resolution.

Training in System Maintenance

Employees need to be provided with the skills and techniques for managing, evaluating and maintaining process performance both in the short run and over extended time periods. Process maintenance activities need to answer questions like: 'Is the process statistically stable and what evidence supports our conclusions?'

The starting point for this analysis is a basic run plot of the key attributes of inputs and characteristics of outputs plotted against the target and acceptable range. This simple exercise will reveal process stability or lack thereof. Other techniques of process monitoring skills include the mean and range chart – X-bar and R – histograms, bar charts, run charts, scatter diagrams, measles diagrams and other graphic techniques – see Chapter 13 for a full discussion of problem-solving tools and techniques. Employees must be trained to use the monitoring information in a timely manner to analyse actual performance against the design expectation and then act upon *important* differences between process design and process performance.

Before any process monitoring analysis can begin, it is important to ensure that the process is stable with no special cause deviations present. This can only be done with adequate history as a histogram or very rigorous concurrent monitoring. Personnel must develop an understanding of the implications of timely process monitoring. If process signals are not acted upon, the company misses opportunities for improvement efficiency, effectiveness and may even increase regulatory exposure by generating incomplete root cause analyses.

The concepts of short- and long-run process capability, C_{pk} and P_{pk} respectively, indirectly corroborate and affirm the effectiveness of the training programme by monitoring the process results. If the training programme is successful, the outcome should be reflected in reduced variability and better centring of the process due to effective and timely problem solving. However, these are more sophisticated techniques with many assumptions of process stability and should be used with care. Additional sophisticated trending techniques can reveal hidden opportunities for improvements and should be used in more mature process management systems. Complex analyses should not, however, replace proven and simple data plotting. The basics must be well understood and must form the foundation for more advanced techniques which assume higher levels of process control to ensure the validity of the results.

Ideally, the process maintenance is practiced concurrently to the processing in order to assess emerging trends as part of the product release process. This was the practice in one of the companies in which we both worked, where current lot release was predicated upon consistency with the previous 25 or more product lots.

If the company's process management programme is relatively new and undeveloped, or if the company is small and feels unable to invest in full-blown PAT or QbD, retrospective analysis is a valuable start, beginning with the basic run chart. If long-term evaluation is done in conjunction with the Annual Product Review (APR) – a regulatory requirement specific to the pharmaceutical industry – the resulting package can demonstrate the overall health of the process in relation to all of the processes present at the manufacturer. The retrospective annual analysis should include the ideas and experiences of the manufacturing operators and laboratory chemists.

Training in Documentation Skills

The final consideration in developing the human renewable resource is to develop and refine communication and documentation skills to clearly and accurately capture process activities. The employee must clearly document the start of the event, describe activities and countermeasures taken to resolve problems, corrective action, and finally discuss problems observed and suggest appropriate preventive actions. In other words, the employee must be able to put in writing a clear, understandable and factual summary of the process event.

GMP requires accurate and correct documentation to allow regulatory inspectors to determine whether or not the manufacturer is producing drug products which are safe and effective. Problem identification and resolution is only as sound as the documented historical record. The adage which is used by regulatory agencies such as the US Food and Drug Administration (FDA) makes the point: 'if it isn't documented it wasn't done'.

Accurate and sound documentation underpins corporate risk-avoidance strategies. So training in documentation and communication skills makes sense on both a business risk level and a process excellence level. The more advanced process management systems can use such tools as trend analysis, Failure Mode and Effects Analysis (FMEA), quality function deployment and other structured evaluations to build a documented record of the correlation of failure potential between the activity and the process. The key is to train employees in techniques of documentation to minimize inconsistency of the written record to the intended outcome of the exercise. Risk analysis is only as good as the accuracy of the documentation from past operational experiences. Therefore, it is important to stress in terms of process documentation that focus must be given to a proper level of trending, analysis and data robustness. Data must be deductive, factual and reproducible, rather than inductive and inaccurate due to faulty logic or assumptions.

Process documentation must be designed to simplify the collection and monitoring of data. The format and content must highlight a specific issue and lead the employee to the root cause. If change to the process is the outcome of a well-documented problem analysis, both the Quality Unit (QU) and regulatory affairs groups must clearly understand the situation in order to promote the change through the proper channels. Without accurate histories of problem resolution, system improvements are difficult to identify, investigate, report or register with the regulatory agencies.

Development and Delivery of Training

A continuing education programme focused on broadening the employee's process view helps to develop better process controls by employees. The outcome of sound employee training in technical skills, problem identification and resolution, system maintenance and documentation is less business disruption. Specific to the pharmaceutical regulations, GMP requires the QU to be involved in the review and development of training materials for personnel.

Since the QU often has broad oversight responsibility and knowledge of statistical techniques, it makes sense to engage the QU in the initial training system design. Further, senior employees should have an active role in the training to impart experience of process performance techniques to more junior employees.

Internal Customers

The aim of a job description should be to empower the operator to be the frontline resource for identifying atypical performance in established physical or operational characteristics. Process handoff is sometimes referred to as meeting the internal customer needs. This theme of the internal customer can and does create a poor understanding of the delivery of process-consistent materials and may not be aligned with the process. As a matter of fact, the sole target of pharmaceutical products at each point in the process should be defined as consistent product performance supported by scientific fact. One outcome of narrow job boundaries is the placement of blinkers on process performance. This can encourage the so-called 'tossing it over the wall' – anything to meet the schedule – rather than providing consistent materials to the next process step.

Predictions versus Historical Data

To understand what exactly constitutes consistency of output, the employee must have a sound and practical understanding of fundamental mathematics, including statistics and probability, basic science and pharmacology. Even more important is the understanding of limitations surrounding the precision and accuracy of the science and pharmacology. We have often observed the careless application of science and statistics as the root cause for poor process management. Care must be taken not to extrapolate beyond reality. Just because a result can be reported well beyond the relevant range of the process design does not mean that the result is important for managerial decision-making.

However, following this approach often infringes and extrapolates beyond a defensible scientific range. Process implementation has moved away from empirically evolved practices which work, but lack a mechanistic model, to statistically inferred mechanistic models that lack demonstrated or practical results. Along with the increased dependence on research modelling, employee training has shifted from at-point decision-making to prediction of future events which may not be valid. Deming said it best: 'The most important things are unknown or unknowable' ([1993] 2000). The unintended outcome of the shift from practical to theoretical is manufacturing chaos and an inability to identify valid process deviations. This state clearly cannot provide consistent materials to the next process step, except by accident.

Conclusion

System maintenance skills, together with problem resolution skills, should provide key insights into inconsistencies of attributes observed and experienced during activities at the specific processing step. Well-trained operators can provide valuable insights into the need for process maintenance and the scheduling of maintenance activities. They can focus the maintenance function through identification of the most to the least prevalent occurrence during the past time period. The reporting should be factual and visual, in a format such as a Pareto analysis – see Chapter 13.

In designing for stable, high-quality process performance, it is important to consider the roles and responsibilities as well as the personnel skills which are likely to be required during day-to-day work effort. Training is the starting point to enhance the innate talents of the employee. This task should be completed very early in the design process. The best situation is to use past experience as building blocks to carry forward in learning new process troubleshooting requirements and new technologies which may lead to altered responsibilities. A subsequent 'gap analysis' should point to the areas of supplemental or continuing training.

Continuing education is the best mechanism for maintaining or improving skill levels within the operation. There are four important sources for continuous education materials:

- customer complaints provide information about product quality problems that escaped the controls of the process;

- internal audits can provide valuable system and process information;

- professional literature provides insights into current trends;

- off-site training can widen experience via benchmarking.

A balance among the four is recommended as the most likely way of meeting the variety of training needs encountered by a firm. Remember, the QU should review all training for adequacy.

In conclusion, the analysis for the *man* element of process design is involved with matching personnel skills to the management and maintenance needs established in the master process design. This analysis is simplified when the primary job role, problem identification and problem resolution, is integrated into the job position. When the responsibilities are clearly stated, the employee must learn to distinguish between process signals that require action and those that do not. Finally, all training should be evaluated and reviewed by the QU to ensure the content of any training programme is adequate in terms of educating personnel in either skills or GMP issues.

4

Machine: The Voice of the Process

If you can't describe what you are doing as a process, you don't know what you are doing.

(W. Edwards Deming, 1900–1993, American statistician)

Introduction

In Chapter 3 we discussed the *mind of the process – man*. In this chapter, we discuss the *voice of the process – machine*. In a practical sense the only way to convert raw materials or intermediate products into a finished product is through a directed application of energy by one or more machines. Successful conversion of raw materials into the tablet or other finished dosage form results in measurable effects on the machine doing the work and is related to the compositional design, which is beyond the scope of this book. The measurement of the dosage form resistance during formulation, especially table production, forms the basis of the precision and accuracy required as a process control. Further, the effects of material conversion can result in direct or indirect forces which must be captured in the control strategy. Variability of the components will change with each new lot introduced to the production process. Measuring the effects of that variability will be presented in Chapter 6.

Directly controllable attributes such as compaction force or granulation flow are measured through transducers or gauges during operation and are capable of being adjusted in response to signal changes. These signals are presumed to have direct impact on the physical characteristics of the drug product. Homogeneous dispersion of active substance, on the other hand, must be measured indirectly by assessing chemical composition.

The precision of machine designs has facilitated high-speed processing, but has simultaneously created an unforgiving and inflexible method of manufacture. The unintended consequences include an inability to isolate problems that are specific to the machine from those related to other process elements. In other words, the root cause is difficult to isolate. The key to successful process management of machines and instruments is the ability of the control systems to accurately sense these forces and attributes to develop the Voice of the Process (VoP) which is highly correlated to quality and recognizable to process operators.

Historically, the VoP was learned by the artisan through lengthy apprenticeship. If a tool (machine) became dull, the process provided feedback to the artisan in three ways:

- increased resistance to cutting or tool chatter (similar to automobile windshield wipers when they hop and jump across the glass);

- sight and feel of the degraded surface texture as the machine tore rather than cut;

- mismatches at surface intersections. If the material was not suited for the purpose, the artisan could find more suitable materials or change the work technique by selecting a more appropriate tool.

This kind of response flexibility is limited with modern equipment such as tablet presses. In a sense, the VoP has been muted as a consequence of precision design and high processing speeds. Separating the correct and meaningful process signals from all other process noise has become a challenging task.

Table 4.1 shows the interdependencies of each of the process steps up to, and including, tablet compression. VoP considerations should build in performance measures that reveal subtle differences only visible at extreme conditions of temperature, pressure or heat. These signals are valuable ways to resolve process machine performance issues.

The ability to hear the VoP via the human senses of touch, sight and sound has been lost or replaced by pseudo-variable process signals. While these pseudo-controls are theoretically feasible, they are not practically applicable to process control strategies for machines. What may not be an obvious outcome of this shift is how often the surrogate techniques fail to accurately characterize the true message of the VoP.

Table 4.1   Generalized control strategy based on VoP

VoP goal: Consistency of ...	VoP strategic activity	VoP controls		Responsible business unit(s)
		Physical properties	**Chemical properties**	
Incoming materials	Supplier audits, sampling plans, quality agreements	Particle size, polymorph, crystal habit, density, melt point, colour, printing, shipping and handling	Assay, identity, impurities, residual solvents, water, specific identity, contamination	Laboratory, quality unit, operations, material management
Granulation and blending	Process validation, PAT	Granule size and shape, sieve testing, laser particle testing	Assay, uniformity of sample	Manufacturing, laboratory, regulatory affairs
Machine set-up and start-up	Process validation, set-up parameters (tolerances), granulation flow, mean time from start-up	Weight of individual tablets, friability, average weight, hardness, disintegration, angle of repose	Assay, uniformity of dosage units, dissolution, impurities	Manufacturing laboratory, quality unit, regulatory affairs

Erroneous Assumptions Relating to the VoP

We routinely observe erroneous assumptions regarding the proper application of controls to achieve VoP. The more common misbeliefs lead to the incorrect application of process quality controls. To be effective in process management, the pharmaceutical process designer must appreciate the following characteristics of any machine or instrument:

- machines are 100 per cent inspectors that affirm process design or reveal process design problems;

- machines are designed to make good products, not bad products or random defects;

- machines create defects at start-up, shut-down or when run beyond the normal maintenance interval;

- machine output is statistically valid only at the steady state.

THE 100 PER CENT INSPECTOR

Machine processing reveals all the subtle cumulative changes and variation present in the system up to the point of processing into final output. In the case of tablet compression, subtle differences in physical, chemical or crystalline properties in approved raw materials are revealed as the powder granulate is compressed under several tons of pressure per square inch. The raw materials may pass all specified parameters and still create problems when combined with other excipients. Important processing attributes related to inherent seasonal variation may not be identified as critical except through machining problems. The compression step can confirm the correct product design of excipient and drug substance composition. Alternatively, it can expose inappropriate combinations of materials by creating defects such as capped or split tablets, even when operating within validated ranges.

Consider, for example, the production of a natural alfalfa leaf nutritional product. This product had been successfully made on a large scale for many years with no machine complications or problems. An unknown change at the raw material supplier resulted in a drastic reduction in density of the main component, which was ignored until final release testing. The raw material was initially approved by the laboratory. It was later realized that density was a critical attribute but was not designated as an acceptance test parameter.

The problem was first noticed at the ribbon blender discharge with a clogging in the ductwork – VoP saying 'big change'. After dislodging the blockage – ignoring VoP – more lots in the campaign were blended with the same outcome. The blended material was passed to tablet compression, where even being pressed at maximum compression force – VoP saying 'big change' – the tablets were much softer than had ever been observed but 'just passed manufacturing specification' and were sent to packaging – ignoring VoP. In packaging, the tablets were dusty, highly friable and difficult to handle. The slot filler had to be stopped for interim cleaning when the powder began to interfere with filling by obscuring photocell light paths, a first for the packaging operation – VoP saying 'big change'. Packaging was continued – ignoring VoP.

Samples were collected during packaging for laboratory-release analysis after the manufacturing campaign was complete. It was at this point that the tablets failed acceptance criteria and could not be released for shipment, and a departmental struggle ensued. An investigation was launched only to discover a change in ownership of the sole source supplier. The new owner blended alfalfa stem, a light porous portion of the plant, with the alfalfa leaf, a denser section. The outcome was the costly rework of millions of tablets, a missed delivery schedule, overtime pay to rebuild the inventory buffer, temporary-worker pay to open packs and remove product and overtime for quality inspection to verify tablets contained no adulterants such as pieces of inner-seal materials, all of which could have been avoided or minimized by listening and responding to the VoP message at the earliest point.

MACHINES DO NOT PRODUCE RANDOM DEFECTS

Machines are designed to produce good products once steady-state conditions are achieved. Machines are not designed to produce random defects. The most common process management strategy until now has been to employ statistical sampling to 'control the quality of the final product'. Sampling as a tool has been used for more than five decades and is deeply ingrained in the pharmaceutical industrial culture. The underlying assumption is that defects are created in a random fashion and are uniformly dispersed throughout the components or finished product. This is untrue for nearly all pharmaceutical processes. Paragraphs 211.184(b), 211.122(a), 211.160(b)(1) and 211.134(b) among others of the US Code of Federal Regulations talk about inspection and representative sampling. The assumption is that verification of outgoing quality can be assessed by a well-designed, representative sampling plan. This assumption is true only if all the following are valid:

- the quality attribute being measured is meaningful to product performance and/or patient safety;

- the method is 10 to 100 times more accurate than the variation of the attribute;

- the meaningful attribute is a function of machine adjustments and not tool design or uncontrolled material characteristics;

- the product being manufactured is a solution where homogeneity is the most likely state. With other forms, such as solids, ointments or suspensions, non-homogeneity is much more likely to occur.

The following example demonstrates the above points. The setting was a supplier certification site audit of a leading aluminium flip-seal manufacturer. Flip-seals are the metallic overseals used to lock elastomeric closures in place on injectable products packaged in glass vials (see Figure 4.1 below).

The process overview presented by the supplier revealed the skirt of the flip-seal was 'critical to performance'. During the audit, a highly precise measuring device for skirt length appeared to be damaged and became a point of focus.

Figure 4.1   Flip-seal for injectable products

Flip-seals are manufactured by metal stamping, using precision-machined hardened steel dies and aluminium foil. The critical variables of the operation are maintenance of the tooling and consistency of foil thickness. The apparently malfunctioning precision device, an optical comparator, was found to have three of the five measurement display windows non-operational, the display lights having been purposely turned off. The reason for this was that the specification for skirt length is target point plus or minus tenths of millimetres (0.1 mm), while the optic comparator is capable of measuring to ten-thousandths of a millimeter (0.0001 mm). The quality director observed that operators were attempting to achieve perfect results by extending the precision of the specification to match to the precision of the comparator, i.e. 0.1000 mm. Consequently, excellent components were being classified as defective, leading to unnecessary corrective and preventive action (CAPA) investigations. The display lights beyond the hundredths of a millimetre place were switched off to re-establish meaningful controls. Many similar situations exist today. Measuring to an accuracy level beyond meaningful control causes needless additional work effort and creates imaginary defects.

DEFECTS OCCUR AT MACHINE START-UP AND SHUT-DOWN

Control of defective product should be the basis of all quality control and quality assurance activity during pharmaceutical processing, but it is not. The simplicity of the observation is overlooked as a critical aspect of VoP design. The characteristics of the start-up and shut-down activities of a tablet press operation, for example, speak to the subtle characteristics of particle size-related flow, consistency of lubrication or other attributes too subtle to be revealed through laboratory acceptance test samples. The machine's voice during start-up is often an accurate and early predictor of what is to come. The same can be said for shut-down, or when operating a machine beyond the recommended maintenance period.

For example, a mineral supplement tablet was failing acceptance testing and was not processing correctly on a unit dose packaging machine. During a 'for cause' audit of the nutritional manufacturer supplying the tablets in bulk, it was suggested that pharmaceutical GMP standards should not be used to judge the manufacturer's operation. However, good process management is not industry-specific.

In reviewing the manufacturing records, the documented VoP revealed the tablet press, a 180-degree design, produced two different distributions of

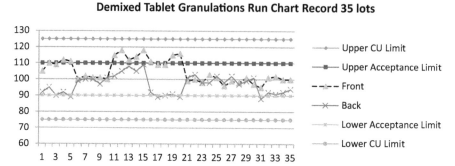

Figure 4.2   Run chart demonstrating demixing of granulate

tablets, the average of which was centred on 100 per cent of the label claim. Further, the distributions were observed to change in a predictable manner.

The process was direct to hopper dry blend compression. The manufacturer received shipments of pre-mixed powder blends from a second company a considerable distance from the manufacturing site. The shipments travelled many kilometres by ground transportation over a highway known to have potholes and exceedingly rough surfaces. The root cause was identified as demixing of the powder blends during transit. The tablet press VoP spoke, or rather screamed, to the operator each time a new container was started, every fifth point on the chart. The data indicates flow problems on both sides, front and back, of the tablet press and even further demixing as two distributions were usually present. The problem had not been recognized since the average was meeting specification. A depiction of just one lot of product is shown in Figure 4.2 above.

This example leads to the next observation; processes must be operating in a stable state for the statistical model to work properly. Violation of this rule ensures that incorrect business decisions will be made as a result of bad information.

STATISTICALLY VALID RESULTS OCCUR ONLY AT STEADY STATE

Pharmaceutical machines are sophisticated, precision instruments. Verification of the current machine characteristics must only focus on the immediate state of control and not attempt to predict the future. Confidence in the future state meeting specifications is limited to a comparison of the present state to historical production successes. In other words, if at the halfway point of a normally scheduled production batch the measures of mean and variability of the current lot are characteristic of past lots, there is a high probability that this lot will complete the production run as designed.

Finished products must be controlled within narrow parameters and have a centrally located target to ensure the delivery of proper amounts of medication. Attention must be focused on differences in performance rather than meeting arbitrarily wide specifications prescribed by referee literature or other universally accepted standards. To do otherwise leads to safety issues or adulterated products with unrecognized process drift or shift. Risk is only minimized and control maximized by proper monitoring of the machine product conversion at clearly identified critical control points. Managing pharmaceutical processes is about creating the correct statistical model capable of verifying good product and sensitive enough to detect even subtle changes. The best process management programmes use human intellectual capacity to design and apply control strategies. Effective control strategies include mathematically based control theory applied in a proper fashion as well as graphic displays to reveal patterns and relationships within the data.

Proposed Solutions

Having exposed the most common false assumptions of machine process controls, we suggest six approaches to overcome common misconceptions and ensure proper control designs for machines and instruments.

CROSS-FUNCTIONAL DESIGN TEAMS

Cross-functional teams must work together to establish the control framework for machines. Within the team, there should be a diverse spectrum related to age, length of service in the industry, technical specialities and awareness of the regulatory framework to integrate theoretical techniques with the maturity and experience of more veteran employees. The diverse balance of experience and understanding will minimize the likelihood of group thinking or fallacies of logic being committed that often lead down unproductive pathways. We recommend a greater proportion of generalist skills within the team, especially in leadership roles. Subject-matter experts can inadvertently limit the scope of machine controls through a myopic and biased view of the issue.

PROCESS OUTPUT BALANCING

Machines and controls must be an integral part of the initial manufacturing design rather than receiving focus as a single piece of equipment. Process design should give consideration to the potential for bottlenecks created by the speed of processing of any single piece of machinery. The entire process cannot operate in a normal manner if one machine is too fast or too slow. In the case of the former, the efficiency of the machine falls below its design capability and introduces variables of material feed rate and stop/start operation. This situation could result in poor quality and high levels of scrap. Additional information on the elimination of bottlenecks can be found in Goldratt's theory of constraints (Dettmer 1997).

CUSTOMIZED CONTROL STRATEGY

Quality control measures must be customized for each product and focus on the correct statistical model that describes input consistency, the unique combination of material properties and operating parameters, necessary to achieve homogeneous dispersion of the drug substance. In other words, a one-size quality control strategy will not fit all products and processing requirements. While different tablet products may share the same tools, the control strategy must consider the unique physical properties of the starting materials, the properties and characteristics of the blended mixture, the nature of control action to be performed at the quality control step and by whom.

For example, the specific control strategy may require the manufacturing organization to assume responsibility for the statistical stability of physical characteristics of tablets including weight, thickness, friability, hardness and visual appearance, such as mottling, picking, sticking, capping or others. The same product control strategy may require the laboratory to verify the statistical stability of the drug substance dispersion and release characteristics.

Control strategy begins with the physical properties of the components themselves and how they combine to create a homogeneous dispersion as well as knowledge of how the homogeneity can be destroyed. Applying a universal standard and control strategy is an invitation for the routine creation of Out of Specification (OOS) events with no clearly defined root cause. For example, if the blended tablet powder has excellent flow properties, the machine may be able to operate at a higher speed than a powder with marginal flow properties. Compression force for a powder blend with elastic deformation excipients may need to be lower or have a longer dwell time to settle the material and prevent the capping or splitting of finished tablets. These factors can only be known through experience and proper team composition, including formulators.

INTEGRATED VARIABLE AND ATTRIBUTE CONTROLS

The quality control strategy for the machine must include VoP measures of both a variable and attribute nature. No one set of measures can adequately describe machine performance in a manner to allow effective problem solving. It is important to include complementary and corroborative measures to describe the current state of processing. Consider the start-up of a tablet press. The machine begins with initial setting and then fine-tuning the travel of the upper and lower punches. Granulation is introduced to the machine and variable measures such as weight, thickness and friability are verified. However, would it not make sense to also have attribute analysis performed or even a time-related consideration of how difficult or easy is process stabilization? Do tablets pick and stick? Is tablet disintegration consistent with the past history of the product? Is the flow at the scrapper blade consistent? Is the active dispersed properly? All of these factors are part of a comprehensive control strategy.

All the required controls currently exist but are not applied in the proper context. The control strategy must be integrated with the input controls in addition to the controls and set-up of the processing step. Table 4.2 provides a brief cross-section of a complete control strategy. There are many ways of determining the voice of the process at any given step. The idea of the control strategy is to identify and institutionalize the proper combination of measurements to expose the degree and nature of variability and locate the point of central tendency of the process design. Some comments are required relating to each of the stages covered in Table 4.2.

Acceptance Testing

Consider industry issues of the widely used control strategy for incoming materials. The sponsor visits suppliers infrequently or only when problems arise. Acceptance controls rely on Certificate of Analysis results to describe physical and chemical characteristics. A legally required minimal identity test is performed, usually limited to generalized wet chemical tests with 'pass' or 'fail' attribute measures. Controls are mostly based on single attribute measures, which are known to be insensitive to change if applied improperly.

Table 4.2   Suggested control strategy for tablet compression

Voice of the process (needs)	Component acceptance testing (attribute and variable control needed)	Granulation and blending (attribute and variable control needed)	Machine set-up and start-up characteristics (attribute and variable control needed)
Homogeneity or consistency	Supplier controls, sampling plans	Process validation, PAT	Process validation, set-up parameters (tolerances), granulation flow
Physical characteristics	Particle size, polymorph, crystal habit, density, melt point	Granule size and shape, sieve testing, laser particle testing	Weight of individual tablets, friability, average weight, hardness, disintegration
Chemical characteristics	Assay, identity, impurities, residual solvents, water, functional group characteristics	Assay, uniformity of sample	Assay, uniformity of dosage units, dissolution, impurities
Responsible for control strategy	Laboratory	Manufacturing, laboratory	Manufacturing, laboratory

The company can be unaware of changes in critical properties. Chondroitin contamination of heparin or melamine contamination of pet protein blends are recent examples.

Granulation

The control strategy for granulation must include variable and attribute measures to verify the adequacy of the incoming acceptance plan. All released materials come into blending and granulation for uniform dispersion of the individual components and conditioning of the particle characteristics to achieve proper machine flow and compression characteristics, and are presumed to be consistent with the validation data. Subtle changes in density, if not assessed, can have major unexpected process implications.

Start-up

Subtle changes in blending/granulation are often exposed at the compression pressures of a tablet press and result in difficult and extended start-up time. The implication is lower yields for each batch that experiences a problem. A novel concept, mean time from start-up, can be a critical variable aspect of the consistency of granulation and finished tablet characteristics.

INDIRECT OVERLAPPING REDUNDANCY OF PROCESS CONTROLS

Each step of the process involves inputs, processing and outputs. The dynamic forces of each sequential step in a manufacturing process can increase significantly, often by factors of a thousandfold or more as the drug product is produced. The acceptance test sample may only consist of 25 or 100 grams of material and is presumed to properly characterize the variability within the lot receipt. This is often not the case. Suppose that sieve fractions of the acceptance sample pass specified ranges but that the actual mean of the supplier's process shifted. Or suppose there is a slight change in density of the principal component of a powder blend. The impact of this variability is likely to be revealed at the blending step through the dynamics that characterize, let us say, a 1,500 kg batch size.

The only manner to resolve the problem would be to accept as valid the analytical result of blending and work backwards to assess particle size measures. At this point, it is hoped that the quality unit would recognize that sieve analysis, a test of attributes, is sometimes insensitive in detecting particle distribution shifts. Alternatively, the quality unit should understand that density can be a critical variable in fixed container blending, such as tote blending, where changes of volume for a fixed weight of dispensed material can make blending ineffective. The conversion of sieve fraction results to an estimate of particle size is required in the former situation. Larger samples to perform density analysis would be required. Both solutions are in response to the VoP considerations during process design.

REAL LIFE

Sometimes, no action is taken, even when materials change dramatically. For example, a contract manufacturing company was producing acetaminophen tablets. The batch size was designed to fill 80 per cent of the available volume of a blending tote and weighed around 750 kg. The lubricant for the dry compression powder blend was magnesium stearate. The process was properly validated and the product was successfully manufactured over time using the original design controls for acceptance testing.

One day, the blending totes were filled as usual but the materials came up to the top neck of the tote – the VoP was yelling 'this is a change; pay attention'. In order to meet the production schedule for on-time customer delivery, the operator literally formed a cavity with a gloved hand large enough to add the required amount of lubricant to the batch. The tote lid was sealed, the tote was hoisted into the tumbling frame and the process was started. The first tumble compacted the lubricant into a sphere the size of a football. By the end of the blending cycle, the lubricant mass was reduced to the size of ping pong balls. The blend was sent to tablet compression. The first tablets stuck to the punches, as the blend was under-lubricated. Tablets had weight variability problems related to poor powder flow and their physical appearance was inconsistent with historical results. The sample tablets failed testing in the laboratory. The product had to be scrapped and a new batch produced.

Conclusion

Since the first use of machines by artisans, many changes have been introduced which improve the speed and consistency of output. Along the way, fundamentals and response techniques to VoP messages have changed from human sensory responses into electrical or mathematical interpretations of human responses. If the artisan's chisel or knife was dull, he could sense the extra force necessary to propel the tool – the machine. The action was to sharpen the tool and return it to a proper condition to perform the task.

Today's pharmaceutical equipment uses instruments to create the VoP for the machine. The challenge of process design management is to select and integrate machine instrumentation that is easily understood and has meaning to the operator in charge of the machine. Such techniques include statistical process control as well as other control strategies presented in this chapter. Instrument controls must not only manage the immediate value-adding conversion from raw material to product but must also provide information about the success of the preceding input process steps. A failure to include process control links between process steps inevitability means a failure to determine a single root cause when problems occur.

5

Method: The Techniques of Process Control

A man who carries a cat by the tail learns something he can learn in no other way.

(Mark Twain, 1835–1910, American author)

Introduction

Methods, according to our Artisan Model, are analogous to the human senses used in the process of creating hand-crafted products. The methods discussed are nearly the same ones that are found in the quality toolbox. There is no need to resort to sophisticated statistical techniques to manage any pharmaceutical process. This is good news for small- and medium-sized companies seeking cost-effective ways to produce safe and efficacious drug products. We continually find improper application of one or more quality tools at the root of failures in the management of process design or implementation. The reason for this misuse is the lack of hands-on experience of the user or designer. Quality tools cannot be applied correctly if the user has no real-life experience in their operation.

The current quality tools, when applied properly, offer precise, accurate, robust and specific control within the relevant range of the process. This is a key concept. In our view, the improper use and application of existing methods are the root cause of many problems observed by regulatory agencies during inspections. The incorrect application of methods has become the reason for programmes such as Quality in the 21st Century, QbD and PAT.

For established products, we advocate the proper application of existing tools as the strategic priority for process improvement. For new products, following the Artisan Model at the design phase is the best way to ensure right-first-time operation. Methods properly applied will solve the regulator's dilemma: if this marketing authorization application is approved, will the manufacturer be capable of consistently producing safe and efficacious medicines? The answer lies in the proper application of well-characterized and well-applied methods to the correct points within the process. Applying methods properly cannot be learned from a textbook. The proper application of process management tools can only be applied after the issues are clearly understood.

Issues Relating to the Proper Application of Methods

This book aims to give the reader insights into the proper application of process controls refined over years of practical experience. The proper implementation of time-honoured techniques complements a solid technical and scientific foundation of process management. Quality-based process management methods and tools are universally misapplied across the industry. A force field analysis in Table 5.1 shows some of the underlying issues that characterize our current state of process management and the difficulties with the proper application of methods.

Table 5.1   Force field analysis on the proper application of methods

Forces for change	Forces against change
Rapid application of novel scientific discovery (new products to market)	• Proving safety and efficacy in increasingly smaller patient populations • Human physiology • Lack of time
Rapid application of novel, high-volume manufacturing techniques (low-cost products to market)	• Scientific and business ignorance • Logical fallacies • Process ignorance • Lack of time
Legal problems	• Scientific ignorance • Lengthy system to update requirements and change laws
Incorrect application	• Lack of experience • Lack of understanding of technique • Lack of understanding of the operating principle
Predictable control of all aspects of the business	• Increased reliance on universal Standard Operating Procedures (SOPs) • Increased reliance on universal computerized systems • Increased logistical challenges • Lock-step schedules

Scientific and business ignorance was beautifully demonstrated in the *Wall Street Journal* article 'New Prescription for Drug Makers: Update the Plants' (Abboud and Hensley 2003). The suppositions, conclusions and implications of this article, which formed the basis of 'new process management strategies' for the pharmaceutical industry, are inductive in nature with comparison to industries that operate on a totally different level of safety and efficacy. If potato crisps cured cancer, they would be regulated as drugs. They don't, so they aren't.

Every programme claims to provide 'the one and only solution' to a firm's process management strategy. It is no wonder that the business landscape is littered with abandoned efforts. It is necessary to discuss the constraining factors in order to present the universal solutions to turn process management towards the proper end goal. Three primary misunderstandings about process management tools, methods and techniques exist today. Some come from institutional memory – old procedures and practices – and some from lack of understanding of content – theoretical foundations – but most derive from a contextual misunderstanding of the process principles to which the technique should be applied.

REPLACING KNOWLEDGE WITH PROCEDURAL CONTROL AND ENTERPRISE INSTANT COMMUNICATION

All process design and process management records must be proactively created and thoughtfully documented. We must distinguish between thoughtful capture of relevant content and excruciating levels of detail that substitute for experience, knowledge or intellectual creativity.

Overly detailed procedures add complexity and frequently fail to deliver the intended results – consistent performance. Some are written in response to a perceived problem or a one-off complaint. Others are instituted for organizational control. In such situations, process signals and process noise can become procedurally intertwined to become a pseudo-voice of the process.

The pharmaceutical industry is in the middle of a major business shift where the big are becoming super-sized through economy of scale strategies. The logic behind this strategy is that larger size will facilitate robust profitability through greater innovation and reduced costs of goods due to better purchasing power. However, the opposite in fact occurs. The larger organization finds a greater need to control the day-to-day operations. This need for control promotes extreme levels of procedural detail to encompass all possible business scenarios. The unintended consequence of extreme detail is the creation of an inflexible operating structure and the adoption of a compliance mindset.

To add to the process management method challenges, communication across business units is frequently left to enterprise models of e-mail based upon presumed similarities of the employee's need for and timely access to business information. Herein lies a barrier to effective process management – how to capture institutional experience and memory into one standardized format while still allowing for maximum use of human intellect. We have found that companies in general do a poor job of this activity, especially when different organizational cultures exist due to mergers and acquisitions. The intangible economic loss of process knowledge and understanding is staggering in terms of regulatory compliance problems.

CONTENT WITHOUT CONTEXT

By content we refer to the academic training or formal study by the person responsible for managing all or part of the process. The academic study of process management methods alone is insufficient to ensure the proper implementation and administration of a process management system in a pharmaceutical operation. Understanding the academic theory does not prevent the user from blindly accepting logical fallacies and in so doing undermining their success.

Much of what detours the effective outcomes of pharmaceutical process management can be traced to logical fallacies of words or perceptions. To paraphrase Haskins (2006), theory often looks good on paper but fails terribly in a real-world application.

Logical Fallacy 1: Belief of Testimonial Evidence

A good example of this is Six-Sigma. Motorola's declared success fuelled a whole new industry to lead companies down a path that is not practically measurable even when using today's state-of-the-art technology. There is much controversy regarding the validity of measuring parts per million. According to the Six-Sigma creators Mikhail Harry and Ronald Lawson, and based upon their experience at Motorola, at the mathematically exact parts per million defect level, which is 4.5 standard deviations, there is an estimated figure of 1.5 standard deviations of error due to long-term system drift. Having the potential to shift the process target by nearly 30 per cent on either side of the label claim, for example, is likely to create false positive out of specification (OOS) results and high levels of ineffective problem investigations.

Logical Fallacy 2: Doublespeak, Jargon and Euphemisms

Concepts are described in fuzzy inductive terms that are often politically correct but result in process chaos. A good example is the concept of multi-tasking. Multi-tasking fulfils the business need to do more with less, but the unintended consequences are organizational chaos and an inability to think analytically. Most if not all pharmaceutical process management issues require considered evaluation, that is, quiet and careful reflection, rather than an automatic response, done in a hurried fashion.

Logical Fallacy 3: Ad Populum, Bandwagon Fallacy

This occurs where there is an appeal to the popularity of the claim with no basis in sound reasoning or argument. This fallacy is the underlying cause for the rapid adoption of so-called 'flavour of the month' programmes that characterized business strategy beginning in the 1970s. To give an example, Quality Circles were adopted by many large pharmaceutical organizations in the belief that tactical teamwork would lead to strategic success on a par with the Japanese automotive industry. The programmes floundered when the American-styled Quality Circle Teams exposed a key difference between Japanese and Western business structures – an unwillingness on the part of the Westerners to delegate authority.

To overcome these fallacies, which ultimately undermine successful process management, companies must rely on employees who are well versed in process content and well experienced in proper process context.

The proper application of pharmaceutical process management methods is grounded in the fact that all aspects of process management are interconnected, directly or indirectly, and are most often applied correctly by veteran employees. For example, the production of a drug substance was transferred to a new manufacturing site from an exisiting site with years of successful process knowledge. During the transfer, long-term employees at the closing site were not consulted for their key insights that were difficult to adequately express in written procedures. The receiving site adopted changes to the process that on the surface appeared to be correct. The results of the first commercially produced batches at the new site showed critical performance differences when these materials were used in the finished drug product. Process management methods must by nature be simple and direct, coming from understanding gained through direct hands-on experience. Any other approach too often leads to chaos and unintended consequences, such as unsolved OOS investigations. Regulatory inspectors do not like to see OOS events.

Let us remember Leonardo Da Vinci's saying: 'Simplicity is the ultimate sophistication'. Process management contextual knowledge gained by hands-on experience opens the door for creative applications of existing process management techniques and in so doing resolves some vexing business issues. It is worth reiterating what we said in Chapter 3: the development of process management methods content must include topics outside standard pharmaceutical training programmes:

- product characteristics must be understood in terms of their clinically intended purpose as well as the health risks to the most vulnerable members of the population in the case of process deviations;

- the relevant operational range of process design must be well understood and characterized to rational levels of detail;

- the underlying statistical model must be easily understood by personnel – *man* – in a manner consistent with the physical and chemical attributes of the *machines, materials* and *environment* being processed.

REPLACING SIMPLE PROVEN TECHNIQUES WITH COMPUTATIONAL ESTIMATES

Recent trends in pharmaceutical process management have mostly been directed towards the statistical modelling of future events. This approach is contrary to the fundamental principles of process management: making good decisions at the point of quality control analysis. In other words, statistics should be limited to affirmation of decisions based on current and historical performance and not for the purpose of accurately predicting future state from the current data set.

Knowledge, understanding and technology interact over time. Knowledge is primarily a function of academic study and resulting facts created during research. Knowledge is perpetuated through books and other written records and provides the foundation for scientific tests of hypothesis. Pharmaceutical clinical studies rely heavily on this principle.

Understanding, on the other hand, is an extension of knowledge gained largely through life experience. Understanding cannot be learned from a book and is knowledge applied, correctly or incorrectly.

Technological advancement results when diverse knowledge is combined in a novel manner, thus opening the way for additional knowledge. At the intersection at any given point of technological innovation, there is a boundary of uncertainty that the new technology will increase knowledge and understanding. In effect, the futuristic modelling of processes extends past the point of factually derived understanding. Also, using modelling incorrectly or as a single solution to all process management problems introduces a host of unpredictable variables that can lead to the Fallacy of Large Numbers; in a large sample, the seemingly impossible is in fact highly probable (Haskins 2006).

A good example of modelling is the use of near-infrared (NIR) analysis. This technology has a very beneficial value to process management, but has limitations that must be understood before it is universally applied to a broad array of process control situations. The technology uses a narrow spectral range of infrared light to analyse samples in their native state. In other words, the laboratory goes to the sample rather than the sample coming to the laboratory for testing.

A qualified NIR instrument does not require extensive chemical knowledge to operate. In very general terms, the operator needs only to understand how to select the proper library reference, locate the probe within the shipping container and start the analysis. NIR is appealing as a way to lower the cost of labour because traditional sample preparation of the parent method, infrared spectroscopy, is replaced. In addition, sample analysis and spectral interpretation by a qualified chemist in the laboratory is eliminated.

However, there are critical trade-offs that must be considered. NIR is a test of goodness, an attribute test. Tests of attribute evaluate samples for a pass or fail determination and are optimally used when there are limited uncontrolled variables. As a method, NIR is sensitive to external process variables such as particle size, particle shape, ratios of ingredients and ambient moisture among other factors, and therefore introduces a level of complexity in the development of a relevant library – lots of time by a trained chemist.

Recommended Strategies

The problem resolution strategies for the previous issues involve simple assessment by qualified and experienced persons and can be accomplished with minimal expenditure. The strategies suggested will begin the alignment of the method to the realities of the process design. All the approaches are based on simplicity rather than extreme levels of detail.

IS THE PROCESS BEHAVING PROPERLY?

The first, second and third rules of process management are plot the data, plot the data and plot the data. When everything else fails, plot the data. All process management techniques are statistical and/or visual in nature. It is important to understand which statistical model applies to the process management system being evaluated. If the data plot looks odd, the statistical conclusions will be wrong.

More often than not, processes involve variable data distributed normally. Variable data have measurable properties. Examples include tablet weight, assay, uniformity of dose or the number of rejected tablets. Failures within this system are predictable and potential problems can often be averted by skilled data interpretation and timely interventions by the operator or analyst. Once the variable is identified, the data should be gathered and plotted. If the histogram does not look like a textbook example, the special root cause should be found and fixed.

DISTINGUISH AMONG COMMON/SPECIAL CAUSE DATA AND SIGNAL/NOISE THRESHOLD

These four concepts determine the rational boundaries of the process and the validity of the data from the process. If the process method designer fails to account for these conditions, the product quality decisions will be incorrect.

The common and special cause data constitutes the precision of the process method. Common cause data are inherent characteristics of the process. Common cause data result when all process elements are functioning within the design parameters. Special cause data result when one or more of the process elements have been compromised or are not performed properly.

Consider tablet compression: when all components meet established specifications, the components are properly dispensed and the tablet press is set up properly, the resulting tablets will meet target weight, assay and uniformity of dosage specification ranges. If the results lie within the historical distribution pattern, the process is displaying common cause variability. Special cause data on the other hand reflect an abnormality in the process performance. Suppose the tablet press was set up incorrectly and produced tablets of two different weights. The special cause data will show increased variability and would be shaped like a Bactrian camel – with two humps. If the special cause was a shortage of a powder blend lubricant, then the pattern would appear to be normal, but would be uniformly dispersed across a wider spread of values.

Common cause signal is a real data point produced at levels defined by the cumulative error within the process. Common cause signals are associated with the inherent variability of the total system and are a function of the design.

Special cause data, on the other hand, are potentially invalid data caused by factors outside the process design. Special cause signals have an assignable reason that is revealed during *careful* evaluation of process data. A common cause and special cause data comparison is shown in Table 5.2 below.

Distinguishing between signal and noise data is a more subtle aspect of the method and addresses the precision of measurement as well as the point of the process at which the measurement is taken. Understanding the signal to noise

Table 5.2   Common and special cause data of tablet compression

Common cause data		Special cause data Scenario 1 root cause: Tablet press set-up		Special cause data Scenario 2 root cause: Shortage of lubricant	
Mean weight	500 mg	Mean weight	500 mg	Mean weight	500 mg
Assay	100.1% LC	Assay	99.9% LC	Assay	99.9% LC
Weight variation	490–510 mg	Variant 1 Variant 2	515–25 mg 475–85 mg	Variant	446–552 mg
Assay	98.5–101.5%	Assay 1 Assay 2	103.4–107.1% 93.2–98.0%	Assay	91.1–106.3%
• Characteristics • Sum total of all imprecision at each handling step • Defines process capability • Data that 'is'		• Characteristics • Single or combination of faults in process design • Unexpected change in one or more system elements • Widens process capability • Data that 'is not'			

boundary comes with experience. Data in the signal region are believable and lead to correct actions in managing the process. Noise data on the other hand are not confirmable and lead to differing conclusions by different people.

Data in the noise region have three basic origins: extrapolation, insensitivity or hypersensitivity of measurement. The difference between signal and noise regions of a method can be seen in Table 5.3, which shows that data validity is a continuum.

For example, if a tablet manufacturing process requires 25 kg of drug substance, the choice of dispensing scale has a significant impact on the signal to noise boundary of common cause data. The only effective way to change common cause signals is to redesign the process to weigh materials fewer times, purchase more accurate weighing equipment or increase the lot size. Table 5.4 demonstrates this principle. Homogeneous dispersion is an assumption.

The same sort of error is present in a laboratory setting with one additional consideration: small mass transfer. For example, if 10 mg of standard is weighed

Table 5.3   Characteristics of signal and noise data

Method	Noise region	Signal region	Noise region	
	Insensitive data	True data	Hypersensitive data	Extrapolation data
Individual tablet weight	± 2 mg Scale 2 mg N=1	± 1 mg Scale 0.1 mg N=10	± 0.01 mg Scale 0.001 mg N=10	± 1.0000 mg Scale 0.1 mg
Average tablet weight	Weight rounded to ± 5 mg N=5	Weight in mg N=25	Weight in 1/100 mg N=25	Weight in 1/1000 mg as calculated N=25
Assay	% label claim 95–105	% label claim 95.0–105.0	% label claim 95.000–105.000	Not applicable

Table 5.4   Process design considerations of measuring precision in pharmacy dispensing

Process step	Scenario 1	Scenario 2	Scenario 3	Scenario 4
Drug Substance	25 kg	25 kg	25 kg	0.025 kg
Scale	± 1 kg	± 0.5 kg	± 0.2 kg	± 0.01 kg
Percentage error	± 4.00%	± 2.00%	± 0.80%	± 0.04%

to a precision of hundredths of a milligram, the accuracy is about 0.1 per cent. However, 10 mg is a very small amount of material. If handling accidently loses half a milligram, an approximate 5 per cent error is present. For the laboratory, the amount of standard dispensed must be sufficient to ensure only minimal loss on transfer. A well-designed process, such as one using QbD, will involve this sort of analysis for all steps within the process to ensure that the cumulative errors during manufacturing are lower than the cumulative errors of the sampling and analytical methods.

THE RULE OF TENTHS PLUS ONE ADDITIONAL DECIMAL POINT

As demonstrated in Tables 5.3 and 5.4, many method options are available to the process designer. The key is to balance the precision of measurement and the consequential noise and signal thresholds to ensure the data from each quality control point are accurate.

Standard data management practice provides for at least one decimal level of precision beyond the single point for variable data. Often, two levels are necessary. Beyond two levels of precision, the user runs the risk of creating false signals. However, remember that the specification does not need to include the precision of the quality control measurement. These considerations are summarized in Table 5.5.

Table 5.5   Rules of division of error in measuring

Plan 1: Next decimal divided by 2 xx.(x/2)	The 4/5 rounding rule Error is approximately 50%	Example: Target: 10 mg Scale : ± 0.5 mg
Plan 2: Next decimal divided in 5 xx.(x/5)	Error is approximately 20%	Target: 10.0 mg Scale ± 0.2 mg
Plan 3: Next decimal divided in 10 xx.(x/10)	Error is approximately 10%	Target: 10.0 mg Scale: ± 0.1 mg
Plan 4: Second decimal divided in 2 xx.x(x/2)	Error is approximately 5%	Target: 10.0 mg Scale: ± 0.05 mg
Plan 5: Second decimal divided in 5 xx.x(x/5)	Error is approximately 2%	Target: 10.0 mg Scale: ± 0.02 mg
Plan 6: Second decimal divided in 10 xx.x(x/10)	Error is approximately 1%	Target: 10.0 mg Scale: ± 0.01 mg

If precision is not balanced within the system to meet the intended purpose, data can and will generate false signals. The worst-case scenarios are shipping bad products to market unknowingly or holding good products pending the results of extensive OOS investigations that lead to no root cause.

The low cost/no cost action to resolve this situation is to map the precisions of methods against the flow of the process and to express the precision of measurement in common terms. Mismatched method precision should be corrected. Be certain, however, to check the regulatory filings to determine whether methods can be changed easily or with great complexity. Changes must be made according to regulatory agency rules.

SIMPLIFY THE SYSTEM AFTER CONSTRUCTING A 'CURRENT STATE' MAP OF THE PROCESS

The mapping exercise provides the opportunity to refine the process and reduce the number of steps in which method error can be introduced. With each unnecessary process step, the reliability of the controls decreases by a power of two. For example, in a pass/fail visual attribute technique that has not been carefully constructed and involving a serial five-step process, the resulting reliability of the overall system is $0.50 \times 0.50 \times 0.50 \times 0.50 \times 0.50$ or about 3 per cent. In other words, the likelihood of being able to reliably release good product to market by this system design is poor.

By reducing the measurement points or increasing the accuracy of the method, or a combination of the two, the system reliability is increased and the user starts to approach the desired state, QbD.

USE METHODS WITH DIFFERENT BASIS IN SCIENCE

The broad array of tools available for quality control method design is a strong characteristic of the pharmaceutical industry. The process management designer should take full advantage of this. Tools available include physical measures, such as weight or time; instrumental methods such as high-performance liquid chromatography (HPLC), gas chromatography (GC) or ultraviolet (UV); chemical methods, such as heavy metal testing or presence of chloride; quantitative methods, such as acid-base titrations or potentiometric titrations; point of use methods such as in-line moisture sensing and NIR; and sorting methods, such as sieve analysis and laser particle diffraction. Method deployment within the process must incorporate dissimilar methods to view the consistency of the process from different perspectives.

Consider the following example: a company must rely on chemical, physical, microbiological and human sensory testing methods to affirm the integrity of the components delivered to goods inwards. This is the only means to establish purity, identity and consistency with expectations. If one element is bypassed, the risk of failure is added to the next steps in the process.

Next, dispensing at the pharmacy depends primarily on gravimetric measurement, in other words weighing, to allocate proper amounts of the material. If the density has not been considered at goods inwards, the consistency of granulation is put at risk.

The same is true for particle size. Blending dynamics is usually fixed and therefore will reveal material dynamics that are beyond the capability of a laboratory sample to detect. By maintaining a 'fixed' process step, the underlying root cause of variability, a subtle change in the raw materials, is exposed. It would be a mistake to alter the blending process parameters since this would only obscure and hide the underlying root cause.

As the blend moves through the process and is compressed into a tablet, chemistry is again required to determine purity and content against known product standards. This is not testing quality into the product; rather, it is applying the proper methodology in an appropriate manner. As we shall see in later chapters, it is questionable whether or not it is good process management to evaluate 100 per cent of the granulation in an effort to predict the future. Predicting the future of a real-life process is risky and overly complex.

START BY USING SIMPLE METHODS AND TECHNIQUES CORRECTLY

One theme of this book is the detrimental effect the Industrial Revolution has had on effective process management as developed by artisan craftsmen. This is especially true in the pharmaceutical industry, where commodity process models are not appropriate for the nature of the business. The only way to overcome this hurdle is to become familiar with the proper application of process methods. Two sets of techniques with seven tools in each group, as shown in Table 5.6, will provide nearly all of the techniques necessary to design and manage a process correctly.

The seven basic tools are already often used by employees in the quality department. However, everyone should be able to use these tools to create an efficient and effective organization. The older process design tools go back to

Table 5.6   Tools of process management methods

Seven basic 'quality control tools'	Seven new process management tools
Control charts	Five whys (from Kiazen)
Histograms	Affinity diagrams
Scatter diagrams	Force field analysis
Check sheets	Matrix diagrams
Cause-and-effect diagrams	Nominal group technique
Pareto charts	Brainstorming
Flow diagrams	Relations diagram (Fishbone)

the 1920s and the work done at Western Electric, Bell Laboratories by Dr Walter Shewhart. In the 1960s Japanese quality experts expanded the process design techniques to include visual methods. The premise is simple: design the system to a specified statistical model and incorporate simple techniques to assess the validity of the process as it operates.

This view is so basic that many pharmaceutical companies overlook proven, simple techniques because they are either not 'exciting' or lack 'research' to prove their effectiveness. Process management is not exciting in itself, except when sustained and predictable profits result. The seven basic tools are used to capture and process data in a mathematical sense. The seven new tools are used for revealing patterns or developing sound root cause evaluations.

These techniques, which are described in full in Chapter 13, should be used in combination, along with the diverse techniques mentioned in the previous section.

Conclusion

The current state of methods used in pharmaceutical processes can be summed up as too much or too little method accuracy and precision at the incorrect control points. Pharmaceutical processes need to find the middle ground between the extremes that prevail today.

On the one hand, using methods of attribute are quick and easy, but lack sufficient precision and accuracy to be meaningful to process management. On the other hand, technology such as NIR is seen as a 'universal method' that is applicable to any conceivable application. It is not.

Methods suffer from a number of challenges that can easily be fixed to result in better and more consistent results. The prescription for improvement includes the following:

- focus on proper application of methods;

- build method redundancy into the system as part of routine operating;

- use different methods to create cross-checking of test results;

- simplify systems by reducing steps and aligning method precision to the criticality of decision-making resulting from the data;

- minimize the number of significant figures capable of the method.

Remember, process management *methods* allow the 'mind of the process' – *man* – to relate to the 'voice of the process' – *machine* – a language that readily speaks to and affirms the consistency of the output product.

6

Materials: The Life-Blood of the Process

A laborer no longer makes whole articles. He receives raw materials, puts
his touch on them, and passes them to another worker in the series.
(John Bates Clark, 1847–1938, American neoclassical economist)

Introduction

Control of materials has changed and requires attention in order to achieve a robust process model. Materials are now sourced globally for economic advantage, but in doing so their characteristics are often altered in unpredictable and sometimes deleterious ways. A brief review of a newspaper or internet newscast often turns up a new compromise to product safety and efficacy as a consequence of poor materials and lack of supplier oversight.

Consider the problems across the pharmaceutical industry from pallets contaminated by fungicide (Sharfstein 2010) to heparin contaminated with over-sulphated chondroitin (FDA 2008). The pharmaceutical industry is not alone in this respect. Mattel, the children's toy manufacturer, conducted a major recall for toys containing unsafe levels of lead in 2007 (Story 2007). Later in 2007, melamine was discovered in animal food, sadly through the death of pets (FDA 2007a).

The purpose of material control in design of process is to identify, characterize and standardize properties that are determined to be critical to consistent end-product performance. Assessment should include both chemical and physical properties. Current guidance for drug products (FDA 1987a) and drug substances (FDA 2004) discuss the topic in the respective sections on materials and material control. Special attention is given in the excipient and Active Pharmaceutical Ingredient (API) sections to providing meaningful physiochemical characteristics of the material to establish a profile of both safety attributes – purity and identity – and process sensitive physical attributes such as particle size, shape and morphology.

The process developer must strive to identify the critical controls for both the excipient and the API. From a process management perspective, lack of control over incoming materials cannot be remedied later in the manufacturing process. In practice, however, project timeline constraints frequently preclude adequate physical characterization beyond compendia monographs. To go further may require additional validation of the methods, and many fast-track firms may not have the resources to do this in a sophisticated way. As a result, post-approval *processing controls* may be sacrificed on the assumption that compendia requirements are adequate and sufficient to ensure final product consistency. The process designer must always consider whether the proposed process control is sensitive to physical characteristics that are not defined by the specification.

Compromises to the Material Selection Process

Three business changes have hindered the ability to select and manage materials used in pharmaceutical processes:

- materials are no longer selected by process operators who possess knowledge and understanding of the effects of physical variability on finished product consistency;

- global supply sources have introduced unforeseeable variability that is uncharacteristic of locally purchased materials;

- global procurement has resulted in unanticipated and increased risks of tampering, adulteration and contamination.

MATERIAL SELECTION

Artisans still select materials for their work by using a number of different techniques. They primarily rely on the senses such as sight and feel to choose the appropriate qualities such as colour or texture.

Pharmaceutical manufacturing with extreme degrees of specialization no longer engages the user in the material selection process. Specialized business functions such as purchasing, seeking to optimize profits, will search the world to obtain the lowest price on procured materials that meet the requirements in compendia.

Generalized standards such as compendia make an excellent starting point in the selection of materials based on legal considerations and chemical purity. In this approach, the chemistry laboratory often evaluates three lots of materials on the assumption that the samples accurately represent the supplier's process capability. The laboratory testing approach is economical but often assumes the proposed material will have exactly the same physical characteristics as the approved material.

One way to verify this assumption is to produce three lots of the finished product at risk at full manufacturing scale. This approach would be an excellent way to demonstrate material performance and affirm the laboratory testing results, but this is a costly way to involve the user. If the materials are not comparable, release to market would be questionable. The process management design team must also consider how the material will be used in a specific drug product formulation and involve the user.

UNFORESEEN VARIABILITY OF QUALITY ATTRIBUTES

In Chapter 4 we discussed measures that are essential to ensure the consistency of materials and accuracy of system controls. The current strategy of global sourcing in many cases works against the consistency of materials and predictable process output. Important attributes beyond the purity and chemical characteristics of the material, often outside of compendia considerations, can be introduced.

The unique chemistry of the local materials, environmental pollutants, increased handling and logistical issues or in-transit temperature variation are some of the factors causing unpredictable variability that can be introduced and can alter material performance characteristics when used in large-scale production. All process steps are interdependent. Slight changes in materials may have significant unforeseen consequences during full-scale production. Several real-life examples of material performance issues are given at the end of this chapter.

INCREASED RISK OF ADULTERATION

Consider some of the current issues faced by the industry. Unfortunately, pharmaceutical products are easily copied and harmful lookalike components can be introduced to the product quite easily. Pharmaceutical products are profitable and can be easy targets for counterfeiting and sale through illegal channels (WHO 2010). The following examples are tragic, all the more so for not being unique:

- adulteration of heparin: chemically similar materials derived from pig leg cartilage were added to the more costly heparin, which is derived from pig intestine mucosa (FDA 2007b);

- substitution of diethylene glycol for glycerol: diethylene glycol is a commonly used ingredient of antifreeze in automobile cooling systems. US drug laws were amended in 1938 as a consequence of human deaths in 1937, but the compound continues to harm patients: Haiti in 1995–1996, India in 1998 and Panama in 2006 (Rentz et al. 2008);

- bovine spongiform encephalopathy (BSE) or transmittable spongiform encephalopathy (TSE) are health risks relating to materials derived from animal sources that are fed with the ruminant parts of other animals. The risk to human health takes long periods of time to show up (FDA 2011).

Identification of source country is a newer consideration in comparison to diethylene glycol substitution but still reflects concerns over the control of materials. Lack of attention to supply chain issues as costs are reduced by aggressive expense management introduces opportunities for criminal activity. Process design must incorporate failsafe, low cost solutions to ensure safety and efficacy

Necessary Process Characterizations for Materials

There are five considerations of material process design analysis in order to provide a complete assessment of material needs:

- physiochemical characteristics;

- shipping, handling and storage conditions;

- sampling plan design and special techniques;

- manufacturing conditioning steps; and

- supplier's process controls.

PHYSIOCHEMICAL CHARACTERISTICS

Physicochemical characteristics include particle shape, particle mass, electrostatic interaction and absorbency. Physical attributes play a predominant role in achieving consistent process performance. Many times, simple physical characterization is not adequately understood or is overlooked in order to meet shortened time lines. The adoption of compendia grade material ensures that minimum standards are met, but in our experience, minimum standards will not effectively ensure proper process controls.

The worst case scenario, from a post-approval perspective, occurs when product development samples come from one of the extreme ends of the supplier's normal process variability range. A member of the quality unit with a basic understanding of development pharmaceutics should be able to identify these conditions during a supplier qualification audit.

Supplier variability can have a dramatic effect on post-approval manufacturing. Sporadic problems during in-process testing, release testing or production processing may cause lost production batches. This is especially true for solid dose products. Random and sporadic quality deviations are the most difficult type of process problems to investigate properly and adequately. Often the root cause comes down to a best guess based on experience, especially if the supplier's process is not well understood. The company can be certain that the problem will occur repeatedly, often without warning, until the physical attributes of the supplier's process are well understood.

SHIPPING, HANDLING AND STORAGE CONDITIONS

The process design analysis should assess the supplier controls, trucking line handling, temperature and humidity controls, storage configurations, length of storage time and the ability of the material to bear top-load weight. Often these realities of the supply chain are not considered important to process success. Consequently, the material may be held in a condition that can alter the physical characteristics. The result would be compromised process performance during manufacturing.

The appropriate controls may include limitations on the material storage racking for heat-sensitive materials, for example, store no higher than 3 metres (10 feet) from the floor. For smaller purchases of materials, the company may need to consider dedicated transport – a more expensive ordering practice – to ensure material integrity. From a process management perspective, the incremental shipping cost may be small compared to the cost of delays caused by OOS investigations.

SAMPLING PLAN DESIGN AND SPECIAL TECHNIQUES

Sampling technique has a significant impact on the testing results and the final accept or reject decision of the quality unit. Consider the example of micronized steric acid where particle size specification is a requirement of acceptance testing. The challenge is to select a representative sample to demonstrate proper processing by the supplier. The sampler must identify a proper location to ensure that the material is representative of the whole batch for the test parameter.

On the one hand, if the sample is taken from the inside corner of the bag, particles may be compressed and may not represent the true particle distribution. The result is an OOS result for particle size. On the other hand, if the sample is taken from the interior of the bag, the material may pass acceptance testing but may result in processing issues if large particles created by rough handling are present and are not broken up prior to use. In either case, process controls are compromised. Only a thorough material analysis, which includes persons experienced in processing use evaluation, would raise this issue.

We endorse the application of rapid technologies, but not in an indiscriminate manner. An experienced chemist must be included in the evaluation of materials should the discussion progress to use of NIR spectroscopy. Process design management must give attention to new variable factors inherent to NIR spectroscopy and the associated risks of indiscriminate application as a universal tool for material identity confirmation.

Experienced operators, chemists and other staff directly involved in the approval or handling of materials are an untapped resource to identify minor, often subtle differences in the properties of materials that can and do play a major role in process variability. The variability of incoming materials serves to increase the complexity of managing the process at later stages.

MANUFACTURING CONDITIONING STEPS

Another consideration of the *material* element of process design is special processing requirements. If handling, shipping and storage can change important physical characteristics of a material, a process control mechanism must be placed immediately prior to use. This is the only certain means by which the process can achieve uniformity.

By including manufacturing handling experience in the material needs analysis, many of the problems related to storage, shipping and handling are rendered moot. The same holds true for acceptance sampling. It may be better to accept the particle size value on the Certificate of Analysis and perhaps a particle histogram distribution rather than risk generating an OOS result for particle size testing.

SUPPLIER'S PROCESS CONTROLS

The final consideration of material process analysis is supplier process control and management. Materials that consistently meet a supplier's statistical design criteria provide confidence in use by the manufacturer in two ways:

- the process was designed with care and due diligence;

- analytical data verify the supplier's claims of consistency.

One approach to determining the supplier's capability is to request a statistical process profile for a year's worth of production data. This provides the process design team with the chance to observe the effects of seasonal change, among other points, on the physical characteristics of the material. These data should be supplemented with a site audit to confirm the level of GMP diligence. The result is a robust analysis of the supplier's capability and a complete evaluation of material requirements.

Specific Examples

MAGNESIUM STEARATE

Magnesium stearate is a commonly used lubricant added for ease of processing during tablet compression or encapsulation. Magnesium stearate from a practical, non-technical perspective is grease in solid form. In addition to routine chemical analysis and surface area evaluation, compendia acceptance limits allow a relatively large amount of impurities (about 10 per cent).

Two groups – the laboratory dissolution chemists and the manufacturing granulator or tablet press operators – are likely to have valuable information about critical material specifications to be considered from a process design perspective. This experience must be used as part of the system controls for materials.

Laboratory experience gained during testing may reveal differences in material texture or dissolution performance. In manufacturing, the tablet press operators and granulation technicians could add insight into the handling, dispensing and storage of the material, which is likely to provide clues about inconsistency of particle size or morphology issues. The process design issues to be considered may include additional analysis not described in compendia or special handling to deagglomerate particles prior to use. This knowledge can be invaluable when setting robust, accurate process controls.

STEARIC ACID

Another commonly used tablet lubricant is stearic acid. Like magnesium stearate, stearic acid is used to keep powder blends from sticking to tablet punches during compression. Stearic acid can be micronized and may be more suitable than magnesium stearate when fine particles are necessary.

Like magnesium stearate, stearic acid can compress under its own weight; as such, shipping, storage temperature and storage duration become important controls. A development customer requested micronized stearic acid from an overseas source. The need was minor, but the only container available was a 25 kg polylined kraft paper bag. From the process design perspective, purchasing a single bag of micronized stearic acid from Southeast Asia and having it shipped by air to the manufacturing site in summertime was likely to alter the physical characteristics. The extent of the problem became evident when the container was sampled for particle size analysis. The bag's content was essentially a solid block and could only be sampled as a lump. Process design teams should have considered the effects of shipping and handling on the material.

Actions Required for Material Process Management

Having defined the current situation and given examples of the implications of not managing materials appropriately, we will now look at a range of actions needed to align materials with process requirements.

INSTITUTE A ROBUST SUPPLIER AUDIT PROGRAMME

Starting around 2007, the world witnessed raw material supply chains that can only be described as out of control. Beginning with melamine in pet foods and extending to pharmaceutical and food preparation ingredients, globally sourced materials have been adulterated and contaminated with toxic materials that have resulted in death and injury. The presence of such compounds evades detection by minimal, non-specific material identification techniques.

Poorly designed or superficial supplier audit programmes only open the door for further abuse by introducing a false sense of security. In our experience, a good audit programme is one in which the auditors are highly educated, greatly experienced and adequately funded. Supplier audit cannot be conducted from the head office using only a paper survey. Audit programmes cannot be designed by someone without a deep level of experience and understanding. Supplier audits are an essential cost of preventing future problems. Additionally, they can also be used to identify opportunities to minimize manufacturing site handling costs.

Audits should not be a 'tick box' exercise. The auditor must understand how materials are to be used in the manufacturing process and be able to identify significant differences between the supplier's control strategy and the manufacturing product control strategy. Bridging gaps between control plans is a positive gain in terms of process controls. These gains must be captured in financially meaningful ways and will be discussed later in this book.

SELECT SUPPLIERS ON THE BASIS OF PROCESS CONSISTENCY

As far back as the late 1950s, W. Edwards Deming was endorsing single source strategy. Unspoken in the discussion was the fact that a single source minimizes the variability of incoming materials. Purchasing on price alone has been shown to be negatively correlated to product processing performance. We have seen, over time, a shift in sourcing from historically leading supply companies in the so-called developed countries to less well-known companies in developing countries. At the same time, according to the regulators, the number of recalls and product problems has increased significantly. For example, the FDA is preparing to issue guidance on supplier management to begin addressing what is considered to be a major problem. Simply put, less expensive materials are often lower in price for a good reason. From a process management perspective, low price and alternate supply sources do not ensure high efficiency in use. On many occasions the consequence is OOS test results for the finished product as the drug product process adjusts to the differences inherent to the new supplier.

DEVELOP SPECIAL MANUFACTURING CONTROLS WITH EXPERIENCED USER PARTICIPATION

Special manufacturing controls may be required in order to ensure that the physical characteristics of the material meet the specification requirements at the time of use. These special controls may include oven drying, sieving or other activities to ensure components are suitable at the time of use rather than at the time of receipt. Complementary acceptance tests must be additionally considered based upon the specific requirements of the process.

The natural tendency of materials to electrostatically adhere, agglomerate under their own weight during storage or absorb moisture over time is ever-present. Each component is different in this respect and must be assessed individually. While performing this step involves an additional labour cost, the savings will be realized by statistically consistent process performance. It is unlikely that mathematical modelling can fully predict the outcomes of storage effects. Process design requires the involvement of experienced manufacturing and quality personnel with knowledge of material texture variability to introduce the user perspective into the selection process and the determination of essential controls. Materials which require this kind of experienced evaluation include:

- micronized excipients that tend to agglomerate with storage, such as titanium dioxide;

- cellulose-based excipients, such as hydroxypropylcellulose, that can be found in fibrous and spherical forms. Further, cellulose-based materials tend to absorb and lose moisture over time and could change size slightly;

- lubricant materials with multiple particle sizes and shapes, such as magnesium stearate;

- active substances where particle size and shape are critical for sterile suspension or inhalation products.

Special handling, such as passing the material through a sieve screen immediately prior to dispensing, ensures that the particle characteristics remains within the appropriate range proven through validation study. The point of use of the material must be known and rationalized within the control strategy. Often experienced operators can tell stories of materials that must be deagglomerated – broken up – before use by hand or other means. The experienced dissolution chemist can speak about the dissolution test differences observed when small lumps of lubricant are present. Acceptance test results are unimportant if manufacturing process controls cannot ensure that materials will meet intended characteristics at the time of use, even if this means increased cost to condition materials prior to use.

CONFIRM THE VALIDITY OF THE SAMPLING PLAN

Sampling a starting material begins with an understanding of the supplier's process capability. From that understanding, the quality control and quality assurance measures can be rationally applied to generate the correct data and place the correct controls to the pharmaceutical process. All good sampling plans accomplish two goals:

- sample analysis is timely and relevant to decisions by the process operator;

- in the case of failure, the non-conforming materials can be effectively isolated and removed.

A well-designed process integrates effective acceptance sampling based on knowledge of the supplier's operation, aligned with production-critical controls. Manufacturing operations and the analytical laboratory must be coordinated in the control strategy.

The quality control samples convey limited information with respect to subtle nuances of material performance at the production scale. In taking samples from the process, it is important to know the purpose of the sample, whether it is for compliance or performance reasons. The quality control sampling plan must establish the sample size necessary to minimize the chance that sample data will lead to an incorrect conclusion. The material sample size should be able to quickly identify systemic quality problems and provide trustworthy data to assist the operator in isolating and fixing the problem.

BENCHMARK BEST PRACTICES OF SIMILAR INDUSTRIES

Best practices are not always found in the most obvious places. Benchmarking is a standard practice for identifying principles and techniques that serve as a foundation for new breakthroughs in thinking. It could be used to identify alternative considerations of material controls.

However, benchmarking is often driven by business 'buzz' rather than scientific need. Without a basis in science, significant risk to material consistency is introduced into the process design. Industries that are not at the forefront of business buzz can actually model and use best practices as these companies practice simple ways by which to get the job done. Effective benchmarking leads to lower regulatory burden, better scientific understanding and higher profits by optimal material qualification.

A comprehensive model for the pharmaceutical industry on the procurement of new materials can be found in the fragrance and flavour industries. The depth of scientific understanding that underlies fragrance component selection is seldom achieved by pharmaceutical API or excipient manufacturers. Information about the safety and consistency of material performance is obtained from a comprehensive, scientifically derived database that has been developed by industry trade groups and serves as a standard for all to use.

During the audit of a fragrance and flavour manufacturer, the scientific assessment of material characteristics was found to be a model of simplicity and effectiveness. Materials are primarily evaluated by physical constants, such as optical rotation, melting point and specific gravity, which are constant functions of a material's purity, among other characteristics. Extensive and costly laboratory preparation is not important as the samples are evaluated in a 'neat' (unprepared) state. Assessment of the finished product still relies on evaluation by a trained sensory panel as differences in odour of a complex system are still not quantifiable by sophisticated chemical techniques.

Conclusion

There are three points to be made with regard to the process control of materials:

- complying solely with compendia requirements and specifications does not ensure the success of a manufacturing process;

- the pharmaceutical manufacturer must select supply sources whose materials perform in a statistically consistent manner as they are processed;

- material characteristics must include 'common-sense' evaluation of handling and storage to assess the need for including special manufacturing controls to ensure that physical properties such as particle size remain consistent over time.

The immediate payback to the organization is a reduced level of problems during post-approval manufacturing. There may be supplemental benefits in that regulatory agencies may accept changes with reduced validation testing.

Component materials must be evaluated across the entire supply chain to guarantee proper controls and acceptance ranges. The analysis should include supplier control information, shipping and handling controls, sampling and acceptance activities and the final manufacturing processing.

When key controls are identified during development, these should be captured in a specification document to facilitate communication to purchasing and the quality unit. The final result of an effective material design analysis is robust process control.

Sampling considerations that play a major role in the effective characterization of component materials will be discussed further in other chapters. In summary, quality control and quality assurance sampling must be carefully applied to processes according to the process design. If not, the process data will be unusable for statistical management purposes. As a consequence, the manufacturer can only react when problems occur; this equates to 'testing quality into the product'.

7

Environment

A pessimist sees the difficulty in every opportunity; an optimist sees the opportunity in every difficulty.

(Winston Churchill, 1874–1965, British politician)

Introduction

The process elements discussed up to this point require a framework within which to operate and this is provided by the final process element: *environment*. Like so many businesses today, the global pharmaceutical industry is driven by economies of scale. We have seen an emphasis on low-cost, end-product-focused control strategies without regard to process design principles. The consequence is an increase in business chaos and turbidity as well as increased risk regarding predictable process performance. These challenges are increased by exposure to natural disasters, political instability, language barriers, dissimilar drug regulations and personnel management. The effort required to create a cohesive business framework is pushed even further by a number of factors: taxation laws, which encourage multinational firms to invest abroad under an economic development theme such as Puerto Rico in the 1970s; prediction of future earnings, which promotes short-term gains, often at the expense of long-term structure; and externally applied 'motivation' techniques to 'do more with less', such as multitasking. Finally, the historic security of long-term productive employment is all but gone due to mergers and acquisitions and the associated reduction in productive work staff.

The chief concern of the *environment* process element is to create a situation in which productivity provides the workforce with a meaningful voice in the design and execution of the process, thereby giving improved purpose to their activities.

There are two broad dimensions, both of which must be considered in order to properly align and optimize the *environment* element in support of the other four elements (*man, machine, method* and *material*):

- the physical environment of the manufacturing operation or scientific laboratories;

- the mental and intellectual environment that accompanies business strategy and the manner in which that strategy is implemented at the operations level.

The physical environment relates to the design, maintenance and control of process air and water; cleanliness and repair of equipment; consistency of power supply; and security of production activities. The requirements are established by local, regional or national laws and governmental oversight plus nature and climate. The physical environment also impacts on controls of machine performance, the precision of methods and the adequacy of storage of materials that are to be used in an approved process.

As understanding and knowledge of the health risks associated with a disease state increase, so does the understanding of the factors that can negatively influence successful outcomes from the medication. An example would be endotoxin levels contained in sterile drug products. Sterile life-saving drugs or admixtures could become lethal, even if they contain within-specification amounts of endotoxin, should they be administered to a neonate population (Garrett et al. 2002). Attention must be given to the systems and procedures of the production facility to ensure that intended user populations do not have special needs that can only be addressed during the design of the process and associated process controls.

The issues of the mental and intellectual environment are more subtle, but carry an equal or greater weight in the long-term success of the operation of the process. Pharmaceutical process operators and laboratory personnel develop a keen understanding of what works and what does not. At this point, a discriminating employee can identify potential problems from experience. Personnel are not intent on performing inferior work when hired. However, the spark of an enthusiastic new employee can be extinguished by a rigid and inflexible organization. As experience on the job increases, employees develop understanding that discriminates between what should be and what is. If the two are not aligned, process excellence can be greatly diminished.

The focus in the environment process evaluation revolves around the human interaction with machines, materials and methods during the course of routine processing operations. The demands placed on the employee must be aligned to the equipment capability or the method design. For example, if the manufacturing batch requires a high degree of precision or accuracy in the weighing of the active substance, the employee cannot be held accountable for poor results in the finished product when asked to use a balance which is incapable of achieving the desired precision of measurement. Likewise, the employee can in no way be held accountable for literally 'sleeping on the job' if an airborne drug substance is inhaled and accumulates at toxic levels in the body. As explained to one of us during facility orientation as a new employee in the early 1980s, respiratory protection had been introduced in that facility in the late 1970s following the discovery of a company employee 'napping' on a bench in the production area of a potent drug – the poor man had inhaled a toxic level of drug dust during routine production and nearly took a permanent nap. Similarly, a poorly configured process consisting of numerous steps and informational barriers will always be slow and incapable of optimal productive output. According to Deming (2000), exhortation will not overcome the systemic design issues.

What are the Challenges?

The design team faces five challenges associated with the *environment* process:

- extended chain of custody for materials;

- rapidly changing global regulatory expectations;

- merger and acquisition – chaos of size, culture and legacy processes;

- uncertainty of employment;

- business strategy based solely on elapsed time without regard to complexity.

EXTENDED CHAIN OF CUSTODY FOR MATERIALS

All process elements are intertwined, inseparable and interact in some manner. A change to one element will have an impact on one or more of the others, either immediately or at some point in the future – although the correlation between cause and effect could be difficult to establish. As components are sourced globally, the process design team must consider the impact of issues such as tampering, temperature controls, adulteration or other ways in which the materials, machines, methods and perhaps people are changed outside of the intended process requirements.

In the case of supplier changes, there is significant pressure in today's fast-paced economy to accept any and all deliveries with the promise of high-quality material. It is the obligation of the purchaser to verify the supplier claims – buyer beware. From the process perspective, a seemingly simple change could result in unanticipated influences on finished product quality that must become part of the design consideration.

From the perspective of the material element, for example, a substitute or replacement component may have a different particle size and crystal shape from those established over time as process-critical attributes. Shipping and handling conditions and controls would need to be defined and understood. If materials are light-sensitive, adequate protection has to be considered for the entire transit time. Seasonal considerations for shipping would need to be understood to prevent freezing or overheating during transit. Bioterrorism, tampering or substitution concerns might introduce the need to seal shipments with security tags. All of these points are to be considered in the design of the process.

A current industry trend is to use contract laboratory services, especially when samples are being provided from another country. The approval qualification of such a laboratory cannot be performed only as a paperwork exercise. The process design team must coordinate expert review of the potential new service provider to ensure that controls, training, insturmentation and the maintenance of analytical equipment meet expectations. Specialized testing qualifications should be incorporated into regulatory documentation for proper communication with regulatory agencies. A low-cost service may not guarantee the accuracy and precision of analytical work. Most importantly, the contract laboratory must be able to effectively troubleshoot and maintain their processes.

The environmental considerations for equipment must include the needs of use and how easily and safely the equipment can be cleaned and maintained. For example, does the equipment have the ability to control dust created during operations or does the process require an inert atmosphere to operate safely and precisely? Are hazardous solvents required for cleaning residual materials?

Finally, second- or third-tier suppliers may be used by the primary supplier and result in unanticipated variation outside of the normally designed process. It is important to understand this relationship to determine if the primary supplier is actually able to produce a consistent product.

RAPIDLY CHANGING GLOBAL REGULATORY EXPECTATIONS

Global pharmaceutical regulation, including application submissions, post-approval changes or lifecycle management issues, has not historically been considered to be part of a process design effort, but it is time to make this change. Post-market change has a strong correlation with continuous improvement efforts as process understanding increases. But even seemingly obvious improvements can be tied up in review for years in some countries and approved almost immediately in others. If company policy is to only implement a change following the final approval, the effect of widely differing approval times is a delay in proposed process improvements. Alternatively, staggered implementation will result in difficult logistical coordination and increased compliance risk if the change is implemented approval by approval.

In the latter case, the manufacturer is obliged to maintain parallel manufacturing processes, one for approved changes and the other for the pending changes, to ensure the correct product is available and shipped to the correct country. This is an obvious increase in the cost of manufacture.

Table 7.1 provides a partial list of organizations that are involved in the conceptualization of drug safety regulations for new and existing pharmaceutical processes, and shows just how specialized the regulatory approval process is becoming. While the global community strives for greater standardization and harmonization, the opposite often occurs as scientific methods are over-analysed into a state of paralysis, both technically and economically.

On the surface, continuous improvement seems to be a natural outcome of new understanding gained during processing. The premise of PAT is largely based on this view. In practice the dissimilar regulatory environment makes improvement difficult and costly to effect. In volume terms, most of the world's drugs have been marketed for years and were developed to the

Table 7.1   Organizations influencing pharmaceutical environment and process management

Organization	Geographical coverage
Agência National de Vigilência Sanitária (ANVISA)	Brazil
Asia-Pacific Economic Cooperation (APEC)	21 countries
European Medicines Agency (EMA)	27 Member States
Food and Drug Administration (FDA)	USA
Global Harmonization Task Force (GHTF)	EU, USA, Canada, Australia, Japan
Health Canada (HC)	Canada
International Conference on Harmonization (ICH)	EU, USA, Japan
Pan American Health Organization (PAHO)	40 countries
Pharmaceutical Inspection Co-operation Scheme (PIC/S)	30+ members
Southern African Development Community (SADC)	15 countries
World Health Organization (WHO)	The entire world

scientific standards of the time. Bringing science to contemporaneous levels is costly and, in a number of cases, may be unnecessary. Often the safety and efficacy profile and use risk are well understood, established and documented, even though the specific mechanism of action is not precisely understood. The key for the process designer is to be broadly aware of the concepts and practices of global regulations to accommodate the post-approval regulatory environment. There is immediate 'return on investment' for understanding process excellence concepts.

MERGER AND ACQUISITION: CHAOS OF SIZE, CULTURE AND LEGACY PROCESSES

Processes operate within relevant ranges of design. Process systems respond only as fast as the constraint (bottleneck) allows. Mergers and acquisitions have the effect of altering the relevant range of design rapidly and consequently the capacity of the newly merged system. The strategy used most frequently is the downsizing of staff, buildings and equipment. We have observed that the chaos accompanying increased organizational size leads to the Gestalt effect, in that the human mind is not capable of ordering or understanding chaos and therefore hesitates. At the time when decisive and purposeful actions must be taken to establish new and relevant processes, the rapidly shifting priorities can stall and paralyse large numbers of employees.

Prior to the mass adoption of computing, mergers and acquisitions were much easier since the companies had only to deal with hard copy paper files. Institutional memory was easy to research assuming that paper copies were filed routinely. Today, much of the critical information is found on digital media. Media systems in the pharmaceutical industry are almost exclusively customized to the unique requirements of a company. Hence, following a merger or acquisition, in addition to merging people systems, data systems also have to be integrated.

This is not a small or trivial exercise. The concern for process management is obscured purpose or data integrity erosion that undermines the ability of the process to perform properly. A significant amount of time can be required for employees to climb the steep learning curve of understanding each other's process design configuration as well as the meaning of the data used to manage process results. Should the company choose to delay the integration of systems or change in a piecemeal fashion, chaos-induced paralysis can result at the operating level. Business results following mergers are mixed, but it is generally believed that on the whole, mergers and acquisitions are not beneficial to shareholders or employees affected by the purchase (Pautler 2003).

With international mergers, another environmental consideration must be factored into the process design – culture. Culturally related issues cover both social mores and conceptual understanding of the legal framework on which many drug laws depend. For example, Asian cultural mores are often based upon trust that is established over many years. There is additionally deference to older persons as a sign of respect for the wisdom of age. The process design team must factor in adequate time during implementation for international teams to develop mutual trust to ensure a sound process foundation is in place. In our experience, it can take up to five years for a subsidiary operation to develop the scientific and regulatory trust of the internationally headquartered development team.

In terms of conceptual understanding, the greatest hurdles we see are:

- the regulatory concept of risk of harming the patient if the pharmaceutical product is produced incorrectly;

- 'perfect' documentation as the benchmark of excellence.

Risk management surrounds the proof of equivalence between scientifically based process data and safety and efficacy profiles determined in clinical study. The two are sometimes difficult to correlate and this results in many 'what if' discussions. What appears to be a positive process improvement can lead to unexpected results in product performance. In one case an exercise to improve the impurity profile of the active drug substance resulted in reduced bioavailability to the patient as the molecule converted from a less stable crystal form to a more stable crystal form, which was difficult for the body to absorb.

The other concept that must be factored into the process design revolves around the misconception that regulatory inspectors expect to see perfect documents. Actually, those we know would prefer to see an effective system with occasional errors that are properly resolved rather than to have perfect documents that fail to reveal the true challenges of the manufacturing system.

Finally, legacy business rules and practices of merged companies can often lead to problems when there are significant differences in the regulatory and quality strategies. One company may follow an 'all-inclusive' strategy where every document related to the process is provided to the regulatory agency. The belief is that the company can never be criticized for failing to inform the authorities of all aspects of the process. Another company may not provide such a level of detail.

Both approaches have serious drawbacks for the process manager and the process integrity. In the case of too much information, every trivial alteration of documents results in regulatory communication, a slow process at best since the regulator is left to sort out critical process parameters from the trivial administrative directives. This is analogous to the fable 'The Boy Who Cried Wolf'. The other extreme leads to great levels of regulatory risk due to the lack of detail required to demonstrate consistency. No one is ever certain what has or has not been communicated and it is likely that changes can occur and finished products can be distributed without the implication of the change on the patient being assessed.

UNCERTAINTY OF EMPLOYMENT

The insecure and transitory nature of employment today has resulted in many of the business survival issues faced in the pharmaceutical industry. As late as the 1980s, pharmaceutical companies often hired with the intent of employment until retirement. However, as technology became more sophisticated, process operations became more dependent on process automation techniques. The cost of production began to increase as the line between theory and practice became blurred. Not only was equipment more costly but the products were more potent and sophisticated. Increases in cost were inevitable.

The minimum academic requirements for new employees rose steadily as basic academic research shifted into industrial research and development laboratories. In the authors' view, history suggests that much of the preference for advanced degrees stemmed legally from the 1962 change in the US drug laws, in which efficacy was added to the burden of proof that was to be submitted to the FDA. Internationally, the Helsinki Declaration carries the concepts of safety, informed consent and ethical practices into research processes. These two standards of safety and efficacy were rightfully enacted to ensure no repeats of events such as the thalidomide tragedy.

Regulatory requirements continued to be compliance-driven until the start of the twenty-first century, when discussion at the FDA and other regulatory agencies turned from compliance to process management. Along the way, mergers and acquisitions created significant business pressure to deliver double-digit returns. The result was 'employment at will' – the mutual lack of obligations of the company or employee for lifelong employment. Psychological theory suggests that people thrive in an environment in which they feel valued and can count on a stable and fulfilling career. It is critical to ensure supervisory leadership establishes a positive environment in the process system.

Early in the twentieth century, human engineering studies, the forerunners of industrial engineering, were conducted by Harvard Professor Elton Mayo (1949) at the Hawthorne Works of the Western Electric Company. His aim was to discover the factors underlying improvements in productivity. Starting with a baseline of 'completed units per day', various environmental factors were changed to study the impact upon productivity.

The study demonstrated that workers excel when supervisory management creates an attentive process environment that is not constantly being altered in random ways such as continuous interruptions, also known as multitasking. Uninterrupted work process rhythm within a well-defined process framework, rather than multitasking, is key to process productivity. The conclusions of this experiment still stand today and must be considered in the process design through the environmental element.

BUSINESS STRATEGY BASED SOLELY ON ELAPSED TIME WITHOUT REGARD TO COMPLEXITY

Intellectual considerations encompassing the environment process design consider how personnel have access to and use the tools to manage their areas of responsibility. Tools are more than computers; they include information that should be readily accessible and available for use when needed without devoting time to seeking and finding it. All processes should be developed within well-defined process boundaries. For example, specifications provide a point of reference to assess whether or not the process performed as designed. Data outside of the boundaries of the specification suggest that the process was off-target or too variable and should be investigated. Data within the historically generated statistical range and within the specification boundaries provide a high degree of confidence that the product meets the design criteria. The personnel on the 'frontline' of the process must be able to quickly determine which case applies. If the data are truly aberrant, then time must be allowed for a meaningful evaluation to be performed. This process cannot be rushed or forced to meet arbitrarily short time lines. This is not to say that time to completion is unimportant, but rather, if the issue is complex, that a superficial investigation ensures that a similar event will occur again.

A tell-tale sign that insufficient design consideration has been given to the environmental portion of a process is the frequency of manufacturing investigations or laboratory OOS investigations. In our experience frequent investigations can truly be considered 'testing quality into the product' and should not be mistaken for the use of chemical techniques to evaluate product characteristics that cannot be determined in any other manner.

Solutions

Now that we have touched on the primary issues relating to properly configuring the environment element of process design, we will look at the recommended ways in which any business can overcome these issues.

MAP THE PROCESS ACROSS THE SUPPLY CHAIN

The old adage 'a picture is worth a thousand words' is important for the team responsible for developing a process or assessing existing processes. The process design team is more likely to use a flow-chart – see Chapter 13 – rather than a picture, but the important point is to accurately convey the manner in which the process is intended to operate (if new) or how it is presently operating (if a legacy system). The flow-chart should be a cross-functional style where the process flows from the top of the sheet to the bottom and from left to right to show interactions between business units and different departments.

The flow-chart can be noted with standard terms identified by the manufacturer, but at a minimum should show where and by whom products are made and packaged; where products are tested for release and stability; who is supplying the drug substance and excipient materials; and, finally, who is responsible for transportation and logistics. The latter should include the party responsible for contracting and coordinating logistics pick-up and delivery schedules. The final version of the flow-chart may be intimidating and unbelievable, but will provide the first steps towards simplification to reduce the cost of handling.

ADOPT HIGH-LEVEL PROCESS SUMMARIES AND MODULAR DOCUMENTATION

One of the easiest solutions to regulatory complexity is to adopt a simple summary table of significant process information. The idea is to summarize, in five pages or less, the principal process design requirements for the purpose of quickly and accurately orienting new employees or understanding the thinking that went into the first generation process.

The summary can form the basis of developing regulatory method or process summaries in which critical-to-quality points are separated from ordinary and routine controls. The Annual Report Guidance issued by the FDA (1994) provides a general model of the approach. The content of the method or process summary should be modified to include process design information related to the five process elements: *man, machine, method, material* and *environment*. It is best to incorporate a principle-driven summary rather than specifics associated with a particular machine or method. For example, if the machine is a brand A High-Performance Liquid Chromatograph (HPLC), then the reference should speak to the characteristics that would apply to this brand as well as equal competing brands. The summary would contain the regulatory content in the first module; the GMP control document would configure the second module; and history of change and approval would be in the third module. An example of such a document is provided the Appendix.

ESTABLISH ROUTINE PROCESS RISK EVALUATIONS

Kaizen watching, described in *Kaizen: The Key to Japan's Competitive Success* (Imai 1986), is a technique that was introduced into the quality toolbox in the last half of the twentieth century. The observations made in Kaizen watching can be valuable as risk-based evaluations of any of the process elements. The principle is to create a 'fresh eyes' view of the organization using experienced employees to assess similar work processes at a sister location. In effect, Kaizen watching is a continuous audit of the consistency of application of the work process using the expert understanding of employees who routinely perform the work.

The value to the process design and management is to identify the obvious, often overlooked differences between process practice within the same organization. Additionally, implementation must be strictly focused on improving process performance and design rather than finding fault or criticizing the process under review. The results of Kaizen watching often reveal the path towards best practice.

HARMONIZE TOWARDS ONE BEST PRACTICE

The differences between processes practised at different sites revealed by the Kaizen watching exercise often reveal no-cost, rapid-to-implement opportunities for improving process consistency. In theory, where two or more sites produce identical products, they should maintain the same controls and collect similar data. However, over time, changes occur for any number of reasons and if these have not been carefully coordinated, they may result in differences that are distinguishable by customers in the end product. When best practice is identified, the techniques should be deployed as an improvement project and captured in the institutional memory, SOPs. For example, by creating a high-level summary of key elements and making this available from a centrally located access point, misperceptions are minimized or eliminated.

Part of the harmonization effort is to introduce more sensitive measures of the control system to ensure that slight changes do not allow the system to drift off-target between sites.

INCREASE PROCESS MEASUREMENT SENSITIVITY

Risk analysis using the 'fresh eyes' observation approach is an important way to identify and direct improvement efforts. Such observations point out areas where existing controls are insensitive or include multiple control points within one broad measure. In the latter case, this often results in process drift which creates unique challenges to lifecycle management improvement. In order to counteract such process drift, the sensitivity of the controls should be increased by subdividing the process element into meaningful subsections.

An example of a broadly applied measure without adequate sensitivity is the final laboratory release test for content uniformity. Without measures of consistency during pharmacy dispensing, batching and blending and dose manufacture, an analytical test that reveals homogeneity problems is difficult if not impossible to investigate for a true root cause. If the pharmaceutical process is tablet compression, powder blend performance tests may be considered. Alternatively, at pharmacy weighing, a record is made of the physical appearance and texture of the material. The subprocess information helps to decompress the problem into more fertile problem-solving areas.

Consider the example of an audit of a contract tablet manufacturer for problems of tablet friability and hardness controls. The control data showed the powder blend fed inconsistently, with variable weight and hardness. However, the test results met specifications and the tablets were released to the customer. It was during unit dose packaging that the friability problem was revealed. The solution was to improve the handling sensitivity of the feed by using a newly qualified force frame feeder. Granulation flow problems were handled more efficiently and friability loss was reduced from >4 per cent to <1 per cent.

FACILITATE INDIVIDUAL PARTICIPATION

The 'fresh eyes' approach means personal involvement. When participation is likely to result in fewer job hassles for the employee, word of one or two successes will result in the level of active participation increasing dramatically. Without calling the technique a quality programme, continuous improvement expectations are automatically infused into the process design. PAT tools and techniques, such as Design of Experiment (DOE), if used during post-approval as well as development activities, will clarify and distinguish the significance of critical quality control points in a meaningful way. The early data generated from improvement approaches can add clarity and focus to research projects as well as post-approval maintenance and operational improvement efforts. However, it is important to keep the improvements within the relevant range of the process control so that the added effort of incremental improvement is not lost to the infinite cost of perfection.

Conclusion

In conclusion, the *environment* element of process design establishes a mental and physical framework in which the business can operate efficiently and profitably. Care must be given to consider the impact of changes to other system elements and how they may show up when least expected and in possibly adverse ways. The environment frames personal responsibility and accountability for the other four elements. If the environment is one of blame and fault-finding, the *man* element suffers degraded performance. If the *machine* operator is not involved in the selection and design of equipment, there is no personal commitment to overcoming operating challenges with creative thinking. When *materials* are purchased without seeking knowledgeable input from the staff who appreciate the details of handling, storage or dispensing challenges, an opportunity is lost to achieve process excellence. Finally, if the *methods* used to evaluate the process are not adequate to accurately assess the process control point, seemingly good decisions will lead to poor results. Processes are interdependent and rely on environmental assessment to establish the horizontal connections that keep business moving forwards.

PART III

Effective Pharmaceutical Process Design and Management

8

Changing the Way We Think

If you want to change the culture, you will have to start by changing the organization.

(Mary Douglas, 1921–2007, British anthropologist)

Introduction

When we started working in manufacturing, there used to be a belief – both on the part of management and staff – that process operators should 'hang their brains on their coat pegs' as they entered the factory. In other words, managers were paid to think, while operators were paid to do what they were told. It was hardly surprising that this engendered an atmosphere of 'us' and 'them' and a disconnect between the process results and the management expectations. If something went wrong, it wasn't the operators' fault; they were just doing what they were told.

In order to bring about effective process management, it is necessary to convert all the 'doers' into 'thinkers' as well. In fact, since the doers are the process experts, it stands to reason that they should be the prime thinkers or problem-solvers. How many times have process operators, faced with an insoluble problem or an ineffective process, been heard to say 'well, if they'd asked me, I could have told them'?

This chapter looks at the culture change needed to turn everyone into problem-solvers.

Methods of Involvement

One of the early ways of involving operators in the management of a company was via the Suggestion Scheme. Popular in the 1960s and 1970s, this was a way in which employees could – anonymously if they wished – make suggestions which, if approved, were acted on by management. There were one or two well-publicized successes, such as the employee who supposedly saved a matchbox manufacturer huge amounts by suggesting the strike paper be applied to one side rather than both sides of the box. However, in most cases, suggestions related to non-process activities, such as holidays or the placement of water coolers.

In the 1980s, when there was much excitement about the 'new' concepts of Total Quality Management (TQM) and World Class Manufacturing (WCM), many companies introduced a number of different types of quality teams as the way of harnessing the expertise of the operators.

The most well known of these was the Quality Circle, in which the team was set up at the behest of management and provided with a facilitator trained in the tools and techniques of problem-solving. Team members usually came from the same production area and the team leader might be a supervisor or an operator. The teams identified the problem(s) they wished to work on, collected data and carried out analyses to determine the best solutions. Typically, these problems would be ones that impacted primarily on the department where the team worked. The solutions would then be implemented by the team members, support staff such as maintenance engineers, or managers as appropriate. As problems were solved, there would be an element of celebration. In one of the companies in which we worked, the team was taken out to dinner by the divisional manager.

A variation on this was the Quality Task Team, set up at the behest of management to investigate and solve a specific problem. Often, these would be larger, cross-departmental teams, led by a manager and investigating problems such as extended delivery times, high reject rates on final release or an increase in the number of customer complaints. In fact, there was nothing new about this sort of team; the only difference was the recognition that the operators may well have detailed knowledge that could be useful in investigation and problem-solving.

Finally, there were the project teams for major activities, such as designing a new factory, redesigning the process documentation or validating the water treatment system. In these cases, operators tended not to become full members of the team, especially when these teams operated on a full-time basis. However, they might be called upon for specific stages, such as stakeholder review of concept designs for the new factory.

Problems with Partial Involvement

While these quality teams enjoyed some level of success, especially at the beginning when there was the novelty of something new and different, there were a number of structural problems. In some cases, the teams grew disillusioned and ceased meeting. These problems were primarily external to the group itself.

Some external problems arose in relations with their fellow operators who:

- saw their colleagues 'getting time off to sit around and talk'; this perception might be removed if problems were solved which benefited everyone;

- wondered why their colleagues had been chosen and not them;

- did not see the 'us and them' attitude being broken down – the quality team members were merely perceived to have crossed the wall and become 'one of them'.

The problems relating to managers were similar and again related both to perceptions and facts. It should be remembered that these quality initiatives were often imposed by more senior managers who had read the latest book, seen the latest TV programme or attended the latest seminar about how successful Japanese manufacture was compared to companies in the West. The promise was high levels of profitability with little effort:

- less senior managers and supervisory staff saw their operators being taken away from production lines with no immediate results or benefits. Coupled with a maintained output target, these middle managers had to find ways of making up the missing resource and only saw the short-term disadvantages of the approach;

- where the teams developed solutions that required resources other than themselves to implement them, this was seen as adding to the problems of the managers rather than reducing them;

- the managers who had initiated the programmes had absorbed the headlines but not the details of problem-solving. In particular, they failed to understand that initial investigation of a problem takes most of the time; once the problem is correctly defined, the solution is relatively quick and easy to develop. They quickly became frustrated at the perceived lack of results from some of the teams;

In summary, the problems stemmed from incomplete culture change, poor communication and an attitude of entitlement rather than complete involvement. Operators were selectively invited or permitted to participate in management-sponsored activities. There was no culture of full involvement by all employees.

Effecting Full Culture Change

Richard Schonberger (1986) summed up the requirement succinctly: solving problems, continually and rapidly, is everyone's business. He recognized that WCM 'makes operators owner of the processes and the first line of attack on the wide array of problems that spring up on any shop floor'. He stated that: 'The manufacturing upheaval may be called a revolution when the last wall, the wall around the operators, is fully breached'.

For this revolution to happen, there are a number of prerequisites: everyone must have the responsibility, the authority and the ability to become a problem-solver. In addition, the role of the manager will alter.

RESPONSIBILITY

It should not be a case of certain individuals being invited to participate in quality team activities. All employees must understand that they are expected, as part of their roles, to carry out not only the direct manufacturing activities but also the indirect tasks such as data collection, gap and drift analysis and solution definition. This should be written into job descriptions and be part of the initial induction into the company.

AUTHORITY

It is not sufficient for the operators to know that frontline problem identification is an integral part of their job. They have to know that they have the right or authority that goes with the bounded job description responsibility. If a problem develops, the true problem-solving approach is to stop the process temporarily, solve the problem and then recommence. In a traditional manufacturing environment, output is everything and stopping the process is seen as a negative thing. This perception must be changed such that stopping the process is seen as a permissible activity; a way of finding an improvement that will make the process run more effectively in the future.

ABILITY

If the operators are the process owners and experts, their ability to run the process is not in doubt. However, becoming a problem-solver requires the introduction of a whole new set of skills. Some of these, the more complex statistical ones, are better provided by statisticians. However, 'hard' skills, such as data collection and analysis, and 'soft' skills, such as working in groups, careful observation or time management, will be needed. These can be provided partly by formal training sessions and also by the use of facilitators.

THE ROLE OF THE MANAGER

If the operators are the process owners, the managers and the other indirect staff will find their roles are also changing. The managers will move towards the role of enabler and facilitator. Instead of telling the operators what to do, they need to make it possible for the operators to do what they need to be successful.

This is not to say that all traditional managerial roles will disappear. While most operators are likely to appreciate the fact that they are fully involved in the problem-solving process, there may be a few who do not want to cooperate and prefer the 'good old days when we just turned up and did what we were told'. Dealing with this may be something that can be done by peer pressure, but there must be a managerial process in place if the problem persists.

The other indirect staff may find their jobs change somewhat; people involved in waste management, inventory handling, order progressing, etc. may find they have less to do. On the other hand, the purchasing department may have an increased workload as the level of communication with suppliers increases. These indirect staff will become 'subject matter experts' supporting the process owners. There is no suggestion that the operators can become experts in everything. There will still be the need for qualified engineers, for example. Engineers will just spend less time dealing with *ad hoc* breakdowns and more time working with the operators and management in improving the effectiveness of the process.

Process Thinking or Product Thinking: A Matter of Perspective

The remainder of this chapter considers two different ways of looking at operations: Product Thinking and Process Thinking. Making the distinction between these two perspectives is key to understanding and properly applying the concepts of process design and management espoused in this book, as well as bringing about the cultural changes described above.

Differences and Distinctions

Understanding the differences and distinctions between Product Thinking and Process Thinking is essential to proper management of drug products. Simply put, Product Thinking focuses purely on product creation. This perspective renders decision-making to one basic question: 'does the product meet specification or not?'. It would be nice if products were this simple, but in practice they rarely are.

Process Thinking on the other hand balances both the macro and the micro factors of a product. It consists of three elements that define critical relationships within a process chain:

- starting materials systems (dealing with inputs);

- product creation;

- final user systems (dealing with outputs).

The relationship between Product Thinking and Process Thinking is shown in Figure 8.1. Process Thinking focuses on continual improvement as a business strategy. Continual improvement implies ongoing evaluation of the gaps between process design and process performance. Process Thinking has been described as a journey, whereas Product Thinking can be thought of as a destination.

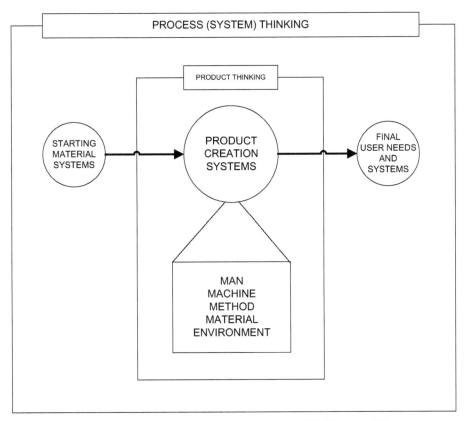

Figure 8.1 The relationship between Product Thinking and Process Thinking

Product Thinking exists within a narrow boundary, where success is defined as conformance with specification limits. There is little continuity within knowledge streams; organizations that practice Product Thinking have to direct high levels of resources at constant retraining. The result of this is a perpetual or discontinuous learning curve.

In stark contrast, the organization that practices Process Thinking achieves effectiveness through an additive process and experiences a complementary or integrated learning curve. See Figure 3.1 in Chapter 3 for a diagrammatic representation of these two types of learning environment.

In a Product Thinking organization, knowledge is often lost at the end of a project. In contrast, Process Thinking teamwork provides depth to the organization by embedding new knowledge after the project is complete.

The regulatory affairs professional who appreciates the differences between Product Thinking and Process Thinking will potentially streamline filings by developing concurrent history. A solid development history will also create opportunities for post-approval improvements. Most importantly, the significant critical variables that ensure safety, efficacy and quality will be understood and articulated in the filing.

The downside of not embracing a Process Thinking point of view can include ineffective Corrective Action and Preventive Action (CAPA), unrecognized trends, the inability to make required changes and missed product deliveries.

Hurdles to Understanding the Process Thinking Point of View

A number of hurdles stand in the way to developing effective Process Thinking. These barriers can be overcome with careful observation, education and improved intracompany communication, resulting in more effective process management functions. However, for this to happen, it is necessary to be able to identify the hurdles in the first place. The main hurdles are:

- lack of business discipline;

- equating product specifications with process capability;

- success by specification alone;

- unstated statistical assumptions;

- effects of cumulative process tolerance;

- legacy business rules.

LACK OF BUSINESS DISCIPLINE

Successful companies demonstrate excellent business discipline. Well-disciplined organizations have the ability to develop goal-oriented action plans, balance conflicting technological demands and effectively disseminate knowledge within the organization – while still having fun. As companies grow, increased attention to business discipline must occur in two areas: technological oversight and ineffective communication.

Technological Oversight

Today's process owner could be overwhelmed by the wide choice of precise analytical tools. The resulting dilemma is how to balance newly found accuracy and precision with project needs and timelines. Let us consider as an example: laser particle size analysis. This is a fantastic resource for the precise analysis of drug substances with solubility and permeability challenges. However, laser technology may be an inappropriate in-process control test to evaluate a tablet granulation process within a high-speed production environment. A set of shaker sieves can accomplish the same goal at a fraction of the cost and time.

Effective business discipline should consider any divergent positions and not automatically default to acquiring the 'latest and greatest' instrument. One approach in resolving this hurdle is to determine if the proposed new technology will:

- streamline the current process by reducing the number of steps;

- meet a changing regulatory requirement;

- improve the specificity of the test result, such as changing from UV to HPLC.

Only if one or more of these criteria is satisfied should the purchase of the new technology be warranted.

Ineffective Communication

In the past 20 years, pharmaceutical companies have grown primarily through mergers and acquisitions. The strategies used are rationalized on 'economies of scale' throughout their research and development (R&D) and manufacturing facilities. 'Economies of scale' is a business concept that proposes that a firm can reduce costs and/or increase productivity as it grows in size. Smith ([1776] 1904) observed that while firms initially benefit by specialization and large scale, there is a point beyond which both become problematic due to delays between process steps or internal coordination problems.

Business discipline in this situation means that the large company must be structured and must operate in a way that ensures proper and timely communications. These communication channels will include a mixture of meetings and other face-to-face interactions, with documented information. This is an important step in keeping all employees heading towards the same goal.

In summary, business discipline in the context of developing Process Thinking relates to all employees being able to make correct choices based on accurate data. The disciplined manager can facilitate teams reaching optimal solutions while at the same time communicating fluidly and frequently to ensure that all employees understand the content and context of their roles and responsibilities within the organization.

EQUATING PRODUCT SPECIFICATIONS WITH PROCESS CAPABILITY

There is a misconception that product specifications and process capability are equivalent quality measures. They are not. Product specifications are a drug safety convention used to ensure product safety, whereas process capability analyses the risk of failure between test data within the specification range. The two concepts must work in concert to affirm that the development process is robust and controlled. Failing to recognize the distinction between the two creates unnecessary risk to product consistency.

Product Thinking, the acceptance of test data by specification ranges only, undermines the theory of Process Thinking, which focuses on process capability and process design. All processes rely on two mathematical conventions to describe the quality of test results: the data mean or average and the data range, including a measure of statistical deviation. By making a judgment on product quality based only on specification range criteria, the reviewer effectively uses only mean data. Consequently, the variability of the data is hidden from view and becomes a risk liability.

One consequence of Product Thinking is analytical drift which remains undetected until a failure occurs. Further, the wider the specification range, the greater the potential risk. Consider, for example, the real case of a modified release product. According to the United States Pharmacopeia (USP), such a product has a dissolution specification of $Q > 85$ per cent at eight hours (USP 2005). For the past two months test values had been progressively lower than the historic 99 per cent mean. However, the problem was not recognized until a value of 83 per cent was generated. The resulting OOS investigation revealed that the dissolution paddle's inert coating had, through wear and tear, disintegrated in an inconspicuous location. The low results were likely to have been caused by interaction of the exposed metal and the drug substance. If the product acceptance had included a measure of process capability, the data would have revealed the trend before the OOS was required.

In summary, Process Thinking recognizes that product specification and process capability are two complementary tools to confirm product integrity through reduced risk. To use only product specification as the acceptance criterion is a Product Thinking point of view that exposes the company to needless process management risks.

SUCCESS BY SPECIFICATION ALONE

Product Thinking does not maximize a product's full expiry period market success. The reasons are varied, but can be summarized as recalls resulting from overlooked, insignificant changes in critical parameters during the expiry period. In this regard, PAT techniques drive Process Thinking approaches to overcome the legacy of arduous, multiple-lot development models. Other techniques such as design of experiments (DOE) are able to leverage process design extremes to maximize the predictive power of smaller data sets. It is critical, however, to fully understand the variability of supply sources before conducting the DOE, otherwise the experiment may be designed suboptimally.

For example, a dual active immediate release dose with APIs A and B was to be transferred to the manufacturing site as part of an Abbreviated New Drug Application (ANDA) approval. The analytical method was supposed to be a validated one. However, the best efforts of the laboratory personnel could not recreate acceptable chromatography. In the end, it was discovered that a forced degradation study had only been carried out on active A. Carrying out a forced study for active B appeared to be unnecessary, since the finished product analytical method was based on the API method for active B. However, active B degraded under stress conditions and created an artefact, which co-eluted with the main peak of active A. It would have paid to know both degradation profiles to identify the problem earlier in the project.

UNSTATED STATISTICAL ASSUMPTIONS

Within every process, two statistical control models coexist. One set of controls is based on continuous statistics and is called variable control. The data generated by continuous statistics have predictive power within a confidence interval. The other set of controls are based on discontinuous statistics and are called discrete or attribute controls. These data have marginal predictive power. Variable controls and attribute controls must be kept separate in order to manage the process properly. These statistical control systems present two more distinct challenges to the development of a Process Thinking approach:

- selecting the proper control model for the data;

- having sufficient precision attributed to variable data.

From the Process Thinking perspective, the primary task of product development should be to understand the basis of controls of the products. Without a stated understanding of the control model, test results may be rendered meaningless. Consider the situation of uniformity of dose. The USP prescribes acceptance in terms of mean value and allowable range of the individual values. The typical range is 85–115 per cent of the label claim for individual test results, which may be too generous for the process design. The process has a great deal of variable latitude in this situation, so it is important for the data to be reported in a variable control model.

If product specifications are written in such a way that the reporting requirement is 'passes test', the statistical model is inadvertently modified to an attribute model. In a worst-case scenario, valuable data about tablet uniformity could be lost. At best, chromatography data may have to be reviewed again.

The second challenge in articulating the control model is to establish proper precision for variable data. One important consideration is how the data and resulting information will be used. For example, if the variable data will be used to establish stability profiles for impurities, then integer-level precision is not appropriate due to extreme errors in the confidence interval. A second consideration is the level of analytical error for the test method. Again, if data need to be expressed in extreme precision, yet the method's intermediate precision – the total of all error – is large, the data integrity is marginalized. In each case it is important to involve, from the beginning, an individual with a practical understanding of statistics.

In summary, Process Thinking ensures the integrity by confirming data are generated by the correct statistical model and, further, that data are relevant and consistent with the error of the testing method.

EFFECTS OF CUMULATIVE PROCESS TOLERANCE

The larger the number of steps in a process, the greater will be the variability which has to be managed. This is because each step within a process contains its own element of error and uncertainty. The Process Thinking approach analyses and accounts for these sources of inherent variability. Process Thinking relies on the Process Development model (McVay 2005) to map the locations of variability and incorporate the appropriate controls for data. On the other hand, the Product Thinking approach does not include such a detailed level of assessment.

Consider the following example of small quantity analytical weighing. When an analytical method requires a standard mass of solid to be added to a volumetric container, the transfer error – the amount lost on manual transfer – will tend to be an absolute amount rather than a percentage. Depending on the required weight of the solid, this error may have a significant impact on the accuracy of weighing.

Table 8.1 presents the general concept of cumulative error on testing results. It shows that, given identical equipment and methods, the impact of unpreventable human errors can be confounding to data sets. A well-designed process will account for human error and will develop ways to reduce the variability to ensure confidence in the final data.

In summary, the Process Thinking approach develops understanding of the cumulative effects of small contributing factors outside of the immediate product analysis and seeks to minimize the impact in a cost-effective manner.

Table 8.1   Example of cumulative error

Standard weight to be transferred	25.00 mg	100.00 mg
Transfer accuracy (mg)	0.50	0.50
Transfer error (%)	2.00	0.50
Balance error (%)	0.05	0.05
Volumetric error (%)	0.01	0.01
Instrument error (%)	0.02	0.02
Cumulative error (%)	2.08	0.58

LEGACY BUSINESS RULES

Process Thinking recognizes that SOPs have a vital function within an organization. The Process Thinking organizations exploit procedural updates even in the face of success. The advantage for Process Thinking companies is a clear history of prevailing thoughts and assumptions about the process. Understanding the past is the best way to anticipate future change. Business rules are made to be updated. Business rules change when either the regulatory environment or the business environment changes.

However, we have observed that formal procedures or company traditions and culture create a significant barrier to Process Thinking. It is far easier to maintain an existing system than to create a new one or even update an old one. Success sometimes breeds conformance – 'if it ain't broke, don't fix it'. This is in direct conflict to the continuous improvement approach which is part of Process Thinking. Additionally, rules which were appropriate when they were first written can drift in the light of new technological innovations or changing regulatory requirements. Change should be inevitable.

Conclusion

Effective process design and management requires a radical change in the thinking of traditional pharmaceutical manufacturing companies. It requires involving everyone as problem-solvers and agents of continuous improvement.

The partial involvement of operators, as witnessed in quality programmes from the 1980s onwards, is not sufficient. Full, effective involvement requires a change not just in attitudes but in practices. Direct operations staff will become frontline problem-solvers, while managers and other indirect staff will be facilitators and subject-matter experts.

Product Thinking and Process Thinking are not equivalent process management strategies. Product Thinking is a limiting approach for process management and can often lead to resistance to change. Additionally, it can result in operations departments and/or the quality units being left to sort out the shortcomings of poor development during problem investigations.

Process Thinking, on the other hand, provides a solid knowledge base of process controls and the relevant aspects of routine controls. The knowledge developed by a sound Process Thinking approach can be a powerful strategic tool that will facilitate continual improvement and reduce risk *when* technology or regulations change.

9

Cause and Effect: Getting to the Root Cause

The cause is hidden; the effect is visible to all.

(Ovid, 43 BC–17 AD, Roman poet)

Introduction

This book is about re-establishing the fundamentals of process management that are sorely lacking within global pharmaceutical operations. Many of the examples and conclusions arise from personal experience and informal corroboration by industry colleagues. From the FDA website, some 72 process-associated recalls were initiated during 2010 and 2011. During the same time, more than 30 warning letters were issued. In our view, returning to fundamentals and practising the basics properly is the best way to reduce these numbers.

We hope this book gives the reader the understanding that each technical improvement has productive and counterproductive aspects. Building a process with focus strictly on the productive aspects automatically introduces the baggage of counterproductive issues in a very benign and hidden manner. The term 'hidden factory' is often used to describe the part of the process characterized by an abundance of counterproductive issues. The greatest of these hidden issues is unplanned re-work, missed schedules and excess buffer inventory to make up for the organizational undertow. We contend that the majority of the 'hidden factory' has its origins in the adoption of standardized parts and mathematical descriptions of dimensions and tolerances. Artisan cabinet-makers, for example, rely on measurement transfer rather than exacting measurement to assure proper fit and finish. The importance of this point cannot be understated. Just because measurement by numbers can be made does not mean that this technique should be used.

How is the Artisan Model related to cause and effect? The model rationally subdivides or partitions the process into manageable components that can be directly assessed for outcomes related to the process design. These elements are universally applicable to every aspect of pharmaceutical operations and provide sufficient detail to manage any operation to the level of compliance sought by the regulatory agencies.

A simple example of a counterproductive work effort is the measurement of tablet diameter as a critical control. Tablet diameter is often incorporated into the production control system specification, and while it is true that the tablet diameter and thickness are important to ensure final tablet weight, the diameter is fixed by the precision of the machining used to make the die. It is important to inform the tooling machinist that the die cavity is to be 9.250 ± 0.005 mm on the inner diameter and it is important to verify the proper die is used during tablet press set-up rather than measuring final tablets. The use of a certified plug gauge by the set-up mechanic is building quality into the process; measuring finished tablet diameter is inspecting quality into the process. This example shows how the hidden factory, and the subsequent dilution of cause and effect, can occur. If the incorrect die is used in the first place (cause), re-work is certain (effect).

Establishing a timely root cause of process problems is at the heart of process management. Cause and effect is the pathway to effective root-cause analysis. Profits are lost each time a true root cause of a process deviation is not effectively resolved. Failing to resolve the root cause at the point of occurrence leads to compound increases in cost as deviations are repeated in the future. Consider an off-specification material used in multiple products. The risk of process failures and deviations to each product increases significantly. Now consider a lean operation scheduled to operate at 90 per cent capacity the entire year to maintain a low cost of goods sold. The financial performance within this hidden factory environment will fail to meet expectations, which in turn will promote poor local decisions about product approvals so as not to delay the shipping schedule.

When the fault is identified as soon as it occurs and actions are taken, the process is operating consistently to the design and at lowest total cost. This point is known in process management as the cause and effect point.

The productive capacity of pharmaceutical companies exceeds the market demand for the finished drug product. So, in addition to bringing the process back to its relevant range, the organization must be able to develop new products to extend scientifically based cures, increase market share and contain costs. The adoption of process management as described in this text will pave the way to effectively gain control of process performance by rational partitioning of the process, which is easily and effectively manageable. Figure 9.1 summarizes the relationship of business objectives as these are cascaded through the organization from high-level inception to the lowest level of process execution. The bridge between purpose and execution is the process. The ability to effectively implement the process lies in the ability to understand the cause and effect of the quality control system.

The assurance of proper performance lies in the process design according to the Artisan Model and the proper application of quality control assessments

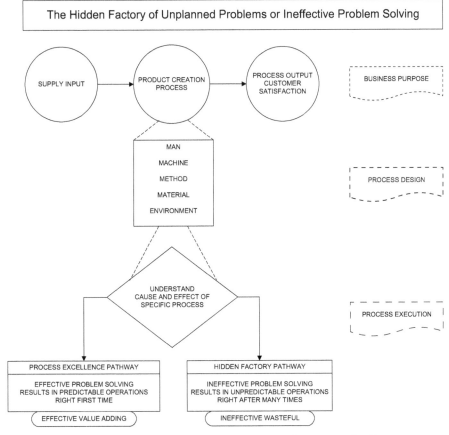

Figure 9.1   **Demonstration of the importance of cause and effect knowledge**

for both point of application and the sensitivity of the quality control measure. When designed properly, production fault conditions can be effectively assessed and mitigated, since the observed effect will in all likelihood have a well-defined cause. We use the term 'fault' to mean transient non-conforming product that is fully under the control of the manufacturer while the effect is being investigated for the root cause. Assessing the production fault should be fairly straightforward with a high probably of success in a timely manner when cause and effect relationships are understood. However, increasing numbers of warning letters from regulatory agencies to manufacturing companies are attesting to the fact that cause and effect is not well understood.

The ideas of cause and effect, as with the other process management tools, are fundamentally common sense. Their success is determined by the experience of the individuals involved in the activity of process design and construction. The approaches are not new, but are configured in a novel manner to add discrimination of detail for the purpose of verification of process performance as the process proceeds as scheduled. The Artisan Model is an important empowerment tool. The operator at the frontline will have the specific tools at his or her disposal to make accurate decisions. Management will be able to plan more effectively based on reliable data from the operational frontline. Customers will benefit from the greater consistency of products and product performance.

What are the Challenges?

There are seven challenges that obscure cause and effect relationships and prevent effective corrective action in a timely manner:

- tossing the process over the development wall;

- transferring statistically unstable processes;

- older processes, designed for compliance, lack relevant history;

- testing into compliance;

- unintended consequences of improvements;

- legacy business constraints;

- presumption of absolute understanding.

TOSSING THE PROCESS OVER THE DEVELOPMENT WALL

Historically, establishing the cause and effect relation of process data and deviations has been difficult. Many older processes were designed at a time when it was acceptable for projects to be 'tossed over the wall'. Development completed their assignment and handed off the process to manufacturing, with only minor levels of qualification. Often absent from the transfer was a comprehensive summary of critical performance parameters, written simply at the machine operator level. This sort of process behaviour still continues today, particularly in larger organizations.

The outcome is that manufacturing is left to resolve the unexpected variability of excipient materials, active substances and environmental controls. The production laboratory may have to modify the control methods to reduce run times. Post-approval regulatory affairs personnel are left to navigate changing scientific and legal requirements with the accompanying implications to product safety and efficacy. Without a clear understanding of the cause and effect relationships discovered during development, post-approval maintenance efforts are slowed and costs increased.

TRANSFERRING STATISTICALLY UNSTABLE PROCESSES

Paraphrasing this point: 'It meets the product specification, so what's the problem?' New products are sometimes accepted when test results meet commonly accepted compendial ranges for assay and uniformity of dosage. If the assay strength target is 100 per cent of the label claim, but the assays of 92 per cent or 108 per cent are acceptable from a regulatory allowance, often the process is accepted, even though it may miss the target by 8 per cent. This is completely unacceptable for process management. Wide variation of the average is the first sign of statistical instability.

Table 9.1 compares acceptable regulatory ranges of assay between two regions. From a strict product compliance perspective, the sponsor is allowed to manufacture product as long as the results lie within the compendial range. The legal framework sets the minimum standards for compliance rather than performance. Compliance inspection is the underpinnings of 'Six-Sigma', 'process excellence', and '21st century product quality' programmes. These programmes are directed towards large-volume statistical evaluations of data during and after manufacture for 'critical quality attributes' and confirmation of process performance.

Table 9.1   Summary of acceptable ranges of product test results

Regulatory test parameter	US compendia ranges			European compendia ranges			Implications for range of results
Assay	90.0–110.0% of label claim (LC)			95.0–105.0% of LC			Accepted range for the average of a pooled multiple-dose sample
Uniformity of dosage	85.0–115.0% of LC (S-1) 80.0–120.0% of LC (S-2) 75.0–125.0% of LC (S-3)			85.0–115.0% of LC			Accepted range for the individual values within a multiple-dose sample. Three tries are provided to pass specification
Dissolution	Average value			Average value			Account for results of both the average and the individual. Three tries are provided to pass specification
	Stage 1 n=6	Stage 2 n=12	Stage 3 n=24	Stage 1 n=6	Stage 2 n=12	Stage 3 n=24	
	+5%	Target	-10%	+5%	Target	-10%	
	Individual value			Individual value			
	Stage 1 n=6	Stage 2 n=12	Stage 3 n=24	Stage 1 n=6	Stage 2 n=12	Stage 3 n=24	
	Target	-10% for 1	-15% for 2	Target	-10% for 1	-15% for 2	

If the product acceptance limits are considered from a statistical ability to hit the label claim target, the realization is eye-opening. Wide variability of the assay allows the mean to drift, thus expanding the extremes of the distribution of individual results. With a wide range of possible results, there is a low probability of successfully identifying the cause that underlies the observed effect. When data are too widely distributed to allow meaningful interpretation, the process performance and financial results suffer. A 'non-statistician' view of process implications to accepting results anywhere within the compendial range with neither centring nor consistency renders statistical analysis ineffective.

If, for example, validation lot one 'passes' assay at 92 per cent of the label claim and validation lot two 'passes' assay at 108 per cent of the label claim, this is a spread of 16 per cent. Now add to this a lot relative standard deviation of 5 per cent at each extreme. The acceptable range is very wide. In other words, the confidence an individual tablet can meet requirements is low. In actual practice, it is unlikely that heavy or light tablets will be sent to market, unless there is intentional fraud being committed, so the actual compliance risk is likely to be small. The deviation or out-of-trend investigation is almost certain to result in a decrease in yield (increase in scrap), which in turn increases the cost of goods sold. The bottom line, statistically unstable processes do not reveal cause and effect other than by random occurrence.

OLDER PROCESSES, DESIGNED FOR COMPLIANCE, LACK RELEVANT HISTORY

Older approved drug products, which comprise a large percentage of marketed medicines, often present unique challenges in determining the cause and effect of a process deviation. Products can have a long history of changes made to improve the process, but the history is seldom documented in a straightforward manner. Complicating the situation is a lack of information on the approach used to create the dosage at the time of approval. Legacy development programmes often relied on the personal experience of the formulator to develop a dosage. Consequently, products were developed more by art than science, since experience revealed what worked and what did not.

Drug product design by art constitutes the principal rationale given by regulatory agencies for adopting quality by design. Drugs could be developed with the goal of passing product specification or meeting a short development deadline, without respect to long-term process output consistency. The approach is similar to a check-box mentality where blinkers are applied to narrow one's focus and understanding. Long-term employees provided a valuable understanding of product history if cause and effect were not obvious when a problem occurred. However, mergers and acquisitions have resulted in the termination of employees with the most knowledge and understanding. This is good for consulting opportunities but bad for firms competing in a global economy where cause and effect hold the key to speed and efficiency. Knowledge and understanding are power to a process design team. Cause and effect solutions to current problems are often hidden in archive information. However, if company document retention policies mandate the destruction of this information for legal reasons, the process design team will need to dig into literature to understand process problems.

TESTING INTO COMPLIANCE

Testing the finished product for compliance was and still is a common strategy for many firms. Physical or chemical testing, when properly integrated within a process, is not a process design flaw; rather, the tests are necessary to match the proper technology to the challenge presented at the control point. For example, chemical testing is the only certain way to prove the identity of two white powders. However, if continual sampling and testing is necessary to find a passing value to resolve an OOS event, this is a problem. The ruling in *United States v. Barr Laboratories* (1993) set the guidelines for new regulations and FDA guidance that required the drug product manufacturer to evaluate aberrant test results before additional sampling could be performed, thus eliminating the practice of 'testing into compliance'.

Frequent laboratory OOS investigation is one of the most certain signals of a process out of control and testing product into compliance. Pharmaceutical regulations rely on product testing as the evidence for demonstrating culpability when rules are broken. The rules and regulations were established to document finished product results as the basis of market approval. The difference between testing into compliance and the appropriate use of analytical techniques is revealed by cause and effect. Figure 9.2 demonstrates the relation of special cause effects, which are outside of the product design, and common cause effects, which are routinely expected to be present. If the system is poorly designed, non-homogeneous products with differing data profiles can be

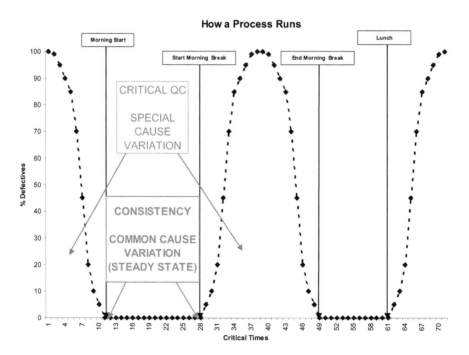

Figure 9.2   Common cause variation and special cause variation

interspersed. Cause and effect properly applied will segregate special cause from common cause and lead to effective problem-solving.

General testing control strategies, primarily the end-product testing of *average* output, are insensitive to subtle changes at inline control points that signal the beginning of a shift or other pattern. Process management by compliance-driven testing approaches is not a sustainable, long-term performance technique; rather, the approach promotes the degradation of quality and profitability. While the concept of validation and process consistency is at the forefront of current discussion, the underlying approach is still voluminous testing. Moving from art to science requires careful study. This is a challenging task, but will ultimately result in better process design.

UNINTENDED CONSEQUENCES OF IMPROVEMENTS

The history of understanding cause and effect has drifted from individual artisan awareness and timely action, such as sharpen the tool when dull, to our current state in which the process is scattered across the organization, making cause and effect nearly impossible to identify. From the Artisan Model viewpoint, cause and effect should be readily obvious at the critical decision point. For example, if wood was not properly dried, it would change dimension even after the product was finished. Improvements were driven to simplify work or solve an immediate problem. However, as organizations grew larger, improvements tended to mask the causes and effects. If a component bulk density decreases, blending uniformity will be changed. The effect may be experienced in manufacturing, but the cause may have started with changing suppliers or not having proper specifications to describe the component attributes.

Sampling plans, starting at Western Electric with Walter Shewhart, Harold Dodge and Harry Romig (Juran 1998), were invented to help understand the statistical nature of cause and effect. Design teams must consider lag in the identification of process shift; drift is often not properly considered when looking at improvements. It is important to recognize that cause and effect has the greatest chance of effective problem resolution at the point in time when it occurs, not hours, days, weeks or months later. As sampling has become more technically sophisticated and large in size, cause and effect is further hidden in process noise. The proponents of these plans have good intentions to improve product consistency but are inadvertently subject to the Fallacy of Large Numbers. Process improvement should not become a rationalization of sophisticated statistical techniques.

LEGACY BUSINESS CONSTRAINTS

SOPs play a vital function within an organization. These document systems (an extension of the *methods* element) provide the framework for design and management of process. Well-conceived procedural systems promote efficiency and the ability to uncover important cause and effect relationships. However, pharmaceutical companies with legacy procedural systems often cannot exploit procedural advantage due to the sheer size and magnitude of organizational inertia.

Business precedents of the acquiring company often constrain organizations from achieving true process control. The effort and cost required to maintain an existing system are often lower than the cost of creating a new system or even updating the old one. Process design employees of the acquiring company are familiar with *their* systems and procedures and often superimpose their approaches on the newly acquired organization.

Dissimilar structures promote a lack of understanding as integration teams force-fit processes to meet financial and efficiency goals stated as the original reason and rationale for the merger. Cause and effect sensitivity is the victim. As pointed out previously, most mergers and acquisitions do not increase shareholder value (Pautler 2003). We contend that this is a function of the processes misalignment and the ensuing handicaps placed on the ability to uncover cause and effect relationships, which are at the root of successful problem solving.

PRESUMPTION OF ABSOLUTE UNDERSTANDING

Understanding the past is the best way to anticipate future change. Evaluation of the past process problems and resulting responses often reveals subtle cause and effect relationships that were not visible at the time. The outcome can lead to smart redesign of the process as causes and effects are revealed with greater clarity.

However, in process management, there is unlikely to be a point in time when perfect theoretical understanding is achieved. Too much emphasis on perfect understanding is counterproductive to process management, as practice lags behind theory and can introduce false security of being in control. This false sense of security violates an observation made by the most likely father of the Scientific Method, Sir Francis Bacon: 'If a man will begin with certainties, he shall end in doubts, but if he will be content to begin with doubts, he shall end in certainties' ([1620] 2000). Success can breed conformance: 'If it is working, why change?' However, this presumes the current system is not broken to start with.

Solutions

We propose eight solutions to the challenges discussed above. Each brings the process design closer to the point where cause and effect can be acted upon in a timely manner. Other approaches are also possible, so this selection should be viewed as a starting point rather than an end:

- organize projects to include representatives from sequential process steps;

- increase process design sensitivity through centred and narrow data;

- identify the most significant controls by DOE;

- initiate a project to capture historically relevant understanding;

- adopt a process performance attitude;

- assess improvement efforts for productive as well as counterproductive attributes;

- re-engineer existing processes or guide new process development using the Artisan Model;

- accept only centred statistically stable data – separate fact from opinion.

ORGANIZE PROJECTS TO INCLUDE REPRESENTATIVES FROM SEQUENTIAL PROCESS STEPS

No process operates in a vacuum or is self-contained. Project teams should represent each element defined in the Artisan Model of process design. This adds process continuity at the design stage. Further, team membership should integrate functions across the product's lifecycle, beginning with late phase II (where an expanded study subject population is used to continue defining the understanding of safety and to start defining efficacy) through phase III (supporting the applications for marketing authorization) and continuing into phase IV (post-approval studies).

This can result in a team of about seven core members, but the benefits of right-first-time understanding of process design limitations, assumptions and desired outcomes outweigh the cost of time spent in a collaborative team setting. The number of steps in a process should also be considered. The greater the number of steps, the more attention must be given to ensure proper team representation. However, in order to limit the team to a manageable size, it is advisable to consider including broad-view generalists as a single point of contact for related group issues. For example, quality assurance, quality control and regulatory affairs could be represented by a single person, as could manufacturing and engineering. When teams become too large, progress often slows in direct proportion to the number of representatives and the accompanying logistical coordination challenges.

INCREASE PROCESS DESIGN SENSITIVITY WITH ACCURATE CONTROL POINTS

The Artisan Model considers sources of inherent variability to be the root cause of unexpected results. Processes should only be transferred from a currently approved manufacturing site to a proposed new site when, by data analysis, the process is demonstrated to be well centred and narrowly distributed around the intended label claim strength. Stated in different terms, the process design should only be accepted if data lie around the specification target (the label claim for finished products).

It is inconsistent and unacceptable for a truly process-driven organization to accept 'passes specification' as a strategy. Missing the stated target is unacceptable practice in process data-driven business models. The one and only way to verify consistency of the initial design is to have well-centred data with a narrow spread of variability. The cost of corrections resulting from unstable process operation is needless expense to the pharmaceutical manufacturer to fix problems when they become large. Small problems require small solutions, while big problems require big solutions. When in doubt about which control is the most important of several under consideration, DOE is a way of identifying and selecting the most important controls with the greatest sensitivity to unintended change.

INITIATE A PROJECT TO CAPTURE HISTORICALLY RELEVANT UNDERSTANDING

An unintended consequence of mergers and acquisitions is that critical understanding and knowledge is either locked away in the archives or is lost through attrition or downsizing. Obviously, the production of approved pharmaceutical products must continue for revenue and profit objectives, but with a loss of understanding, the complexity of the task of managing the day-to-day process as well as regulatory affairs is increased significantly. A good step is to locate and catalogue historic documents that form the platform of the current process design. Often, this effort is bypassed on the presumption that there is insufficient time to perform process archaeology to catalogue historic milestones. We propose the opposite view – there is no reason to delay this exercise. Do the work correctly now or redo the work later. At stake is the sacrifice of the future process capability necessary to meet global product demands on time.

ADOPT A PROCESS PERFORMANCE ATTITUDE

We have observed two basic attitudes towards process management of pharmaceutical products. The first is a conformance or compliance mindset. The second is a performance-driven mindset where continuous improvement is based on historical facts and an understanding of product development issues. Attitude is an *environmental* issue and it rests with senior company leadership to establish the tone. The solution is to incorporate or add an unambiguous policy stating that all business systems, and primarily operations-related activity, will have two criteria on which to manage their operations: average (time, cost and output) and normal variability (of time, cost and output). Further, should the average point or variability deviate more than a statistically determined norm (effect), the cause will be evaluated and acted upon, even when results meet specifications.

ASSESS IMPROVEMENT EFFORTS FOR PRODUCTIVE AS WELL AS COUNTERPRODUCTIVE ATTRIBUTES

It is important not to accept group thinking in which dissenting voices are muted. For process management to be successful, theoretical foundations must be solid and experienced understanding must be used as a counterpoint of strategic discussion. There is a significant difference between theory and experienced understanding, as one of us found when presenting GMP training some years ago in a Middle Eastern country. The industry professionals were highly educated and could always be relied on to bring out at least one reference paper or guidance document that the trainer had not seen. This was initially daunting until it was became apparent that while their theoretical knowledge was very high, their experience in the application of the theory was minimal and it was here that the trainer was able to provide added value. Process design management must balance the two characteristics to ensure that relevant points of design are considered.

The pharmaceutical industry sometimes relies more on theoretical considerations than experienced understanding. While it is not the topic of this book, we propose that much of the rapid rise in the cost of discovery and production of pharmaceutical products is directly correlated to this shift from experienced understanding to largely unproven sophisticated statistical theory. Another variation on a theme of group thinking relates to the precision and scale of measurement to manage a process. Operational excellence is not rocket science. We cannot emphasize this point enough: on many occasions the simple solution is the best.

Continuous improvement and process excellence programmes that rely on extreme levels of measurement accuracy, such as Six-Sigma, should be scrutinized prior to adoption. For example, it is well documented that parts per million quality is achieved at 4.5 standard deviations (sigma). Six-Sigma programmes appeal to the perfectionist in us all by incorporating an estimate of error of 1.5 sigma. The counterproductive aspects of Six-Sigma are the exponential increase in costs of upgrading measurement precision plus the introduction of significant amounts of process noise.

For example, a company seeking routine parts per million systems may spend 700 per cent more for analytical equipment if the choice is to purchase a high-performance liquid chromatograph with coupled mass spectrophotometer (HPLC-MS) rather than a simple ultraviolet-visible spectrophotometer (UV-Vis). Selecting the higher cost machine when the drug product is well characterized, stable in storage and has no impurity and degradant concerns is not fiscally prudent. The same consideration should be given to use of PAT in manufacturing. PAT techniques can generate a tsunami of data which can hide cause and effect. PAT should be a solution to a problem, not a solution seeking a problem.

RE-ENGINEER EXISTING PROCESSES OR GUIDE NEW PROCESS DEVELOPMENT USING THE ARTISAN MODEL

Quality inspection programmes have always existed. Most use a common approach of measurement and assessment after the fact. The Artisan Model changes the inspection-compliance paradigm, which often works unproductively against cause and effect efforts. The Artisan Model approach reverse-engineers the Fishbone Diagram technique in a unique way to guide the development of process elements. A well-integrated design matches cause and effect with sample control points during operation. Deviations from process design will result in an accurate and timely cause and effect signal. The deviation can be effectively evaluated for impact on drug product or drug substance quality and thus can ensure proper and timely corrective action. Any alterations to the process that arise from re-engineering must be a collaborative effort across the product processing system.

ACCEPT ONLY CENTRED STATISTICALLY STABLE DATA – SEPARATE FACT FROM OPINION

Cause and effect is the byproduct of effective and relevant common-sense statistics generated from a stable process. As a process is evaluated either when new or as a re-engineering effort, the one certain way to ensure effective analysis of cause and effect is to validate and accept only those processes that demonstrate statistical stability. This ensures the validity of the data. Data certainty makes it possible to prioritize risk-based decisions for action. The action required is to establish a written policy to mandate the acceptance of statistically stable data as the foundation for process excellence.

The second element of this change is to use something like the 5-Whys approach when examining deviations. This is a tool which asks questions not just at the superficial level but digs down through the layers to identify true causes. Each time an apparent cause is identified, it is interrogated further. For example, if the floor in a plant room is seen to be wet, the question is asked: why? A pipe was leaking; why? A gasket has perished and has not been replaced; why? The plant room is not covered by the Preventative Maintenance (PM) programme. So the floor is wet due to an inadequate PM programme. Subtle change within systems can often alter the intent of the process design.

The critical examination of deviations often delves into sublevel nuances that previously were unknown to the process design team. The technique is fully discussed in Kaizen (Imai 1986).

Conclusion

Understanding cause and effect provides the most fundamental level of confidence that a process has been properly designed and is consistent with the principles of operation. When the inevitable non-conformance occurs, it is the understanding of the relationship of cause and effect that guides the corrective action and preventive action necessary to correct the system design or take other actions that ensure product consistency. The Artisan Model facilitates this understanding through the use of rational partitioning of process elements. The same Fishbone Diagram attributes used to build the process will also be used to evaluate non-conformance incidents. We propose process design by reverse engineering the Fishbone technique as the basis for the Artisan Model of process development.

Cause and effect is often hindered by legacy practice and the rate of change that accompanies mergers and acquisitions. Counterproductive results often occur when the business need for 'immediate results' takes precedence over the right level of process understanding (Begley 2011). Well-designed and configured processes gain their speed through efficient and effective design rather than the after-the-event accumulation of facts unrelated to the success of process performance. Inspection is counterproductive if the user is not absolutely certain that the effect perceived from aberrant data is actually a signal of a specific cause.

Many investigations are unsuccessful and consequently have resulted in significant financial fines and consent decrees. This should not be part of the cost of doing business and can be changed by the increased process management discrimination possible by the development of knowledge framed by the Artisan Model and the resulting success of effective understanding of cause and effect.

10

Corrective Action and Preventive Action: Fixing the Inevitable Oops

Failure is success if we learn from it.
(Malcolm Forbes, 1919–1990, American publisher)

Introduction

Up to this point, we have been concerned with designing and managing pharmaceutical processes for performance and results. In Part III of this book, we have been looking at the strategic considerations that should become part of the final system design process. A robust CAPA programme facilitates systemic change to more closely align process performance with process design. Today the technique is all too often applied *after* a problem is retrospectively recognized. As discussed in Chapter 9, recognition of a problem as it happens gives the process owner the advantage of timely evaluation.

The CAPA process should be applied at the point when an 'external to the system result' is revealed. At this instant, the most effective solutions are realized. The challenge faced by pharmaceutical companies is not to create all-encompassing levels of statistical data to describe all process outcomes, but rather to effectively transform existing data into meaningful information. Meaningful information provides for meaningful CAPA activities.

What are the Challenges?

Four fundamental problems must be considered and resolved to ensure that CAPA activities are beneficial in identifying and resolving root-cause process deviations:

- viewing deviations as isolated incidents or events;

- inappropriate method design – lack of data relevance;

- limited investigation time;

- lack of verification after implementation.

VIEWING DEVIATIONS AS ISOLATED INCIDENTS OR EVENTS

CAPA efforts should be directed at understanding the interrelated steps of the process that play a part in the OOS investigations. If the OOS is considered to be a single, one-off incident, it becomes difficult to successfully resolve the problem. Many apparent solutions present themselves, but often these actually address effects rather than the underlying cause. We have seen that many pharmaceutical OOS investigations treat problems as a single isolated event and subsequently flounder as data cannot easily be correlated to the root cause. Unfortunately, regulatory inspectors observe ineffective problem resolution during a comprehensive review. When the inspector identifies the problem – and the company has not – the trust between the pharmaceutical company and the regulatory agency is damaged. The outcome of lack of confidence in the manufacturer is predictable.

An approved marketing application infers excellent controls and deep process understanding on the part of the process sponsor. In other words, the manufacturer is publicly declaring its ability to consistently produce the drug product. Poor CAPA investigations and continuing problems during production, however, tell a different story. On the extreme side, some regulators would consider this situation deceitful. Effective CAPA investigation can avoid public embarrassment and financial consequences.

The most effective CAPA efforts result when the process is engineered and controlled according to the rational partitioning of its components. The Artisan Model provides a framework in which to gain control of process data and information. If the process is older and was designed only to meet specification acceptance criteria, CAPA efforts can be arduous. Much of the understanding of process parameters is missing, even if the information is sitting in a local warehouse.

If the process is newer, then the deviation investigation could use Ishikawa's Fishbone Diagram (see Chapter 13) to reveal the interconnectedness of the system elements that relate to the problem's solution. Rational verification of the solution is also required and could use the 5-Whys approach (Imai 1986) to affirm the conclusions before putting the final CAPA report into the file.

INAPPROPRIATE METHOD DESIGN – LACK OF DATA RELEVANCE

CAPA comes into play when a confirmed or suspected – hypothetical – product failure has occurred and the manufacturer must eliminate or mitigate the resulting risk to the customer. When the failure is real, the solution is conclusive with a well-defined root cause. When the failure is hypothetical, the solution may be inconclusive or elusive. We refer to the dividing line between real solutions and statistical possibilities as the signal-to-noise (StN) boundary of a process. Successful CAPA investigations derive solutions from the signal region of a process and not the noise region. Method validation approaches described by the International Conference on Harmonisation (ICH) or major compendia describe the StN boundary by the terms Limit of Quantitation (LoQ) and Limit of Detection (LoD) respectively.

There are several basic quality control considerations that underlie effective process management and consequently the success of CAPA investigations and interventions. First, process quality control points should deal only with real process signals. The StN threshold distinguishes relevant data and not-so-important data. The StN delineates the edge of instrument capability (*machine*) in combination with the variability of sample preparation (*method*). Figure 10.1 shows the relationship of signal to noise – and process needs. The process design team must carefully assess the precision of technology necessary to provide sufficient sensitivity to ensure the integrity of the data at the lowest total acquisition cost.

In the laboratory, for example, the process design team could be faced with a choice of instruments for analysing drug potency within a stated budget. Four choices are considered: titration; thin-layer chromatography (TLC); UV-Vis; and HPLC. Each has advantages and disadvantages, but the final decision must consider the StN region and factor in how this will affect the ability to perform analyses, the robustness of the measurement – error proofing – and how the level of precision can support future CAPA investigations.

Colorimetric titration is accurate, but is dependent on the mechanical skill and patience of the analyst in identifying the end point. The cost is the lowest of the choices, especially if performed in standard laboratory glassware. Titration often has a wide StN junction that must be taken into account.

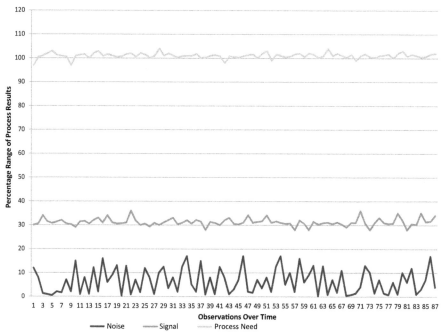

Figure 10.1   Relationship of signal-to-noise and process needs

TLC introduces the ability to detect multiple compounds, but long-term statistical trend analysis is sacrificed and the StN point is sometimes difficult to distinguish as it is broadened. CAPA investigation is hindered for this reason. The cost is higher as more chemicals must be compounded and more time must be spent by chemists and technicians on preparing solutions.

UV-Vis is a faster technology and is sufficiently accurate and of the proper data type to support trending and CAPA investigations. The cost of the instrument increases significantly, but the sample preparation and analysis can be automated easily at a moderate cost. The instrument excels at speed and precision to perhaps 0.1 per cent. For release to market, assay and uniformity of content, when there are no concerns relating to impurities or degradant compounds, UV-Vis methodology provides sufficient StN discrimination between the technique capability and the target measurement to be valuable for CAPA efforts.

Finally, HPLC is most costly, both for instrumentation and labour, but the most precise, with ability to analyse for the presence or quantity of compounds in the parts per billion range. For routine release, the capability is thousands of times more accurate than necessary for drugs with label claims of 1 to 1,000 mg or more. In other words, is a result of 100.0 mg of active substance per tablet less adequate than 100.000250 mg per tablet when the daily dose is 200 milligrams per day? The ability to measure 250 parts per million precision comes at a high cost in terms of labour and instrumentation. The StN point is substantially below the threshold necessary to perform process management and CAPA evaluations.

LIMITED INVESTIGATION TIME

Effective CAPA investigation work takes time. How much time can the pharmaceutical company afford to spend in performing an effective CAPA investigation? If the company does not make time to perform flawlessly the first time, is the same company likely to rationalize the incremental cost of time and labour to correct the problem?

The slowest and most extreme CAPA investigations occur when a problem is only identified after the product has left the manufacturer's control. When product is in distribution, CAPA investigations are known as recalls. A pharmaceutical manufacturer could require months, or even years, to complete a recall CAPA.

The other extreme – and the ideal – would be a CAPA that is generated from a process designed following the Artisan Model, where the problem is identified as it occurs. In this case, the time to complete the CAPA would be reduced to hours or days.

For example, one of us was asked to participate in the final stages of an OOS investigation into an abnormally high result for one out of ten samples analysed via HPLC. The facts included the following:

- reagent standards were prepared correctly;

- calibration and system suitability were proper for the HPLC;

- assay was perfectly centered and within validated variability;

- one out of nine uniformity of dosage results was 5 per cent higher than all other doses;

- all equipment was properly calibrated and within the normal range.

The OOS and subsequent CAPA work (about two days by the laboratory analytical team) had not revealed a clear root cause. Two possibilities were under consideration. The first was sample preparation, which could not be verified as the sample preparation was discarded by the glassware cleaning technician. The second was a fault within the injector. The question 'what evidence would support injector fault?' directed the investigation to the sample holding magazine. Review of the tray revealed a damaged septum on the sample in question. This observation brought out the fact that the HPLC used was capable of holding a drop on the injector needle. The drop size estimates showed that this amount could account nicely for the high analytical value. With a clear root cause, the single abnormal point was discarded as the corrective action. A preventive action was to train the other chemists in the importance of reviewing and understanding the process elements – in this case *machine* and *materials* – at the beginning and at the end of the process run.

In this real-life example, the laboratory fortunately recognized the non-conforming result a short time after it occurred. If this same situation had not been recognized until weeks later, the investigation would have required significantly more time to evaluate because the critical cause (the damaged sample vial) that resulted in the effect (too much sample was analysed) would not have been available. The burden of proof to establish a root cause could have taken significant amounts of time and resources to test hypotheses of a root cause.

LACK OF VERIFICATION AFTER IMPLEMENTATION

CAPA investigations often deal with randomly generated failures or failures that can only be verified following an extended period of time, such as allowing for inventory turnover. The cause and effect details at the time of occurrence are erased by the time between the event and its recognition. The corrective action is typically the short-term priority, since the deviation results in delays in product distribution or possibly a recall.

To satisfy the business imperatives, the CAPA investigation ends after identification of the most plausible root cause. The preventive action – what should be done to prevent future occurrences – is therefore based on a hypothetical root cause. Hypotheses should always be proved by scientific study. As such, the preventive action should be designed to gather scientific evidence to confirm the hypothesis. There are several important implications, all of which involve time plus a process capable of identifying a point when the hypothesis can be verified.

As an example, one of us was involved in a CAPA for customer complaints of short counts in a product packed in blister packs. Sometimes more unethical customers attempted to receive free product through a customer complaint, so it was important to look at the nature of the complaint and ask if this was feasible considering the validated control systems.

The specific manufacturing line involved included an in-line weigh checker, so short counts should never occur. However, the data frequency and the manner in which complaints occurred showed an odd pattern of occurrence. Up to the point where we became involved, the CAPA concluded 'lack of training' was the root cause. If this was true, then after the remedial training session, the problem should not arise again.

The only means of gathering data to verify the effectiveness of the CAPA was to know how long it took for a product to leave the manufacturing facility and travel through the distribution chain to the retail sales level. Comparing production start date for the lot in question and the date of the first complaint was received revealed an approximate five-month interval. In other words, preventive actions could not be confirmed as effective until at least five months after they were completed.

Additional complaints for the same reason were received after the implementation of the preventive action. This resulted in a follow-up audit that revealed the true root cause: a reduction in the length of the transport belt prior to the weigh checker resulted in cartons being placed on the balance platform before the scale could stabilize. On average, 1.5 cartons were occasionally being weighed at once. This led to rejections. When cartons were opened as a 'bad unit', the personnel observed a full package. This led to mistrust in the validated weigh checker and the work procedure was unofficially changed to accumulate rejected cartons and work them into the queue for case packaging when the blister filling machine was down for maintenance – thus keeping the line working at peak operating percentage, a measure of management scheduling success. A small percentage of boxes were actually short filled, but were sent to market as if they were full.

Solutions

CAPA evaluation must be timely and decisive. Timely does not imply performing a sloppy investigation and, as we noted, spending inadequate time considering the related elements of the process is a waste of time and ensures that the problem will arise again. Several concepts outline appropriate actions that must be integrated within the CAPA procedure:

- identify all impacted products and contain immediately;

- evaluate the design controls;

- decide on the action;

- change the system controls, but only if warranted;

- monitor the new system controls for effectiveness.

IDENTIFY ALL IMPACTED PRODUCTS AND CONTAIN IMMEDIATELY

Two categories of corrective action plans must be considered. The internal CAPA is for problems that are still within the control of the manufacturer and will be referred to as internal capture. The external CAPA requires more logistical coordination as the situation can involve a recall or voluntary market withdrawal and will be referred to as external capture. In either state, the primary objective is to protect the patient benefit-to-risk ratio or profile. This analysis must, of course, include consideration of benefit/risk included in the labelling, such as indications, contraindications, patient population or adverse events. In order to fully consider the risk to the health of an already compromised patient, the CAPA must use meaningful data to assess the extent of the problem.

The better of the two situations is the internal capture where the organization still maintains control of the product before it is distributed to the market. Internal capture provides some time to develop and perform a controlled analysis of the problem using pre-defined statistically based sampling approaches. Internal capture is the most certain way to protect the interests of the patient as the CAPA evolves. With manufacturing records at hand and a well-conceived sampling plan in place, a highly credible action plan can be developed. The action plan should not only look at the lot under scrutiny but should also trace backwards to cover other lots that may have used common drug substance lots, excipient component lots or even the same process equipment. A good instructive framework of the issue should be found from the historical review. A competent and honest appraisal should reveal whether or not the problem is the result of subtle drift or if it is a recent shift in quality. Retained product samples will provide additional information and should be used to help bound the situation as to what the problem is and what the problem is not.

External capture is the more challenging CAPA to resolve as product is in the market and identifying product samples for analysis is difficult at best. Further, the manufacturer must often act quickly to protect patient safety. Gathering accurate data is the challenge. The process design team should include a risk contingency plan after the fundamental process has been developed and is in its early stage of production. Response must be rapid and decisive. Sampling for meaningful data is challenging as there are no assurances that the product in the market has not been subjected to adverse storage conditions. Withdrawal is an effective – and usually mandated – albeit costly way to ensure that only safe and effective product is present in the market.

In either an internal or external capture, the CAPA plan must ensure that only reliable data sets are analysed. Reliable data sets will effectively differentiate characteristic data, results which are consistent with the process design, from valid data that have a root cause outside of the process design. For example, if the drug product is a hard-gelatin capsule and a complaint is received for 'capsules being stuck together as a single mass', then performance of the filling equipment does not need to be checked. Further, for external capture, the manufacturer must learn why the quality control system failed to properly identify the situation as it developed, should the problem be proved to have originated at the manufacturer.

EVALUATE THE DESIGN CONTROLS

Data analysis during a CAPA evaluation should consider the boundaries of practical possibilities to define what the problem is but, equally importantly, to understand what the problem is not. This concept has its origins in the Kepner-Tregoe technique for problem-solving (1981). Bounding the problem helps to clarify the signals from the noise to more rapidly understand the immediate situation. The data must be evaluated objectively and without bias. The original process quality controls must be reconsidered. After all, the problem was not identified at the point of occurrence. The investigation should focus on the inherent precision and accuracy assumptions of the process quality controls rather than relying on finished product specification limits.

Four areas of the process should be the focal points of the investigation. The CAPA should consider control of components during dispensing, production process controls, sampling plan sensitivity and laboratory analytical results.

In considering the cumulative impact of the precision and accuracy of the current systems, attention must be given to both the centring and spread of the data distribution. Further, it is advisable to include the retrospective evaluation of change controls that have been made. There are sometimes changes in data that result from integrating an approved change control to the system. This is especially true for change controls that involve drug substances. Subtle and sometimes unknown changes in starting materials or raw materials can alter drug substance crystallization or even the polymorphic form. Both situations will have some effect, good or bad, on the process. Experienced drug substance chemists recognize that consistency of product is a function of trace impurity chemistry characteristics, more so than stoichiometric chemistry.

DECIDE ON THE ACTION

The actions taken must favour patient safety. For external failures, notification to the regulatory agency is expected. When speaking with the regulators, opinion is not relevant and will damage the credibility of the final outcome. The CAPA decision is complicated in today's pharmaceutical business climate. In nearly every country, the risk of being taken to court is growing and the outcomes are carrying process management further into the realm of predictive statistics and further away from functional simplicity. Whatever the final outcome, the resulting decision must be consistent with the scientific facts generated throughout the product's lifecycle, including clinical data, non-clinical data and commercial product test results in addition to the CAPA data generated for the specific investigation.

The final action plan should be captured in the appropriate format, using word processing or spreadsheets as appropriate to facilitate nimble communication. We recommend organizing the CAPA into a three-column comparative table structure that takes the reviewer through the issue in a logical manner. This approach is simple yet effective. The emphasis is on the functionality of the investigation rather than on the format of the final report. Three columns and a few pages should be the extent of this exercise.

For pharmaceutical companies that have already jumped into the Common Technical Document (CTD) format, the manufacturing process, specifications, methods and in-process controls make an excellent starting point for guiding efforts to determine the root cause. The advantage of this approach is the consistency with the CTD and the scientific content. Table 10.1 shows an example of our CAPA investigation organizer.

Table 10.1 Example of laboratory analysis using the CAPA investigation organizer

Scope and History of this investigation: Laboratory analysis of XYZ tablets. The product has a 5 year history of highly consistent analytical test results. The past 10 lots have a process mean of 100.3% (RSD 0.5%); Uniformity of Dosage for the same lots has a mean of 99.9% (RSD 1.2%).

Problem statement: Content uniformity analysis for product XYZ lot ABC analyzed on 24-June-2011 had 3 results outside acceptance criteria limits of 96.0—104.0% when analyzed by method 1234.05 Rev. 02. Test data from tablets 3, 7 were high; test data from tablet 8 was low. Other analytical values appeared lower than normally expected.

Registered In-Process Controls	Investigation Findings	CAPA Summary
Working standard concentration: 1 mg/ml	Standard preparation 100 mg weighed into a 100 ml volumetric	Procedure followed. Proper error of drug substance weight to concentration used. Area count of the chromatogram is consistent with the past 10 lots. UNLIKELY ROOT CAUSE
Reference standard concentration: 1 mg/ml	Reference preparation 10mg weighed in weigh boat and transferred to 10ml volumetric.	Questionable final concentration of the reference standard. Chemist instructed to save cost and stretch compendia standard. Standard is dusty and was weighed under a negative pressure hood for safety reasons. Reference standard is a strong UV absorbing compound. Unrecognized loss during transfer likely. POSSIBLE ROOT CAUSE
Sample preparation: 1 tablet in 100 ml volumetric	Standard preparation 100 mg weighed into a 100 ml volumetric	Procedure followed. Area count of the chromatogram is consistent with the past 10 lots. UNLIKELY ROOT CAUSE
Dilute with mobile phase and mix well	Records of mobile phase preparation document proper preparation. The same lot of mobile phase was also used for product X with no OOS results.	Procedure followed. System suitability of individual components solutions appears normal. UNLIKELY ROOT CAUSE
Place into clean analysis vials with septum. Place into HPLC tray and analyze	Record of HPLC run show all system suitability analyses, standards, blanks and samples were analyzed.	Procedure followed. All data points within the HPLC run appear normal and consistent with the past 10 lots of product XYZ. UNLIKELY ROOT CAUSE

Table 10.1   Continued

NO REQUIREMENT TO INSPECT TRAY FOLLOWING ANALYSIS	Records of HPLC run show all system suitability analyses, standards, blanks and samples were analyzed. The septums in samples 3 and 7 were damaged and dislodged. Sample 8 appeared visually normal.	Verification of instrument is not routinely part of the procedural verifications at the end of analysis. Process management of analytical results should include verification of condition of *machine*, and *material*. POTENTIAL CAPA ACTION
NO REQUIREMENT TO COMPARE CONTENT UNIFORMITY WITH INTERMEDIATE PRECISION OF METHOD VALIDATION Method validation intermediate precision: 0.9%	Analytical results were analyzed for variation and mean recovery against intermediate precision of the method validation. T-test of sample mean result indicates statistically different results compared to previous 10 lots. Mean was 102.4%. The area count was statistically different than the mean area count of the last 10 lots. RSD of sample was 2.3%. RSD of sample without vial 3 and 7 was 1.8% RSD.	Verification of data variability is not routinely part of the procedural verification of data integrity. Process management of analytical results should include verification of performance of the *method*. POTENTIAL CAPA ACTION

CAPA Hypothesis: 1) Injector needle is not consistently piercing septums, leading to inconsistent volume. ACTION 1: Replace needle
2) Insufficient reference standard is being weighed to negate slight handling losses. Concentration of the solution is suspected of artificially elevating tablet test results.

CA Summary: Damage to septums observed on vials 3 and 7 is sufficient to disqualify analysis. Per procedure 1AJE.04, 10 tablets are to be analyzed after HPLC needle retrofit. Standard is to be prepared by weighing 100 mg of reference into a 100 ml volumetric. Results will be compared to previous 10 lots and to the method validation. Hypotheses will be affirmed if no damaged septums are observed and test results are statistically no different when compared to the method validation. Investigation will be expanded to manufacturing if standard data is still inconsistent with validation results.

PA Summary: Laboratory procedures are to be revised to include responsibility to review all aspects of HPLC prior to initiating analysis and at the conclusion of analysis. The analytical procedure will be revised to prescribe minimum and maximum weights of standard to be used in order to minimize variation of weighing and transfer. All other analytical procedures will be evaluated for possible inadvertent weighing variability and will be revised to include minimum and maximum weight to be used in standard preparations.

CHANGE THE SYSTEM CONTROLS, BUT ONLY IF WARRANTED

The CAPA investigation must consider the history to determine if a product defect is process noise or process signal. If this is not done, the generated solution may not resolve the problem. The system controls should only be changed when the failure is a confirmed process signal or the process owner chooses to upgrade equipment to better match the process needs. Remember that effective quality control systems are simple, not complex. They should be based on 'yes or no; right or wrong' data to facilitate quick and accurate decisions. Action should be taken in a timely manner if a shift in the centring or the variability of the process is confirmed. Timely identification will be close in time to the cause and effect point – where the data are most reliable. Given current technology, keeping processes simple and accurate can be challenging. Too much randomly generated data will only obscure the control and can lead to unrecognized change signals.

MONITOR THE NEW SYSTEM CONTROLS FOR EFFECTIVENESS

When changes to controls are the confirmed solution of the CAPA exercise, the failure loop must be closed by a follow-up assessment. The timing is critical to establish meaningful and timely assessments of long-term success. The new controls must be integrated and monitored for adequacy and could sometimes require validation to demonstrate the effectiveness of the change. The company should not overlook the CAPA activities as an opportunity to simplify the controls or even move towards simple proven techniques such as a run chart, in which data are plotted to show trending and variation.

Validation could involve the verification and incorporation of long-term trending of current controls to assess the stability of the system before and after the change. A chart, rather than a sophisticated statistical analysis, is worth a thousand words. Long-term monitoring using simple charts is an effective way to visualize a trend before a process failure requires the use of a CAPA investigation.

Conclusion

Understanding the sensitivity of process controls by the StN ratio is key to performing a successful CAPA exercise. The StN of a process is similar in concept to the Limit of Detection (LoD) and Limit of Quantitation (LoQ) of a method validation.

Lot sampling for release often lacks adequate precision to identify long-term trends. Proven process management tools such as a run chart and histogram will overcome the limitations of isolated, lot-based quality control sampling for evaluation. Several considerations of problem definition and resolution will make CAPA more effective and proactive. A well-defined problem from a properly designed process is half-solved due to the accuracy of the data. Many CAPA investigations are ineffective because statistical methods misdirect problem efforts down a single path based on mathematical averages.

CAPA investigations should rely heavily on the experience of the lead investigator to focus the investigation in the right direction. If the data show the problem to lie within the 'noise region' of the process, it is up to the process owner – management – to resolve. Either the system must be changed, often a capital investment, or the specification must be relaxed to allow for the characteristic defect levels. It is up to the CAPA investigation to sort out the signal from the noise in order to properly resolve a problem and improve the overall quality control system.

11

Process-Driven Quality Systems

The system for causing quality is prevention, not appraisal.
(Philip Crosby, 1926–2001, American author on quality)

Introduction

In the pharmaceutical industry, there is a legislative imperative to satisfy all regulatory requirements relating to the safety, quality and efficacy of the product for the protection of the patient. As such, the first purpose of a quality system is to comply with the letter of the law – doing things right by analytical testing. However, for effective process management, it is also important to comply with the spirit of the law – doing the right things by process design.

The quality systems of many companies focus only on the first aspect, the letter of the law. Such a product-driven quality system is based on the belief that the product will be of sufficient quality and will comply with regulatory expectations provided that all procedures and tests are followed to the letter. Missing is the spirit of continual improvement and process excellence, which is characteristic of process-driven quality systems. Product-driven systems will invariably fail to remain current with GMP, as will be shown later in this chapter.

Older established organizations in particular tend to exhibit such product-driven quality systems. They need to be re-engineered and mapped to incorporate the systematic quality controls within the process boundaries and quality assurance measures of peripheral systems outside of the immediate product process controls. For example, if quality control measures do not exist for Heating, Ventilation and Air Conditioning (HVAC) systems – *environment* – and products are sensitive to heat or humidity, new controls will have to be developed and monitored via manual or automatic systems. Further, quality assurance measures and reports will have to be developed to link HVAC controls of the system to demonstrate that environments are capable of controlling not only ambient temperature and humidity but also airflow, thus preventing adulteration of product. The resulting changes will move the company closer to twenty-first-century process management expectations.

For business organizations with new and evolving systems, early-phase projects should have input from 'process knowledgeable' employees who will guide system development along a process-balanced path with appropriate levels of control. The result should therefore be 'right-first-time' outcomes.

The content of the process design elements has been covered in earlier chapters. Essentially, the quality system must integrate *man* (people, skills and training), *methods* (techniques of analysis and process evaluation), *materials* (active, excipient and packaging components used to create dose forms), *machine* (processing and control equipment for producing and analysing the dose) and *environment* (the building, support systems and managerial skills necessary to ensure employee awareness and to operate in a clean facility). The result will be quality systems that comply with both the spirit and the letter of the law.

Quality Control and Quality Assurance

We start by reviewing the concepts of quality control and quality assurance in order to define the interaction between them. We focus on the functions of each within the context of process design and management. We do not address the issues of departmental titles or roles within the organization.

In order to makes sense of process design and management and to facilitate effective process improvement, it is important to understand the basic differences between quality control and quality assurance. Understanding the possible business limitations of confusing the two is also important for a regulatory professional as they guide CMC changes along the regulatory and GMP content line to reduce future company risk.

Quality controls are the points designed to reveal deviation from the purpose and design of a process from a statistical or cosmetic perspective. Quality control is directly accountable for allowing the process to proceed following assessment. In any process design, there are a host of choices on which way to develop quality controls. Quality controls apply to all five of the process elements:

- *man* – training records, academic qualifications, specific to the problems the person is hired to solve or the solutions the person is expected to provide in a continuous improvement mode, etc.;

- *machine* – speed, frequency of preventive maintenance, pressure, electrical resistance;

- *material* – grade or unique characteristics, physical condition – compendial, crystalline, fluffy powder, white, without dark specks, etc.;

- *method* – precision, accuracy, robustness, appropriate technology, sampling, special controls such as hydrolysis for hygroscopic material or timely freeze drying for lyophilized products;

- *environment* – oxygen suppression, nitrogen blanket, yellow light, low-moisture HVAC, personnel encouragement and development.

Quality assurance is the action of reviewing the quality controls to verify or confirm the veracity and accuracy of the system after the event. Quality audit, efficiency opportunities and comparison of state of the art versus current state can all be triggers for continual improvement in conjunction with quality controls. Table 11.1 lists some of the key differences between process quality control and process quality assurance.

Table 11.1   Comparison of quality control and quality assurance

Quality control	Quality assurance
• Collection, generation or management of data • Determining the risk within the process based on existing and current technology • Taking immediate action to ensure that the process meets design requirements • Measurements or limitations of physical parameters such as time, temperature, pressure, electrical conductance or colour that convey process success or failure • Measures should be simple and leave no room for interpretation • Product controls are expressed in a specification • Process controls include manufacturing records, procedures and guidelines, as appropriate	• Evaluation and appropriate communication of the effectiveness of quality control efforts • Results should be used to improve the process rather than as a means of criticizing individuals • Relates to administrative overview of process quality control • Oversees company-wide improvement efforts • Analyses should have predictive characteristics • Assessment of risk in the letter and spirit of the laws

Quality assurance provides a second and unbiased view of the process and takes on the responsibility of certification of results based on considered assessment of performance against controls. It also provides independent evaluation of the causes of customer complaints.

For example, think back to the case quoted in Chapter 10. A customer complaint was received about a blister pack where some of the blister pockets were missing. This should not have occurred since there was a validated weigh checker in line that was designed to remove underweight cartons. During the investigation, it was realized that an approved change made to the quality controls had voided the validation of the system. The change had been to reduce the dwell time for the carton on the weigh scale for productivity purposes. The unintended consequence was that the scale did not have a chance to settle before the following carton was presented for checking. The cycle time of the two cartons was insufficient to allow the balance to stabilize. However, the weight now exceeded the allowable range and both cartons were being rejected – creating false negatives. This led to personnel bypassing the scale altogether and thus sending failures to market.

Effective Quality Controls Equal Effective Process Management

Quality controls should be simple and the way to ensure their simplicity is by designing them into the process before starting; retrofitting is never a good idea. Effective quality control should be factored into the process design as each of the process component resources – *man, machine, method, material* and *environment* – is configured to meet a business purpose and necessary sensitivity.

This section will discuss effective quality controls from an experienced, hands-on perspective. There are plenty of FDA presentations (Famulare 2007; McNally 2007; Nasr 2006) and considerable management literature (Bolton 1990; Siegel 2003; Wheeler and Chambers 1992) which describe the theoretical outcomes and mathematical considerations underlying process management and quality controls. These references may be reviewed in order to gain additional understanding of the theory and application of effective quality control and process management.

Quality controls are the points within the process where actual performance is assessed against the intended performance of the process design. The outcome of the quality control examination is a decision to either progress the workflow towards completion or to stop the process to problem-solve an observed deviation. The in-process controls specification document is therefore the measure against which the quality control test data are evaluated. Under a process-driven quality system, this evaluation would look not only at the mean of the data but also at the variability between different data points. The interpretation of the data will only be effective in a situation of process knowledge and understanding. There will not be a 'one-size-fits-all' result applicable to all products and processes. To this point, the following six considerations are a start in establishing an effective quality control programme.

RESULTS MUST BE JUDGED AGAINST THE PROCESS DESIGN CRITERIA

Under a product-driven control system, the decision on whether to accept a set of test results is taken following comparison of the test data with the limits in the pharmacopoeial monographs – the legal referee method. This is not acceptable under a process-driven control system.

Every process must include capable, validated tests and statistically meaningful sampling plans for verifying the intended target mean of the process. The allowable variation of the process will be made up of the intrinsic precision of the equipment, the purity of the materials and the technological basis of the methods selected. Compendial standards are good science within themselves. However, in our experience, most are too broad to support the process excellence theoretically achievable by today's technology platforms such as HPLC for sample analysis and highly precise balances for drug substance weighing.

Automatic acceptance of compendial standards will tend to lower the level of outgoing quality. A wide compendial specification range allows the process owner to accept off-target test results providing the mean lies within the compendial range, a *de facto* legal limit of release. Consequently, the off-target test sample will not automatically prompt a process investigation to determine the root cause as to why the process missed the intended target value. The outcome is increased variability of process results and an accompanying reduced quality of product.

TESTS MUST ALIGN TO THE DESIRED CONTROL

The quality control test plan must be aligned to the type of data generated at a given step of the process. Further, data management and interpretation should be consistent with proven quality practice.

There are two general purposes for generating quality control data. The first is to evaluate the mean of the sample against the intended target for the process. A test of the process target would involve a composite sample over a defined short period of time. The result of this test will assist the machine operator in deciding whether or not the process mean has shifted or drifted from the intended target. If it has, decisive action must be taken to consider the implications of adjusting the process mean. In other words, machine adjustments should be made only when there is a high degree of statistical evidence to support such action. For example, this is the seventh sample in a row where the current sample average is higher than the preceding sample average, or a test value outside of historic +3 or -3 standard deviation limits is observed. These situations are well documented as strong evidence of the process mean changing from the intended target.

The second purpose of generating quality control data is to evaluate the variability of the individual values that comprise the mean. The same considerations of sampling and data evaluation as discussed for the mean result apply.

Mean and variation data should be evaluated according to proper data management techniques. Again there are two general characteristics to be considered. The first deals with absolute data, which is sometimes called variable data. Absolute (variable) data must be traceable to a reference standard and are derived from tests such as assay, content uniformity, impurities and tablet mass. Management of absolute data is best achieved with tools such as the X-bar (mean) and R (range) charts, typically referred to as statistical process control (SPC). The purpose of absolute data is to develop statistical evidence that the mean and variation lie within normally expected process design ranges and limits. It is absolute data which are most often used to identify within-lot and between-lot variability.

The second type deals with relative data, also called attribute data. Relative data have no reference standard *per se*. However, they provide highly relevant information about subtle changes in input materials or finished product outputs that cannot be determined directly by the evaluation of variable data. Examples of relative data include visual descriptions of colour, excipient textures and crystal appearance or dissolution results for the final grand average for each lot of finished product. Management of relative data is best accomplished through run charts or control charts of attributes, such as c, p or n-p charts. Relative data provides critical information about the overall consistency of the process, with the key purpose being to identify subtle variability between lots.

TESTS MUST MEASURE ONE DISCRETE OUTCOME OF A PROCESS ELEMENT

In designing an effective process, quality control data have two primary objectives. These are firstly to identify and secondly to resolve problems that are foreign to the process design. Any resulting action to change the operation of the process must be supported by a high degree of statistical certainty and must be factually driven, whether the data are variable or attribute in nature.

For a quality control data point to be meaningful, the test must evaluate only one process element. A process action may involve several sequential manufacturing steps and more than one of the five process elements – *man, machine, method, material* and *environment* – but taken as a whole, there should be one unique quality control test data set to speak to a unique root cause related to one process element. Therefore, placement of the quality control test point according to the process design elements is very important.

For example, think again about the case quoted in Chapter 10 where an analytical value generated by the HPLC for a content uniformity test was found to be OOS since it was above the maximum limit. The problem-solving investigation did not reveal an immediate root cause as two process elements, *machine* (HPLC) and *material* (drug substance content), were involved in the test and either or both could have contributed to this problem. The analyst had failed to inspect the septum of the HPLC sample vial – machine performance – prior to or after evaluating the test data. By failing to review the potential quality control data from the HPLC, the problem had two potential root causes: either a machine problem or product formulation problem, with only one set of data – the content uniformity result – to distinguish between the two root causes. Fortunately, the instrument injection tray had not been discarded and subsequent inspection of the vials revealed the sample needle of the HPLC had failed to pierce the septum of the vial with the high analytical values. Therefore, the most likely root cause resulted from the instrument placing an 'extra drop' of sample into the injector. The brand of HPLC was known to introduce that 'extra drop of sample' into the injector due to the design of the instrument. In other words, the septum was critical to the performance of the content uniformity analysis for 'wiping off' excess sample from the injector needle. Had the sample tray been discarded without identifying the sample vial problem, the OOS would have had an indeterminate root cause. This identified an additional control point to be factored into the process design.

TEST SAMPLES MUST BE CAPABLE OF DETECTING A CHANGE IN MEAN OR VARIABILITY

Samples must be representative of the material and be of adequate size to allow detection of a change either in the mean or in the variability. Often insufficient time is spent on the determination and identification of adequate sample plans that develop controls specific to the process. Commonly accepted sample plans derived from compendial plans – for example, ten tablets for stage 1 of content uniformity or six tablets for stage 1 of dissolution – may be selected out of convenience or cost considerations. These sample sizes may be adequate relative to the specifications published in the compendia but may be completely inadequate to manage the mean or variation of a particular process.

There are two general types of sampling. The first is random sampling which is aimed at detecting defects generated and distributed randomly throughout the final product. Such defects are supposed to have a statistically equal chance of being identified in the quality control sample during acceptance testing. We would propose that there is only one system that meets this definition: a completely fluid system such as a pharmaceutical water plant or fluid bed granulator.

The second type of sampling is termed continuous process sampling in which the samples are representative of the process activity and are taken at times both during normal operation and when the process is not running normally, such as start-up and shut-down.

The premise of a continuous process sample is that a machine does not intentionally produce defects when it is running normally. Instead, defects are generated during defined periods of time and are introduced to finished products in a non-random fashion. Industry spends countless amounts of money to prove that a normally operating piece of machinery runs per design with high-quality output. However, not as much time is spent in ensuring that quality control procedures adequately isolate and remove materials from abnormal operating conditions.

The following example will illustrate this point. Printed folding cartons – secondary packaging – were found to pass the incoming quality tests. Lot sizes were large and the sample size was equally large. However, during production, cartons were sometimes found to be glued together and thus unable to be opened, or not glued and thus unable to hold together during high-speed operation. The result was damaged equipment and poor supplier relations.

The root cause was found to be occurring during carton machine start-up and shut down times around mid-morning breaks and lunch breaks. The machine was not cleared during shut-down for break and the glue dried on the in-process cartons. The quality control sampling, being a random plan, did not automatically isolate potential defectives at start-up following breaks. Random sampling by the customer is often inadequate to manage the quality of a discrete process at the supplier.

DECISIONS MUST BE SIMPLE

Testing of quality control samples and evaluation of test data are intended for the manufacturing operator who has to decide whether to continue with the process or temporarily halt it pending problem resolution. Stated differently, the quality control sample asks the questions 'Has the mean changed, yes or no?' and 'Has the variability changed, yes or no?'. Decisions should be simple without a set of complex rules reflecting a myriad of theoretical possibilities, including those generally outside the process design range. Complex investigations should be handled by the quality assurance functions of an organization based on the identification of a problem when testing the quality control sample.

TESTS MUST CONSIDER BOTH THE CURRENT STATE AND THE PAST

Finally, process evaluation decisions must consider the current state of sample data as well as the historical performance of the process. Samples must monitor both the within-lot variability and the between-lot variability. Robust quality control plans should include within-lot quality control approaches, such as X-bar and R samples, and between-lots controls, such as run charts and attribute charts of non-variable data. Robust process management truly requires both to complement the quality programme.

Determination of Appropriate In-process Control Limits

The determination of appropriate in-process control limits assumes that the process is reliable and robust. Sources of input variation to the process should be identified and controlled. Without control of input variation, there can be no confidence in the reliability of the process. Control of input variation should be directly correlated to resulting process variation. When input variation is allowed within controlled limits, processes should in turn be reliable and robust.

Processes may then be characterized in order to set appropriate control limits. Processes should be adjusted when it is appropriate to adjust but left alone when they exhibit normal variation. How many times have we seen operators 'tweaking' processes – eroding quality – when test results show truly normal variation? Each time the process is adjusted, the mean will move and hence the recording of variation will no longer be valid.

There are many references, including those given earlier in this chapter, describing the appropriate determination of control limits that have been published both within and outside the pharmaceutical literature. Use of the methods described in these references, at levels appropriate to the intended outcome, is highly recommended. The ramifications of *not* setting appropriate control limits or of setting the same limits for all products/processes when true differences exist are significant.

Common Hurdles to Effective Quality Control and Quality Assurance

Implementing effective quality control and quality assurance measures requires significant business discipline, which can be defined as allowing sufficient time to develop and understand process assumptions, characterize important procedures, establish relevant controls and verify assumptions with data. This general understanding of quality control and quality assurance is important throughout an organization in order to provide a basis for understanding the risks built into the process described in a CMC filing. Failure to do this could mean delayed approvals due to regulatory questions about controls.

In this final section, we will describe several common areas of challenge and offer quality technique ideas that will move the company past the hurdle and closer to a quality system that conforms both to the letter and the spirit of the law.

THE QUALITY UNIT IS RESPONSIBLE FOR PRODUCT QUALITY

In this situation, the quality unit's practice is directed towards police-like activities of catching employees who fail to follow procedures or who fail to complete records. Certainly, not following procedures and not completing documentation are significant GMP problems. However, the quality unit may become so busy with enforcement that it becomes blinkered and fails to recognize when the procedure is based on obsolete technology or antiquated techniques or process assumptions. As such, the quality unit may fail to facilitate updates and changes to the process.

A second possibility is that the quality unit assumes a quality control function within the process. In this case, the most likely outcome is the opposite of good quality. Problems occur due to operator inattention and lack of due care, since the most appropriate individual is external to the decision to be made not accountable for the quality control outcome.

As a result of this hurdle, meaningful system improvement will never occur to update outdated, obsolete process assumptions. At the same time, the responsibility for high-quality product is shuffled between the quality unit and operations departments.

A possible solution to this hurdle can be found in process mapping. By using this technique, responsibilities can be clarified and controls placed at the correct stage of the process. Proper accountability can be established.

ADOPTING INDUSTRY STANDARD ATTRIBUTE SAMPLING PLANS

A second barrier is the wholesale adoption of attribute acceptance sampling plans, such as Military Standard 105D (ANSI-ASQ Z1.4). This standard served business well for many years, but is generally inappropriate in today's high-speed manufacturing environment. However, it continues to be used in critical quality control and quality assurance points without proper verification or validation by the user.

There are two basic issues that require careful consideration prior to the implementation of attribute sampling plans. Firstly, the plan is used for sampling attributes and measures of goodness, and is not intended for quality control or quality assurance measures that involve numbers. Secondly, the incoming population is presumed to be homogeneous, which in turn ensures the ability to take a representative sample. With these risks, the plan is still used. The specific reasons vary, but in general terms, the mention of Military Standard sampling plans halts regulatory questions about the statistical appropriateness of the plan.

A possible solution to this hurdle can be found in supplier audits. Supplier process knowledge is absolutely the best manner to establish representative sampling and will also foster communication with a key contributor in a company's success.

'WE HAVE NEVER HAD AN ADVERSE REGULATORY INSPECTION'

Another barrier relates to the culture of the company, which inhibits fresh ideas presented by new employees. This culture can be encouraged by complacency in the situation where there has not been a USFDA 483 observation or the equivalent from European or other international regulators during facility inspections. The result is the continued use of obsolete or ineffective quality control or quality assurance practices.

A possible solution to this hurdle is to positively solicit observations and suggestions from current and – in particular – new employees. The use of Kaizen watching (Imai 1986) provides a means to improve the effectiveness of quality control and quality assurance within an operation. The value of a fresh pair of eyes is to observe the obvious which is often overlooked by people who are too familiar with a situation.

IGNORING 'TRIVIAL' MARKETING COMPLAINTS ON VALIDATED PROCESSES

Every product failure generated from a validated process should be investigated to define the root cause. From a process management perspective, every market complaint is a new piece of evidence that suggests quality control and quality assurance may be compromised. Often, there is no significant impact on the safety or efficacy of the dose, so the issue is overlooked. For example, we have seen a batch of approved stickers for materials stored in the warehouse rejected for being 'the wrong shade of green'. No possible risk to the product or the patient existed; the complaint was truly trivial. Nonetheless, all failures should be reviewed, a root cause established and controls altered to prevent future occurrences.

A possible solution to this hurdle is to develop a process-sensitive customer complaint system to identify profitable business efficiency issues. This requires an understanding of product movement through the supply chain, also called inventory turnover.

MANAGING RISK AS A POST-MORTEM STRATEGY

Accepting 'after-the-fact' process deviations under a risk management strategy compromises the integrity of quality control and quality assurance practice. Accepting risk management as a post-approval technique automatically builds failure into the process. Poor quality analysis at the finished dose stage is counterintuitive to good and robust development activities.

In the context of process management, acceptable risks should only be debated during the process development phase. In doing so, the development team must recognize and analyse quality control alternatives. Risk analysis during development is an appropriate and important way to balance alternative quality control and quality assurance approaches to ensure the precision and timeliness of data and maintain a history of decisions for future improvement purposes.

A possible solution to this hurdle is to build continual improvement expectations into the process design. PAT tools and techniques, if considered during development activities, will identify critical quality control points, where the speed of the result is of the essence. Additionally, process improvement should be included as a means to update the controls when technology changes in the future. Remember that one size does not fit all, so the application of any quality control measure must lie within a relevant range of data needs.

Conclusion

For effective process design and management, it is necessary to take a process-driven approach to the quality system. Companies will have to overcome legacy constraints – outdated cultural approaches – to achieve quality control and quality assurance consistent with the final desired state of compliance outlined by regulators in current and draft guidance and to achieve effective process design and management.

Effective process management begins with correctly identifying both the quality control and quality assurance points of the process. For companies that run regulatory-approved processes, the best way to analyse the quality control and quality assurance requirements and responsibilities is to conduct a process-mapping project as part of a re-engineering activity. For new organizations, an employee who is literate in process management should be included as part of the development team.

As process development progresses, it is important to evaluate the risks of alternative quality control choices and record the final outcome as a starting point for future improvement activities. Finally, risk management is a tool to be employed during early development debate rather than as a post-approval manufacturing analysis technique. It is important for all employees to have a basic understanding of effective quality control and quality assurance outcomes in order to ensure that reliable product quality will be a routine part of a product's lifecycle.

12

Statistics and Decision Boundaries: Data Certainty

I can prove anything by statistics except the truth.
(George Canning, 1770–1827, British politician)

Introduction

Statistics and statistical techniques provide the verification of conclusions drawn as the result of careful and thoughtful study. This is an important point that we have seen frequently overlooked. Statistics should affirm the conclusions of existing knowledge-based decisions or provide the framework for the study of hypotheses to understand relationships that make up the scientific foundation for future conclusions. It is tempting to jump right in and analyse data to determine conclusions about the subject at hand. This approach often results in misunderstandings or misleading conclusions as the analyst fails to check the system construct or design. The data may appear to reflect one set of rules and conditions when in fact the system design has a completely different objective. An excellent example is the calculation of C_{pk}, or the capability of the process. C_{pk} can give the impression that all is well when in fact the opposite is true. Misinterpretation of data often occurs when the first qualifying rule of C_{pk} is violated: the process is performing normally. If you believe that committing this error is isolated to new inexperienced analysts, think again. Forgetting the basics is a problem for even seasoned professionals.

Process management relies on statistics to assist shop-floor personnel when they encounter unexpected events and situations. The experienced operator often recognizes the problem as it evolves and can make an 'intelligent evaluation' from past actions. However, when it is time to discuss the factors and reasoning behind taking specific actions to ameliorate the problem, it often comes down to using the numbers as supportive evidence. As pointed out in Chapter 5, a well-designed process control method provides high confidence in actions taken at the correct time and in the correct measure. Experience-based decisions supported by timely data, accurately analysed, is a potent strategy. A well-conceived statistical control plan should exhibit correct process decisions and answer the following questions: is the process performance consistent with the design and are actions taken consistent with statistical evidence?

Further, statistics provides mathematical discrimination of the average or variability when comparing two events. This is important as a concept for the design of continuous improvement programmes. The value of using sound hypotheses and alternatives is that relatively small data sets can reveal differences that otherwise may not be seen. This is good news for smaller firms without large amounts of money to throw at the problem. Commercial software programmes are available which are exceedingly powerful and easy to use. No longer is it vital to know how to perform specific calculations or memorize tricky formulae.

Our discussion of statistics will cover neither the sophisticated analytical procedures nor the fundamentals of probability that underlie statistical modeling. Rather, we will concentrate on the common-sense approaches to statistics that can be understood and appreciated by all employees and management. We intend for statistics to be correctly applied and in the proper measure to ensure that truth of the science, rather than accuracy of statistical technique, is the end result. When the techniques are practised correctly, the employee can directly benefit by working within smoother running processes. No longer do unexpected events have a significant impact on operational performance.

Closely related to statistics is the concept of decision boundaries. All processes have limitations and upper boundaries of performance. Continually high output performance at the maximum theoretical capacity will work counterintuitively to undermine the effectiveness of decisions and actions. Decision boundaries define the edges of process performance on either side of the point of central tendency (mean) of the data set. Outside of the decision boundary, also called extrapolation, data projections and conclusions can be very suspect, especially if the system that initially generated the data cannot maintain the *exact* conditions over the period of time covered by the extrapolation estimate.

Situations where extrapolative estimates are beneficial are stability studies. Great care is taken to control the storage environment temperature, humidity and light exposure during the life of the study. Early data estimates are possible as many of the pathways to forming degradants are described in first-order linear models. The decision boundary of product stability study is narrow and well defined. The product dose form is fixed and cannot change physical attributes, as the product is held within a protective container. Stability chambers often have continuous power back-up in the event of loss of line power. Samples are evaluated on a rigid test and report schedule.

On the other hand, a situation where extrapolative estimates are very suspect is real-time release (RTR). Of greatest concern are solid dosage forms such as tablets or capsules that seldom behave as a purely fluid process. The level of control that is achievable on modern equipment still lacks the consistency and certainty at full scale required to make predictive estimates of product potency for release purposes. In-process production is a dynamic system rather than a static system, such as is found in stability. Stability samples are assessed for several fundamental points: loss of potency, gain in degradants, physical deterioration or change. In-process analysis must cope with components that can change flow characteristics by particle attrition or unexpected and unspecified characteristics of the starting components. Understanding the underlying principles to be applied at a control point is best accomplished by experienced process employees. Applying the incorrect controls or applying the correct control method at the incorrect location is a recipe for unresolvable OOS events.

What are the Challenges?

There are eight challenges that result in inaccurate or misleading data from statistical analysis. The discussion in this section presumes that data and statistics are used in human clinical studies and post-approval manufacturing controls. The statistical challenges all relate to the confusion of scientific truth rather than the pure theoretical practice of statistical mathematics and include:

- forgetting data always represent a human life;

- blind data mining for management guidance;

- over-analysing or under-analysing data;

- preferring complex mathematics over simple diagrams;

- lack of knowledge, context or both;

- form/format over function;

- rationalizing data as a means to an end;

- extrapolating data in a dynamic system.

FORGETTING DATA ALWAYS REPRESENT A HUMAN LIFE

It must never be forgotten that in phase I, II and III clinical studies, each data point represents a patient. In particular, mathematicians who may not be trained in medical sciences or drug product production techniques may not be fully aware of this reality. An extreme example of the ethics surrounding statistics and the link between data and patients is found in the question of whether data gathered by the Nazis during the Second World War from their medical experiments should be used or not.

Evaluation of data must be performed with the consideration of the intended outcomes and goals of the study. To do otherwise is an invitation to a protracted discussion of the most relevant statistical approach to assess the data. When this happens, unfortunately, opinion and personal preferences are introduced into the decision-making process. We have observed this on numerous occasions. To paraphrase, we can't see the wood for the trees. Evaluation of data with the purpose of 'statistical accuracy' navigates a fine line between benefit and risk for a patient. This is why it is so vital to understand the purpose and objective of the study so as to ensure that the data generated and statistical evaluation are aligned to the end point, which is often a 'best guess' on the researcher's part.

BLIND DATA MINING FOR MANAGEMENT GUIDANCE

One of the unintended consequences of moving away from principle-based process design, as described by the Artisan Model, is the reliance on statistics to determine the priority and strategy of process management and subsequent improvement programmes. We often see companies adopt in-vogue quality and process management programmes on a logical fallacy of 'Irrelevant Appeal to Authority', where acceptance is based solely upon adoption by 'peer' organizations. For example, if 'big pharma' is using a continuous processing approach, it must be good and we should therefore accept the approach. This practice leads to firms blindly accepting their existing data as 'statistically stable' without actually verifying this to be the case. For example, many Six-Sigma programs quickly introduce the use of C_{pk}, P_{pk}, regression analysis and other statistical techniques to examine process performance. This approach puts the 'cart before the horse' and leads to more chaos rather than greater simplicity and clarity. The reason for the chaos is that the user fails to assess the stability of the system that generated the data being analysed.

The risk of data mining, simply put, is that the evaluator has no understanding of the systemic controls and assumptions that underlie the data. Without a clear understanding of the meaning of the data, effective analysis, which should target the truth of the scientific evidence, is not possible to determine. All retrospective programmes must first understand the nature of the process and the data generated before launching full scale into an analysis of data in an out-of-context fashion. A simple example is the performance of a dual-head liquid filling machine, each head containing multiple delivery nozzles. Data mining may show the process to be capable with a good C_{pk} value and therefore to be considered for reduced sampling as a means of cost reduction. However, if either side of the machine is independent in set-up or performance, the ability to control the fill is compromised.

OVER-ANALYSING OR UNDER-ANALYSING DATA

Statistical analysis can become very tedious. Error and risk can be partitioned in any number of ways. In the most basic context, there are alpha and beta risks. Each risk and its determination follows a prescribed set of statistical rules and assumptions. If any rules are violated, the subsequent analysis will be flawed. For example, if one is measuring fill volume of injection or weight of a tablet, a normally distributed population would be an assumption. If, however, the injection filling assembly consists of ten displacement pumps, each of which are independently calibrated and can meter individually, then the assumption of a normal distribution may not be valid. To evaluate the 'average fill' has no meaning unless the individuals are verified independently first to ensure that all ten pumps are statistically indistinguishable. The same can be said for a 36-station tablet press. The use of averages to control multiple source data presumes that the individuals are similar in all respects. If C_{pk} is calculated without understanding the nature of individual similarity, conclusions on capability may be invalid. This is an example of under-analysing data.

Suppose, on the other hand, that each filler head is evaluated independently of the other nine. If the units are evaluated for process control and capability, the sensitivity to control the individual unit may result in erroneous conclusions of process control. To control the individual unit may require a method that is precise to hundredths of a millilitre or thousandths of a milligram in the case of a tablet. This level of precision in measurement is likely to be found within the noise of the process. The measurement error increases with decreased sample size. Using the average of a population sample improves the precision necessary to understand process drift or process shift within the design boundaries. The measurement error decreases with the increase of the sample size. Both individual and average measures must be balanced to ensure that data resides within the relevant range.

LACK OF KNOWLEDGE, CONTEXT OR BOTH

Two parties, the data owner and the statistician, must have knowledge and contextual literacy to ensure the integrity of the statistical evaluation. The owner must be completely knowledgeable about the context of the data being evaluated and also must be literate in the terms and techniques of the statistician. Understanding the context includes being able to discuss goals sought, the scientific background of the need for study to be conducted and the control decisions enacted as a consequence of the data.

The statistician, on the other hand, must be completely knowledgeable about simple and sophisticated statistical techniques and must be literate in fundamental pharmaceutical science and process data usage, otherwise conclusions are likely to be incorrect. Level of experience plays a critical role in overcoming this challenge.

Often, skills are transferrable across business models. For example, accounting for a self-employed statistician or a research scientist follows the same basic rules defined by regional and international third-party standards organizations, such as Generally Accepted Accounting Practices. Understanding the science of handling money is universal in many respects and intent is generally simplified for minimal use of scientific evaluation. However, in the pharmaceutical industry an added legal and regulatory burden of intent must be considered. It is intent that makes mutual understanding and knowledge critical for the successful use of statistics. Intent includes both scientific veracity and evidence of safety and efficacy. The outcome of a statistical analysis should be closely linked to scientific truth and the accuracy of the data without reference to the individual or individuals evaluating the data.

Simplicity in data collection and presentation is a necessary first step. We have seen companies with data plots that reveal multi-modal distributions or sampling design issues performing C_{pk} on the advice of a consultant. On one such occasion, the business owner was asked about decisions derived from the data. It quickly became obvious that the person handling the data lacked a fundamental understanding of statistical techniques and the decisions required with respect to the product. The exercise created significant non-value-adding chart maintenance work but did not improve the overall quality of decision making.

FORM OVER FUNCTION

When form and format are the first consideration of statistical analysis, it can result in blind adherence to theoretical statistical rules. Analysing data in a narrow context restricts discussion of data that do not exactly fit the expected model and eventually skews the conclusions. Techniques exist to deal with aberrant data. The outlier's test is used to 'scientifically disqualify' data that cannot be explained any other way. However, one must be concerned about a fallacy in the logic of false implications. The data may in fact be correct and reveal a systemic flaw that is a random occurrence. Our contention is that at the time the data were generated, a cause-effect control point should have revealed the issue. If not, the process design should be carefully evaluated. Often significant time has elapsed, so it is just as easy to explain away the data by a regulatorily acceptable means than to undertake a lengthy and often ineffective OOS investigation. This effort is to the detriment of the integrity of the Artisan Model.

RATIONALIZING DATA AS A MEANS TO AN END

Personal biases and perceptions can reduce understanding of process controls and the downstream issues that result. Pharmaceutical processes, as stated previously, are interconnected in such a way that lack of understanding at one point can affect results several steps removed. It is important to keep in mind that the intent of the action is a key consideration in managing drug product processes. In the USA, intent is a key element of drug laws. For example, if individual tablet potencies exceed specifications and a within-specification average potency is used to release the drug product, the intent is to hide the variation through statistical data treatment.

Data rationalization through the use of statistics can often have negative effects on the ability to manage a process within the intent of the law. Any statistical analysis that does not link data decisions with the consequences for safety and efficacy will inevitably raise questions from regulators. For example, a company wishes to remove an approved control from the dossier for good reasons. If the proposal to delete the control only discusses the consistency of the control from a historical perspective without respect to the impact on the final drug product, it is unlikely to be approved. All process systems are intricately linked and joined together. A change to a control must be assessed not in terms of consistency and predicatibility within itself, but rather in terms of how the consistency of the control relates to the consistency of the end product.

Another frequently seen logical fallacy for the use of statistics as a means to an end is called the positive outcome bias. Consider the example of red wine consumption. The data set for the various statistical evaluations is most likely a universal pool. Those who wish to evaluate red wine as a positive benefit to health will stress the anti-oxidant and resveratrol content of a glass. Both indications are suspected of supporting cardiovascular health. Those who wish to evaluate red wine as a significant detriment to health cite liver disease, breast cancer, migraine headaches, drug interactions and fetal health risk. All of these adverse effects are also a part of the universal data pool. Each group uses statistical analysis as a means to an end and in so doing completely confuses everyone who is statistically challenged.

Statistics should be used as a tactical verification tool rather than as a means to draw conclusions when experience is limited to theoretical knowledge.

EXTRAPOLATING END POINTS OF A DYNAMIC PROCESS

The final challenge to properly applying statistical analysis relates to the use of extrapolation within a dynamic process. By dynamic process we do not mean degradation of a drug substance or colour changes of solutions when exposed to sunlight; rather, we are talking about taking data during the active production of pharmaceutical dosage forms and using them to adjust the process to meet some future uniformity goal. Extrapolating future control results is bad practice and is at the edge of introducing a logical fallacy of doublespeak jargon. Extrapolation should be used only in very specific situations where a few variables are closely monitored and controlled over a narrow range. The best example is stability study. Another example is drug substance synthesis where the solution reaches reflux. The action of reflux is a universal characteristic within a narrow boundary.

Applying extrapolation as a process control is contrary to all knowledge gained since Francis Bacon proposed the scientific method, which separated good scientific practice from bad, and Walter Shewhart proposed the economic control of quality by improving decision making at the point in the process designated as the process control.

Solutions

We propose six solutions to the challenges discussed. Our intent is to ground statistical use in the proper application of process control decisions. While statistical theory is fascinating and stimulating, beyond the simple tools of process management covered in previous chapters, complex mathematical techniques lend little in the way of benefits in a manufacturing environment. Manufacturing processes operate best when decisions are prompt, accurate and meaningful. When the here and now is controlled according to the process design, the output of such a process is very likely to meet all design and quality attributes.

The six solutions are straightforward and easy to convey to employees, even those without a fundamental mathematical background:

- clarify the purpose before starting;

- map the current process as configured;

- plot the data, plot the data, plot the data;

- estimate the bounds of reality from experience;

- be both a teacher and student;

- data mine for new opportunities.

CLARIFY THE PURPOSE BEFORE STARTING

The lessons learned from experience serve as a starting point to properly implement process management. It is first and foremost necessary to state the assumptions of the statistical model and the anticipated outcomes of the analysis before beginning any statistical evaluation. Without this basic step, the likelihood of initial missteps is greatly increased. The point is to verify that the process meets the assumptions associated with the specific statistical technique. For example, if the data model is presumed to follow a normal bell-shaped curve, then it is important to understand the symmetry and normality assumptions of the plot. For processes such as tablet weight, the distribution is bell shaped provided that each tablet press station is not statistically different from all other stations. Under this consideration, sampling will ensure randomness and operate as a continuous distribution.

There are processes, such as drilling holes into solid material or filling single-use sterile injection vials or ampoules, that do not follow a normal distribution. A hole can never be smaller than the drill bit. The fill must factor in overage beyond the label claim to ensure that the entire dosage content is available for administration. The same condition exists for weight-sorting equipment. Incorrectly configured reject limits can produce a skewed distribution. The assumptions from the initial assessment must be challenged in a business-respectful way.

MAP THE CURRENT PROCESS AS CONFIGURED

Any interactions of preceding or subsequent steps must be factored into the statistical analysis. Throughout this text, we have discussed the direct and indirect cause and effect relationships that exist within a process. It is important to have a clear understanding of the process as it is configured to reveal potential influences on the statistical analysis. This exercise will also begin to clarify the decision boundaries that surround the specific data control point.

Problems must be solved in a one-to-one approach: one problem, one data point, one solution. Frequently, multiple control points, whether or not these are identified in process documentation, will be present within the problem. Consider, for example, where the density of an excipient is likely have an adverse impact on the consistency of blending and tablet compression but is not identified as an incoming component acceptance criterion. If problems are encountered during tablet compression, the solution may only become visible if the investigation traces backwards to discover the root cause. Large-scale problems may result in a faster investigation as the tablet press data are likely to point to a radical change in an excipient component. But what happens in the case where the excipient moves from one side of the acceptance range to the other. The material would pass specification, but the tablet press operator might struggle in an effort to produce a consistent and homogeneous finished product.

In this case, the investigation might not reveal a change in manufacturers of the excipient if the material is purchased directly from a broker warehouse. These issues can, for the most part, be overcome by understanding the process influencers prior to performing statistical analysis.

PLOT THE DATA, PLOT THE DATA, PLOT THE DATA

Data may be absolutely correct; however, relevant information may not be readily apparent if the numerical data within a table are not presented graphically. A simple histogram plot of the data often reveals information and patterns that are difficult to grasp from static tables of numbers. At a glance, an experienced employee with a contextual understanding of statistical analysis can quickly determine from a histogram whether the data can be analysed effectively if there only one underlying distribution of results. Remember, data that does not look correct probably is not.

A second simple data presentation is a run chart in which values are plotted against time. Whereas the histogram may require experience to understand many of the issues, the run chart does not require experience to understand trends or results. If the chart line is rising on the 'Scrap material' chart, it is readily identified that something has changed. This recognition may then result in a more defined statistical analysis to affirm the point in time when the change was first evident to the control system.

All statistical evaluation presumes consistency of process at the unit dose level. Simplicity in collection and visual presentation on a meaningful scale are necessary first steps to developing confidence in the validity of the data set.

ESTIMATE THE BOUNDS OF REALITY FROM EXPERIENCE

We have seen statistical analysis taken outside the relevant range of the process design without any recognition on the part of the user. The most frequent violation is exceeding or under-reporting the significant figures of a particular piece of data. When this happens, the conclusions become unreliable and can either lead to unnecessary investigation or no investigation at all. Properly applied, relevant range accounts for cumulative errors of measurement at each step, the number of significant figures as well as rounding. Estimating reasonable boundaries of data is one of the valuable employee attributes gained from hands-on experience. Identifying controls that are either too sensitive or insensitive avoids lengthy and costly investigations based on data that have not withstood the test of experienced evaluation.

BE BOTH A TEACHER AND STUDENT

Process excellence is the result of careful, considered and constant evaluation of data. Presuming complete knowledge of a process introduces blinkers that lead down a path of erroneous assumptions. Open discussion from different perspectives is the best guard against data myopia. Interchanging the view by assuming the role of either teacher or student facilitates open dialogue and active listening. This approach provides focus on important issues that must be considered from more than one point of view in order to properly clarify the purpose and boundaries of the data.

DATA MINE FOR NEW OPPORTUNITIES

Data mining is a fairly new concept that has only recently become widely available with the advent of low-cost computer hardware and software. We use the term 'data mining' to mean the random searching of large data sets to identify trends, patterns or relationships without a pre-determined goal or problem to be resolved. Data mining differs from research in that the former seeks guidance when faced with lack of understanding, while the latter is a structured capture of information that is germane to effectively understanding the boundaries and assumptions of previous research work. Data mining has a place as a tool to identify opportune areas for adding to the overall body of knowledge, but potential findings need to be followed by careful study under controlled experimental conditions.

Data mining should not be used for finding and applying identical solutions that have been used at other organizations, no matter how similar the appearance of the problem and no matter how much the need to provide a rapid solution to a vexing problem. As pointed out by the Scottish poet Andrew Lang, the unsophisticated forecaster uses statistics as a drunken man uses lamp-posts – for support rather than for illumination. The reason others' solutions should not be applied in an identical fashion is simple: there is no assurance that the data were generated via a controlled well-designed protocol. The company systems, procedures and staff would have to be identical between both firms for there to be any sort of correlation to the final outcome. Given that these considerations are impractical, we recommend that process design teams focus on understanding the statistical principles required by the specific system within their organization.

Conclusion

The practice of statistics carries with it both risk and reward. Processes that are designed without regard to data integrity and quality may show all the signals of a process in control when exactly the opposite is occurring. On the other hand, companies that spend longer on the design of the process in order to define the boundaries, ranges and expectations of the process's performance may be rewarded with accurate identification of emerging trends or prompt, effective resolution of problems that are external to the system design.

The increasing use of computer software has made it easy to exceed the threshold of meaningful data precision. In so doing, process designers must be careful to not violate the points made in this chapter. Specifically:

- the process design team must not forget that statistical data and the conclusions derived from the data have a direct impact on the patient;

- business must always rely on human judgment to ensure that both the intent and results of the process are consistent with legal requirements;

- statistical analysis must be balanced so that the controls and decisions are relevant across the system design boundaries;

- the use of statistics must first consider function and understanding. Simple pictures are in many respects more powerful than complex sets of rules and the accompanying assumptions. With a picture, even one that requires interpretation, understanding can come more quickly;

- extrapolation of data for the purpose of predicting accurately a future event can do more harm than good. Controls should be stationary fixtures within a dynamic system.

Many excellent statistical texts are available as an aid to understanding how a statistical concept applies to a given set of assumptions. Our purpose was to discuss statistics from the viewpoint of proper and improper use within pharmaceutical systems.

13

Problem-Solving Tools and Techniques

A man should look for what is, and not for what he thinks should be.
(Albert Einstein, 1879–1955, German theoretical physicist)

Introduction

This chapter looks at some of the tools and techniques that can be used to carry out root cause analysis and examines how they can be used within the context of pharmaceutical process management.

Some tools and techniques, of which there are many, are simple qualitiative ones requiring little more than common sense for their effective use. On the other hand, there are some highly complex quantitative ones requiring an understanding of statistics or at least the services of a tame statistician. Space dictates that this chapter only provides an introduction to these tools and techniques. The aim is to highlight the different facets of the toolbox rather than turn the reader into a master craftsman. Reference is made to source materials and further reading.

The choice of which tools and techniques are presented is an arbitrary one, based on common usage and our preference. In each case this chapter provides an overview and some background. We then use a pharmaceutical example or case study to demonstrate the use.

Root Cause Analysis

Root cause analysis is an approach to problem-solving which leads to the identification of the true (root) causes of a problem rather than addressing the obvious symptoms. Its purpose is to eliminate the cause and thus to prevent any reoccurrence.

The following points sum up what has been discussed in the preceding chapters:

- to be effective, corrective measures must be aimed at the root cause of the problem, not at its symptoms;

- a systematic approach must be taken to analysing the root cause of a problem;

- decisions must be based on scientific evidence, not on suspicions, suppositions or 'gut feelings';

- for most problems, there is rarely one single cause but a variety of different causes contributing to the overall problem, and therefore the problem may need to be reviewed from several different angles;

- root cause analysis and problem-solving is not a one-off activity but is an integral part of the quality improvement programme;

- an effective CAPA programme requires a successful root cause analysis system. We are therefore discussing a major part of the quality management system.

Root cause analysis should be carried out as a two-stage process. To begin with, the problem needs to be identified and defined. Only after that can the second stage, problem analysis, be carried out.

Tools and Techniques for Problem Identification

If a problem-solving activity is centered on a symptom, it is likely that the wrong problem will be 'solved'. That is why identification and definition of the problem is so important. This stage of the process often takes longer than expected. In fact, if it is done properly, it may well be the longest part of the whole process.

BRAINSTORMING

Brainstorming is a means by which collective experience is brought into the problem-solving process and is a way of generating large numbers of ideas rapidly. It works best when done by a group of people rather than an individual, since several people working together and thinking laterally are likely to come up with more ideas as a group than the total gained by adding their individual lists together.

Suppose someone is asked to list all the possible uses for a paper cup as a new business market (a common warm-up exercise for brainstorming). They might come up with five suggestions quite quickly, or even ten. After that, most people find it a struggle. On the other hand, if everyone is shouting out their ideas and they are being recorded on a flipchart, one person's off-the-wall suggestion might trigger other ideas from other members of the group. For example, the suggestion 'false nose' might lead to other suggestions such as 'part of a mask', 'part of a collage' or 'hat for a doll'.

Brainstorming requires a facilitator who writes the question on the flipchart, records all the answers from the group and makes sure that the rules of brainstorming, as shown in Table 13.1, are followed. Members of the group either take it in turns to make a suggestion or just shout them out as they think of them. The latter approach is more spontaneous but harder for the facilitator to record.

Table 13.2 presents an example of a brainstorming session held by a group investigating ways to increase the productivity of a packaging line. Some of the ideas, such as working 24/7 or abolishing tea breaks, are obviously impractical, but they have led to others, such as staggering tea breaks and reducing changeover times, which can be investigated further and may well result in the desired goal.

Table 13.1   Rules of brainstorming

* There should be no criticism
* Freewheeling is encouraged
* Concentrate on getting the maximum number of ideas
* Record every idea, even repetition
* Incubate all the ideas; do not reject anything out of hand

Table 13.2   Brainstorming – example

Question: In how many different ways could we increase the productivity of the XYZ tablet packaging line?
• Make the operators work 24/7 • Employ more operators • Increase the number of packaging stations • Reduce tea breaks to 5 minutes • Abolish tea breaks • Reduce lunch break to 15 minutes • Stagger breaks so the line does not stop all day • Improve the changeover process so down-time is reduced • Work with suppliers to improve quality of packaging materials

FLOW-CHARTING

When a group of people are working on a problem, the more complex the situation, the less likely it is that any one person will understand the full system in operation. Even with relatively simple situations, it is frequently the case that people think they know what is going on but then find that things are not exactly as they thought they were.

Flow-charting is simply the activity of breaking a process into its constituent steps and drawing them in sequence. Different types of step (action, decision, waiting, etc.) are denoted by specific symbols, as shown in Table 13.3. Flow-charting is very effective in ensuring that everyone has the same picture of what is happening and is investigating the *same* problem. It is the recommended first step in many activities such as risk assessment or validation planning.

Table 13.3   Typical flow-chart symbols

Process step	□
Decision	◇
Internal storage	⊟
Documentation	▱

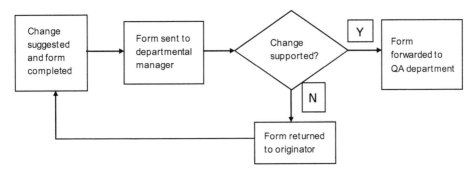

Figure 13.1   Flow-chart for change control initiation

Having identified and drawn out the current process steps, it may be appropriate to prepare a second flow-chart; this one would show the ideal future situation. This is called imagineering and can be an effective way of immediately identifying the parts of the process which most need to be addressed.

Figure 13.1 shows an example of a flow-chart for the first few steps in the journey of a change control document. It can be seen that after the first two steps, there is a decision point; the subsequent route depends on the decision taken. It either proceeds through the rest of the process or is returned to the originator.

CHECK SHEETS

Having drawn out the process (including identifying the boundaries and scope), the next step is usually to start collecting data. This can be done by a simple sampling technique: using a check sheet. The purpose of this is to count how many times a particular event (or events) takes place in a given time period to see what trends exist, if any. The rules for the effective use of check sheets are shown in Table 13.4.

Table 13.4   Rules for effective check sheets

- Full understanding by everyone of what is being measured
- Samples must be representative as possible
- Sampling should not interfere with the job itself
- Sampling should be from a homogeneous population

Table 13.5   Check sheet for source of errors in manufacturing records

Department	July
Warehouse	
Manufacture	xxx
Filling	x
Packaging	x x x x x x x x x x x
QC laboratory	

Table 13.5 shows an example of a check sheet used by document reviewers to record the reasons why manufacturing records are not approved first time round by the Quality Assurance department.

An alternative approach to the check sheet is the so-called 'measles diagram' where the flow-chart is marked with a red coloured X at the problem point. The diagram begins to look like a disease state after a while. This is a great way to present the problem pictorially and works particularly well where there are language barriers and only simple good/bad concepts are understood.

STRATIFICATION

One of the rules of effective check sheets is that the population being sampled should be homogeneous and generated from the process steady state. However, that is not always the case, even if it may appear so at first view. For example, if a machine is frequently stopping and starting or if there is a high turnover of personnel, it is difficult for a process to achieve steady state. Where there are different classifications of data within the same population, a further refinement can be used by means of stratification. When this technique is used, an initial conclusion, drawn from a check sheet, might well be shown to be false and an alternative will need to be formulated. Table 13.6 shows 12 months of data arising from the check sheet exercise described previously.

At first sight, it can be seen that the problem lies in the packaging department. However, the department consists of five identical filling lines. In order to identify the true nature of the problem, the data were further analysed. As Table 13.7 shows, the situation is not as simple as previously concluded.

While a table is an effective way of collating and displaying data, for more complex situations, visualization by chart is helpful. Figure 13.2 presents the above data in a different format.

Table 13.6 Collation of check sheet data over 12 months

Department	J	F	M	A	M	J	J	A	S	O	N	D
Warehouse	0	0	0	0	0	0	0	0	0	0	0	0
Manufacture	2	1	1	0	0	1	3	0	0	1	1	1
Filling	1	1	1	0	1	3	1	0	2	1	1	2
Packaging	8	12	7	19	6	15	11	8	10	14	12	9
QC Lab	0	0	0	0	0	0	0	0	1	0	0	0

Table 13.7 Stratified check sheet data

Department	J	F	M	A	M	J	J	A	S	O	N	D
Packaging totals	8	12	7	19	6	15	11	8	10	14	12	9
Team 1	2	3	1	3	1	2	1	0	1	1	0	0
Team 2	1	2	1	3	0	1	2	1	1	0	0	0
Team 3	1	2	1	2	0	1	2	1	1	0	2	1
Team 4	1	1	1	2	1	3	1	1	1	2	1	2
Team 5	3	4	3	9	4	8	6	5	6	11	9	6

Teams 1 and 2 appear to be improving, while teams 3 and 4 are unchanging. It is some operating characteristic of team 5 in which the true problem resides. Whether this is due to poor training, lack of supervision or another reason

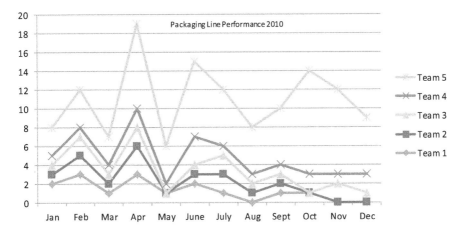

Figure 13.2 Stratified data presented in chart format

(maybe this line is located in a different room without windows), it is apparent that the root cause of the problem is to be found in this team. As such, trying to effect improvements in the other teams (or in the other departments) would not be necessary or appropriate.

NOMINAL GROUP TECHNIQUE

It is sometimes the case that a number of problems are identified at the same time and none in particular seems to take priority. In this case, the choice of which to address first can be a fairly arbitrary one. Using the qualitative nominal group technique ensures that the problem chosen will be perceived to be an important one by the group as a whole, even if not for all the individuals. Table 13.8 shows the steps to be taken in carrying out the nominal group technique.

In Table 13.9 we see the results of a nominal group technique exercise one of us carried out at a recent training seminar. Taking the opportunity

Table 13.8   Steps in the nominal group technique

- List all the problems (in no particular order)
- Problems are scored by each individual in order of importance
- If n ≤ 10, score rank each problem (n, n-1, n-2, etc.)
- If n ≥ 11, score rank only the top 11 (11, 10, 9, etc.)
- Add up the scores for each problem and the one with the highest score is the one *in the opinion of the group* that is the most important to solve

Table 13.9   The nominal group technique on topics for training seminars

Topic	1	2	3	4	5	6	7	8	9	Group
CAPA	6	8	6	9	5	9	9	6	3	**61**
ICH Q8	7	6	8	2	2	1	4	5	7	42
Validation	2	5	4	6	6	6	7	9	1	46
Statistics	8	3	9	7	4	8	6	6	9	**60**
QC	4	2	3	4	7	5	3	7	4	39
APR	9	9	7	8	3	7	5	4	5	**57**
Training	5	7	1	3	9	2	1	8	2	38
Cleaning	3	1	5	1	8	3	8	6	6	41
Water/air	1	4	2	5	1	4	2	7	8	34

presented by a room full of industry professionals, we brainstormed the most useful seminar topics for pharmaceutical technicians and supervisors. Having compiled a list of nine options, we scored them individually and calculated the group favourites.

The conclusion from this admittedly rather unscientific survey is that hot topics that provide the greatest value for training seminars were CAPA, statistics and APR.

PARETO CHART

A more quantitative approach to deciding which problem to address first can be obtained by using a Pareto chart, also known as the 80/20 rule. The problems are measured against a single system criterion and are listed in descending order. The measurements might also be recorded as a cumulative list. The most important problem *according to the chosen criterion* will be found at the top of the list. The relative importance of the problems can be seen even more clearly if the data are presented graphically. Figure 13.3 shows an example of a Pareto chart constructed from the causes for rejection of ampoules analysed at the end of batch filling. It can be seen that 40 per cent of the categories, under- and over-fill (2 of 5) result in almost 80 per cent of the defects (752 of 1,000).

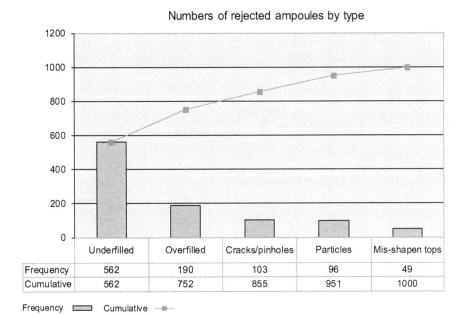

Numbers of rejected ampoules by type

	Underfilled	Overfilled	Cracks/pinholes	Particles	Mis-shapen tops
Frequency	562	190	103	96	49
Cumulative	562	752	855	951	1000

Frequency ▭ Cumulative ─▪─

Figure 13.3   Pareto analysis of ampoule rejects

Table 13.10   Steps in the construction of a Fishbone Diagram

- Write the effect or problem in a box on the right-hand side of the flipchart
- Draw a horizontal line from the centre of the box across the paper; add side-branches (or ribs)
- Identify suitable categories (subgroups) of cause and label side-branches
- List the causes on the sheet under the appropriate category

FISHBONE DIAGRAM

This technique has a number of names in common usage. It was originally called the Ishikawa diagram after Dr Karou Ishikawa, who has been referred to in earlier chapters. It is also called the cause and effect diagram since it is used to organize and structure possible causes for a given effect (or problem). Its most popular name comes from the shape that it takes in its construction – that of a fish skeleton. Table 13.10 shows the steps in construction of a Fishbone Diagram.

The Fishbone Diagram is a more structured form of idea generation than brainstorming, since it identifies a number of categories or subgroups under which the various ideas are grouped. These are often standard sets such as the process elements we have used throughout this book (*man, machine, method, material* and *environment*), although they can be completely new groupings if more appropriate.

In Figure 13.4 some of the possible causes for increased breakages on a liquids filling line are analysed using the Fishbone Diagram.

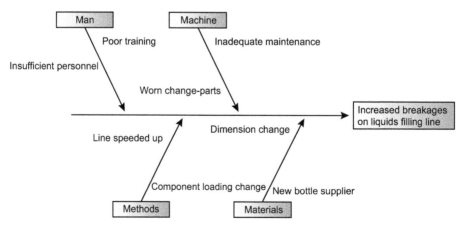

Figure 13.4   Fishbone Diagram for breakages on the filling line

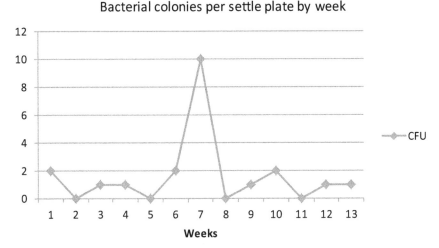

Figure 13.5   Run chart for settle plate results

RUN CHARTS

If a series of measurements are taken over a period of time, they can be simply recorded as numbers in a table. However, it is much more powerful to record them on a run chart as a series of individual readings. In this way, true trends (as opposed to simple variations) can be observed. These trends may be positive, showing that the process control is improving. Alternatively, they may show that the process is running out of control and the situation is getting worse.

Figure 13.5 shows the record of bacterial colony-forming units growing on settle plates used to measure environmental conditions in the changing-room of an aseptic manufacturing suite. It can be seen from the chart that the result in week 7 was a one-off incident rather than part of a trend.

Tools and Techniques for Problem Analysis

Having identified the problem to be investigated and collected appropriate data, the next step is to analyse those data to fully define the cause of the problem (as opposed to the symptoms).

Some of the tools discussed previously in this chapter, such as Pareto charts, Fishbone Diagrams and run charts, can also be used in problem analysis. However, there are other tools in the toolbox that should also be considered.

Table 13.11   Steps in the construction of a histogram

- Divide the possible range of results into appropriate, discrete steps
- Count the number of results falling into each step
- The discrete steps are recorded along the x-axis of the chart
- The number of results within each step is recorded on the y-axis

HISTOGRAMS

A histogram is used to display in the form of a bar chart the distribution of results obtained for an individual data measurement. For example, in the case of specifications for packaging materials, each dimension will be stated with a target value and an acceptable range of variation around that target. Plotting the results of incoming quality control measurements will show the level of variation within a batch and may highlight possible process problems, even with batches which are approved for use. Table 13.11 shows the steps required in constructing a histogram.

In Figure 13.6 we can see the histogram for the distribution of fill volumes for a batch of 2 ml ampoules, with a target fill of 2.1 ml and an upper and lower limit of 2.2 ml and 2.0 ml respectively. The results show a normal distribution around the target volume and confirm that all results are within the permitted

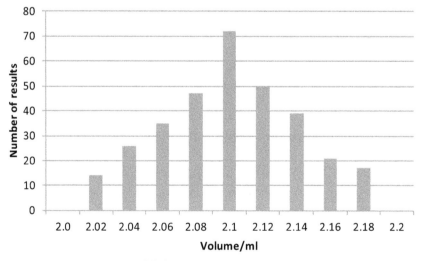

Figure 13.6   Histogram of fill volumes

range. When the distribution is not normal, statistical techniques will not be effective. In such cases, the options are to use qualitative methods such as fishbone analysis or split the population down into its component parts, which should show the normal distribution of variations.

SCATTER DIAGRAMS

Scatter diagrams are useful where there is a possibility that two variables within a process are connected and that changing one will have an effect on the other. This tool will not prove that changing one variable has an effect on a second variable, but it can demonstrate a relationship between the two. Table 13.12 shows the steps in constructing a scatter diagram.

The closer the correlation between the variations in the two variables, the more likely it is that there will be a relationship. Figure 13.7 shows two scatter diagrams based on measurement of activity for an API stored in an unheated warehouse. The measurements were taken over a period of 24 months and in environmental temperatures ranging from 0°C to +25°C.

It can be seen quite clearly that there is a negative relationship between length of storage time and activity of the API. Logic would suggest that the percentage activity reduces with time rather than the other way around. On the other hand, there is no relationship apparent between percentage purity and the temperature at which the sample is taken. Problem-solving would first focus on factors other than temperature.

This tool does not always provide evidence of cause and effect; in the example given, it is a reasonable assumption. However, there may be instances where both changes are the effects of an external cause. In this case, the scatter diagram provides a pointer towards a relationship, but additional work, maybe with DOE, would be required to confirm the true nature of the relationship.

Table 13.12   Steps in the construction of a scatter diagram

• Allocate the variable suspected to be the cause of the change to the x-axis
• Allocate the variable suspected to demonstrate the effect to the y-axis
• Collect 50–100 paired data samples and plot on the graph

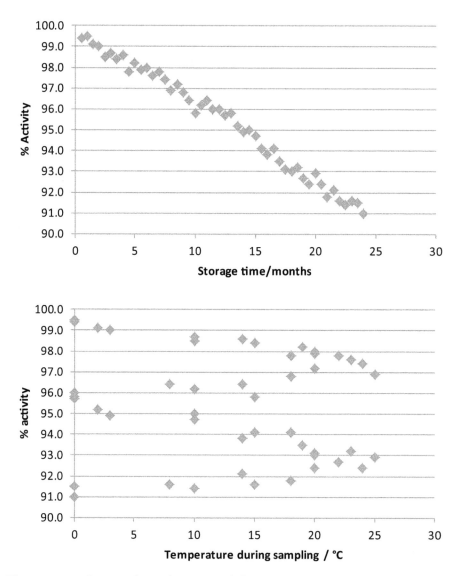

Figure 13.7 Scatter charts for API activity

CONTROL CHARTS

Control charts are used to display test results relating to an individual parameter, such as bottle height, fill volume or tablet weight, to determine whether the process is under control from a statistical point of view. The control chart is a current point in time taken at defined points in time during lot manufacturing

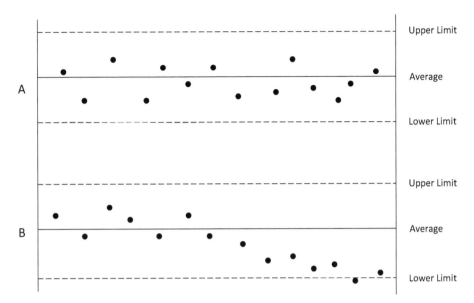

Figure 13.8   Control charts for vial fill volume

activities. It is annotated with the process average or target, and the upper and lower control limits obtained from sample analysis. In some cases, the control limits are subdivided into the action limits and additional alert limits which are added within the range.

Figure 13.8 shows two control charts for the measurement of vial fill volume over time during the manufacture of a batch of product using two different machines.

Both machines exhibit variations in their data. However, it can be seen that on machine A the process is stable, whereas on machine B there is a definite trend towards the lower limit and hence intervention is required to bring the process back to centre.

PROCESS CAPABILITY (C_{PK}) AND PROCESS PERFORMANCE (P_{PK})

Demonstrating that a process is under control, as shown above, is based on representative results taken from a stable process. However, it does not confirm that every unit produced – whether it is a bottle of liquid cough suspension, a vial of liquid for injection or a blister pack of individual tablets – will be produced in conformance to the customer's requirements. To determine confidence of meeting customer expectations requires calculation of process or performance capability. Capability indices are calculated which allow the distribution of the process results to be compared with the limits of the specification.

Process capability and performance only consider common cause variation; they do not work when special cause variation is present. As such, confirmation that the process is statistically stable is a precursor to using this tool.

Process capability and performance can be used in circumstances where the data collected in any set of measurements exhibit a normal distribution. Under these circumstances, the process can be defined in terms of the mean and the standard deviation.

The process capability index – C_{pk} or C_{pm} – is an immediate, short-term measure, while the process performance index – P_{pk} or P_{pm} – presents the long-term view. They are calculated by comparing the variability of results with the product specification. The results are displayed as a histogram which predicts what proportion – if any – of the total output of the process will be outside the specification limits.

Measurement should be made under conditions that demonstrate normal variations in all the process elements. The process mean and standard deviation are calculated. Process capability, which can be determined with as few as 17 data points, is calculated by comparing six standard deviations with the required specification. Figure 13.9 shows process capability assessments for vial fill volume on two different filling lines.

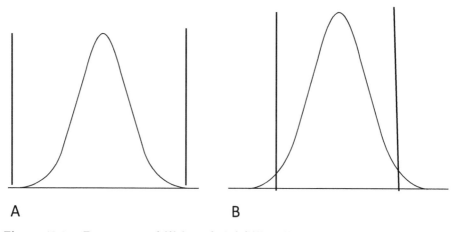

A   B

Figure 13.9   Process capabilities of vial filling lines

On filling line A, six standard deviations fall within the control specification limits and the process is capable of conforming to requirements. On filling line B, part of the six standard deviations falls outside the limits of the specification and some under- or over-filled vials could be expected to be produced.

FORCE FIELD ANALYSIS

It is likely that reducing or eliminating a problem will require an element of change. For any change, there will be a series of forces driving it forwards and another series of forces restraining it. These will include forces relating to money, time and especially people. While some people positively welcome change, for others it can be a time of threat or fear.

The examination of these forces was developed by Kurt Lewin into force field analysis (1997), which can be used in two ways:

- to decide whether a proposed change is possible and feasible; and

- to decide how to facilitate the change in the most effective way.

Table 13.13 shows the steps in setting up a force field analysis.

Table 13.13   Steps in the construction of a force field analysis

- Ensure the proposed change is clearly defined and understood by everyone in the same way
- Draw a vertical line down the centre of a flipchart sheet
- List the positive, driving forces on the left-hand side of the sheet, with arrows pointing to the right
- List the negative, restraining forces on the right-hand side of the sheet, with arrows pointing to the left
- Score all forces between 1 (weak) and 5 (strong)

In Figure 13.10, the line in the centre represents the status quo and the extreme right-hand side represents the required situation.

To determine feasibility, scores are summed for the drivers and for the restrainers. A feasible change is one where the former score is higher than the latter one.

Different lengths of arrow can be used to represent different strengths of force. In order to move from the status quo to the required position, it is

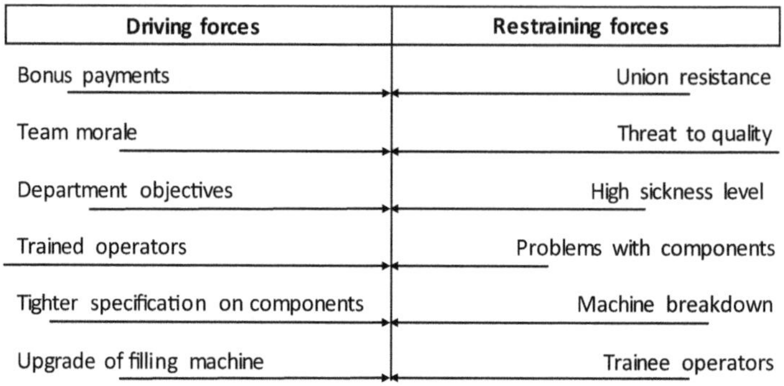

Driving forces	Restraining forces
Bonus payments	Union resistance
Team morale	Threat to quality
Department objectives	High sickness level
Trained operators	Problems with components
Tighter specification on components	Machine breakdown
Upgrade of filling machine	Trainee operators

Figure 13.10   Force field analysis of upgrading a filling line

necessary either to strengthen the driving forces or – more often – weaken the restraining forces.

An example of a force field analysis for upgrading a filling line and increasing productivity is shown in Figure 13.10. In this case, the relative strength of the forces is demonstrated by varying the length of the line.

Conclusion

In this chapter we have reviewed a range of tools and techniques which can be used for problem identification and subsequent resolution. All will tend to be more effective if used in a group or a team, rather than by an individual, since the former will have more knowledge and experience of the process and/or the problem than will the latter. The choice of team or individual is determined by the speed of response required.

Problem-solving should be carried out in a number of steps:

- problem identification – what is the priority issue to be resolved;

- problem analysis and definition – what is the true cause of the problem, rather than the symptoms;

- problem solution plan – if the first two stages have been carried out effectively, this will be the easy part.

Like any toolbox, there are a range of tools or instruments that can be used. The most appropriate for the job will depend on the situation. Choosing the most appropriate one is a matter of experience.

14

Reducing Risk: The New Paradigm

There are risks and costs to a program of action. But they are far less than the long-range risks and costs of comfortable inaction.

(John F. Kennedy, 1917–1963, American President)

Introduction

In the 1980s and 1990s, the word most commonly on pharmaceutical technologists' lips was validation. There was a huge debate over what it was, how it should be implemented and whether enough was being done to satisfy the regulators. From the start of this century, there has been a similar debate, but over a different word: risk.

There are many different ways one could define risk, but in the concept of pharmaceutical manufacturing, it may be considered in three ways: patient risk, operations risk and hypothetical risk.

Patient risk is the one of concern to the regulatory agencies. It relates to maintaining the clinically established profile of indications and the process performance identified during development to ensure a safe and effective pharmaceutical is prescribed to the correct population. Operations risk is concerned with economics and supply of the product where and when needed. It is related to sampling, analysis, production, alpha and beta risk of data, selection of equipment and so on. This is often a driver for deviations from the regulatory dossier that concern the regulators. Both these types of risk are critical and must be assessed and managed appropriately.

Hypothetical risk is more contentious. It results in 'what if?' questions which are one of the leading drivers of increased cost in our industry today. Hypothetical risk is the concern of well-intentioned theorists who take second-guessing to the extreme and thus drive businesses down a continuous research path. Throughout this book, we have emphasized that effective process design and management require full understanding and appropriate controls of the five process elements: *man, machine, method, material* and *environment*. However, for all processes, there is a relevant range of operations. Outside this range, data and decisions are not reliable and change with each new query of the same data set. Investigation of hypothetical risks is probably subject to the law of diminishing returns.

In this chapter, we are going to look at how process management can be used not only to increase product knowledge but also to reduce risk to the quality and safety of the pharmaceutical by reducing variation. Greater consistency will thereby benefit the health of the patient by strengthening clinical understanding of indications and contraindications of the product. However, to start with, we need to examine some key changes that have taken place within the industry in the past decade.

Throughout the preceding chapters, much of what we have said could apply to any manufacturing industry, although our examples have all been drawn from the manufacturing of pharmaceuticals. However, in this chapter we are going to concentrate on specific changes that have taken place in the pharmaceutical industry over the past decade. We will look at the twenty-first-century pharmaceuticals initiatives and the guidelines and changes in behaviour that have arisen out of them.

At the start of the twenty-first century, the pharmaceutical industry was facing a number of key issues relating to manufacturing. As levels of regulation continued to rise globally, the costs of developing and manufacturing finished pharmaceuticals increased, even in the traditionally low-cost regions of the world. This was exacerbated by the fact that the manufacture of APIs was coming under the regulatory spotlight for the first time in many countries.

The resulting increase in demand for assessment of market authorization submissions and inspection of manufacturing facilities against the regulations under these changing conditions placed a huge burden on the already-constrained resources of the regulatory agencies.

From the industry point of view, multinational companies were increasingly turning to third parties to manufacture for them under contract or licence. Since many of the contract acceptors are located in traditionally less-regulated locations such as India and China, the complexity of the supply chain increased significantly.

In terms of technology, innovation was stifled and continuous improvement was not evident in many companies as the boundaries of scientific understanding moved ever closer to the region of hypothetical risk. In some cases, companies were unwilling to run the risk of failing to comply with regulations and tended to resist all change once a process had been validated. In other cases, the companies wanted to change but found it difficult to explain effectively the clinical implications of the scientific innovation in order to ensure a meaningful, timely and relevant review. Additionally, since most products are out of patent and many have been around for more than 20 years, innovative change becomes a major event to update years of inaction. Change has a cost. For example, to validate a chemical synthesis can cost several million euros and approval globally can take two years. This is quite a steep cost to fix a process that may not be broken.

Twenty-First-Century Initiatives

In August 2002 the FDA launched *Pharmaceutical cGMPs for the 21st Century: A Risk-Based Approach*, which was later expanded to embrace pharmaceutical quality, of which cGMP (current GMP) is only one element (FDA 2004).

This initiative was an attempt to address the key issues referred to above. The limited FDA resources were to be used to address the most significant patient risks, which were identified primarily as relating to the manufacturing process. These risks would be identified using Quality Risk Management (QRM). For example, a company producing injectables by means of aseptic manufacturing would expect to be high on the inspection priority list, especially if the company or the product had a history of high levels of complaints or recalls. On the other hand, a company which manufactures oral solid dose products, with well-established stability profiles, would be a much lower priority, especially if the company had a good track record.

Regulatory agencies also made it known that they expected companies to take a scientific approach to GMP and to use concepts of risk management and quality systems to bring an environment of innovation and continuous improvement to pharmaceutical manufacturing.

This adoption of a 'science- and risk-based approach' was not limited to the companies regulated by the FDA. The same terminology is now being used globally, not just in Europe and Japan – which together with the USA make up the major part of the pharmaceutical market in value terms – but also by regulatory agencies in other regions as well – which constitute the majority of the global patient population.

It is fair to say that almost ten years on, both the industry and the regulators are still working through the process of defining how the concept – the so-called New Paradigm – works in practice. This is one of the reasons why we are writing this book: to provide the specificity of actions that other quality and process techniques have been missing. The scientific approach and rational partitioning of the process elements found in the Artisan Model of process design serve such a purpose.

New Terminology

Within the science- and risk-based approach, there are a number of concepts which are new to pharmaceutical manufacturing in form, if not function. Not all of the New Paradigm programmes are new *per se*, so there may be opportunities to learn from other industries which are already further down the road than we are.

For example, the 'Advanced Ship Notice' concept from logistics/supply chain study can be applied to the quality control laboratory. By connecting the purchasing group with the chemists, the latter are able to proactively manage the logistical challenges of release testing for priority, cost reduction – no more expediting charges – and meeting internal customer service goals by having timely access to expected delivery dates.

QUALITY BY DESIGN (QBD)

QbD is the principle that has been implicitly underpinning much of what has been written in the early chapters of this book. Adding to existing experience-based understanding and learning about the unique process attributes during the development stage, the sponsor will develop a full understanding of the critical process parameters and critical product attributes. The continuous expansion of knowledge and understanding leads to a more controlled and cost-effective manufacturing process and a safer, quality product.

DESIGN SPACE

It is impossible for quality to be inspected into a product at the end of a process no matter how sophisticated the reject inspection system. It must be incorporated at the beginning. However, it is important to remember that applying chemical analysis to positively identify and distinguish two different white powders or analyse a tablet for homogeneity or strength against the standard is not testing quality. Such examples comprise smart process design by incorporating scientifically based methods at the correct process control point. This is in contrast to the company which requires multiple re-tests to get the right numbers to justify release of tablets with lot assay of 92 per cent and a relative standard deviation of 6.5 per cent. The former is smart process management and quality by design. The latter is on the edge of fraudulent manufacture.

For pharmaceutical manufacturing, both product and process should be substantially developed before submission of an application for a marketing authorization. Traditionally, this has involved developing a manufacturing methodology where each process parameter is defined individually within a fixed range of validated values and then, ideally, never changed beyond the established range without prior regulatory approval. This of course depends on the input materials being consistent in physical and chemical characteristics. As is so often the case, unexpected change in the input all but ensures an increase in the risk of failure when operating within the validated range. Operating the process within the validated specification range as submitted in the dossier is the regulatory agency's assurance that the clinically generated data are still valid. Change of any sort can have and has had completely unexpected consequences on safety or efficacy.

The concept of design space is that process parameters do not exist in isolation. Design space is defined as 'the multidimensional combination and interaction of input variables (e.g., material attributes) and process parameters that have been demonstrated to provide assurance of quality' (ICH 2009).

By understanding the process from the point of view of a combination of the variables *man, machine, method, material* and *environment*, it is possible to have predictability in the manufacturing process which is science-based and permits changes to be made without the need for continual regulatory approval. The design space is proposed by the applicant on the basis of their development work and must then be approved by the regulators before the process can be operated in this way.

PROCESS ANALYTICAL TECHNOLOGY (PAT)

While design space is relevant during development, PAT is a tool for the manufacturing phase. It involves in-process testing, either in-line or off-line to provide servo-feedback loops for the purpose of adjusting the process to achieve effective measurement of a sensitive end point. PAT may be a more effective way of ensuring quality than by sampling and testing the finished product. However, it is assumed that in-process testing with resulting massive data sets has a direct effect on the final dose critical quality attributes. We have found this to be true for processes that mimic a fluid system. PAT is appropriate for the end points of drying. It may be less effective where large numbers of variables are involved, such as in direct-to-compression dry formulations, since the situation may be too complex to determine root causes for problems.

REAL-TIME RELEASE TESTING (RTRT)

This approach, based upon parametric release principles pioneered for terminal sterilization processes, means that product batches can be released on the basis of PAT and other data collected during the manufacturing process, rather than on finished product testing. This is a concept that has been used in the medical device industry for many years, but is just being approved for select dosage forms within pharmaceutical manufacturing. As with PAT, the application must be considered from all views prior to acceptance. RTRT can only be applied to processes where the surrogate control point has an unequivocal cause and effect outcome.

For example, measurement of elapsed time at target temperature and pressure has been used to release terminally sterilized – autoclaved – parenteral dosage forms. This overcomes the problem of testing for sterility at release, which is known to be virtually ineffective except in the case of gross levels of contamination. The science that underlies the foundation of RTRT is well-known physical constants, such as the latent heat of saturated steam and the microbial death rate at elevated temperature, F_0. If a process does not follow such physical laws, it may not be possible to identify quality problems and hence RTRT would not be an appropriate method of product approval.

International Conference on Harmonisation of Technical Requirements for Registration of Pharmaceuticals for Human Use (ICH) and the New Paradigm

Earlier in this chapter, we discussed some of the key issues facing pharmaceutical manufacturing today. These issues are particularly challenging for a multinational company wishing to market its products globally. The varying regulatory priorities and stages of development of the industry in different countries, each with its own specific technical considerations, resulted in a combination of requests that made it impossible to put together one single dossier that could be used to submit an application for a marketing authorization in all countries. Completing the documentation became more difficult and time-consuming than manufacturing the product. Furthermore, it was not easy to develop corporate operational procedures that would be appropriate throughout all the factories within a multinational company.

As far back as 1990, a move was made towards harmonizing the registration requirements with the establishment of the International Conference on Harmonisation of Technical Requirements for Registration of Pharmaceuticals for Human Use (ICH). When the ICH was set up by the USA, Europe and Japan, its brief was to be a joint forum between regulators and industry to harmonize and organize scientific information for the safety, quality and efficacy of medicines. Standards developed within the ICH became mandatory for companies selling products in the three regions and were accepted as best practice and therefore desirable in many other countries as well.

However, in 2003, the members of the ICH started to look at how the science- and risk-based approach to pharmaceutical manufacturing could be harmonized from the outset, rather than developing in different ways in different parts of the world.

This project was expanded over the next three years until in 2006 it was defined as a search for continuous product and process improvement brought about by the use of pharmaceutical and manufacturing sciences. The objectives were defined as:

- a transparent science- and risk-based assessment approach to dossier submission, review, approval and post-approval changes;

- manufacturers empowered to effect continual improvement throughout the product lifecycle and supply chain;

- more efficient and effective regulatory oversight.

The project has been running for nine years and the output so far is three sets of optional guidelines adopted and a fourth currently being developed.

ICH Q8 PHARMACEUTICAL DEVELOPMENT

ICH Q8 was adopted by all three ICH regions in 2006. It relates to the development stages of the product lifecycle and specifically the scientific content of section 3.2.P.2 of the common technical document (CTD) for regulatory submissions. It has relevance to manufacturing since this is the stage of development during which product and process understanding are accumulated or built upon. However, it is beyond the scope of this book.

ICH Q9 QUALITY RISK MANAGEMENT

ICH Q9 was adopted by the USA and Japan in 2006 and within the EU in 2008. It is a detailed introduction to QRM and offers a generic framework which companies can adopt and adapt, together with examples of where QRM can be used across the product lifecycle. It also provides an overview of some appropriate tools for different circumstances. We will return to QRM later on.

ICH Q10 PHARMACEUTICAL QUALITY SYSTEM

ICH Q10 was adopted by the EU, the USA and Japan during an 18-month period between July 2008 and February 2010. It addresses the implementation of a pharmaceutical quality system and follows the pattern of the ISO 9000 quality standards. However, it is not the intention of the regulators to establish a system for Q10 accreditation. When an inspection team considers a company's quality system, it will do so within the context of a normal GMP inspection.

ICH Q11 DEVELOPMENT AND MANUFACTURE OF DRUG SUBSTANCES

ICH Q11 is in the early stage of preparation (June 2011). It deals with the development and manufacturing of APIs.

MANDATORY VERSUS OPTIONAL ACTIVITIES

There are some elements of the new paradigm that may be considered as requirements while others are optional. For example, being able to demonstrate good product knowledge and process understanding would be an expectation of all assessors reviewing applications for marketing authorization. However, the use of the approaches outlined in ICH Q8 to define the design space for a new product is optional, even though it can be expected to lead to a reduction in regulatory burden.

The use of a QRM approach is mandatory. For example, within the EU, the wording of Chapter 1 of GMP has been amended to make this clear. However, use of ICH Q9, or any specific tool for that matter, is optional. For example, it is a regulatory requirement to carry out an assessment of risks associated with a new piece of equipment as part of the planning of its commissioning and qualification; the choice of the methodology used to carry out this assessment is up to the company and will depend on a number of factors, including the complexity of the equipment and the prior experience and knowledge available to the team.

The requirement for companies to have a quality system is mandatory. This is covered specifically in the EU GMP text, in Chapter 1, and also in 21 CFR 211 in the USA. However, use of ICH Q10 to develop this system is optional.

On the basis of doing what is needed to demonstrate compliance with GMP – but no more – many companies are adopting a 'wait and see' strategy in relation to the optional elements. In some cases, this is due to a belief that the new approaches will have more costs than benefits, while in others, it is a reluctance to make any significant changes in operational methods until the reactions of the regulators have been tried and tested.

Having said that, the regulators from the three ICH regions have emphasized their support for this new approach and are collaborating with industry in determining how it should be implemented. This collaboration is being achieved through joint activities with non-profit-making organizations such as the ISPE (International Society for Pharmaceutical Engineering) and the PDA (Parenteral Drug Association). We hope that this book adds to the debate by providing a new approach to achieve the specificity of actions that underlie the successful management of risk in operations and clinical efficacy.

Quality Risk Management

Risk may be defined as the possibility of suffering harm or loss or being exposed to the possibility of suffering harm or loss. Risk is the potential for harm based on the existence of an actual hazard. For example, a hole in the road is a physical hazard that exists. For a cyclist, there is a risk that he or she might ride across the hole, catch the wheel and fall off. The hole is a certainty; riding across it and falling off is a possibility.

In the context of pharmaceutical manufacturing, the focus is on risk to the patient. Risk, for a given dosage form or drug substance class, is a constant from the regulator's perspective. Aseptic fill poses the most risk to the patient's safety from process failures. Opiate drugs have a constant high-level risk of addiction, which is independent of process performance.

For any particular hazard, the level of risk can be defined as the product of three factors:

- the impact value or how serious will be the effect if something takes place;

- the probability of occurrence;

- the probability of detecting the problem before harm occurs.

The use of terms such as 'factor' and 'probability' seems to imply that we can take a quantitative approach to risk. It is certainly true that, on occasion, quantitative measures are used. However, care should be taken in doing this. In other words, if you are going to use numbers, make very sure that you understand fully what they mean to a patient in a compromised state of health.

In order to identify what action, if any, should be taken to mitigate a particular risk, we need to make a judgment on the criticality of each case. Qualitative terms such as 'high, medium and low' are often used at this point for initial assessment.

In general terms, a risk that has a high probability of occurring and which will have a high impact will be judged as unacceptable and must be eliminated, for example, genotoxic chemicals used to make a drug substance. At the other end of the scale, a hazard which has a low probability of occurring and which would have a low impact anyway will be judged as minor and often subordinated to more significant issues.

The concepts of high, medium and low are situational variables. A risk with a 1 per cent chance of happening would imply low probability. However, if a new pharmaceutical was found during pre-clinical trials to have a 1 per cent probability of killing the patient, this would be considered as high and would normally result in the tests being terminated.

In managing risk, it is sometimes possible to impact directly on the hazard itself. However, in most cases, it is the cause of the hazard that must be addressed and there may well be more than one cause for each event. If there are multiple causes, then it may be necessary to develop more than one strategy for managing the risk. For example, DOE is an effective tool to assess the sensitivity of change in factors that underlie multiple hazards. Similarly, there may be multiple outcomes from a single cause. If the situation is too complex to deal with in one go, then it should be broken down into manageable discrete parts and each one addressed individually. Yet again, we see the value of the Artisan Model.

ICH Q9 Risk Management Model

One of the key parts of ICH Q9 is a risk management model which can be used to manage risk within any organization. The emphasis and the time spent on each element within the model may vary with each situation, but a robust process will include consideration and documentation of each step. The model can be seen in Figure 14.1. A brief overview of each step is presented here, but the source document is an easy read and we recommend it for further study of this topic. One important point of application of risk management, the design of process in the light of risk management principles, must begin with the end in mind, according to Stephen Covey in the text *The 7 Habits of Highly Effective People* (2004).

INITIATE THE PROCESS

Possible steps used by decision makers to initiate and plan a risk management process may include defining the risk under investigation, gathering background data, defining the methodology to be adopted and identifying the team and leader.

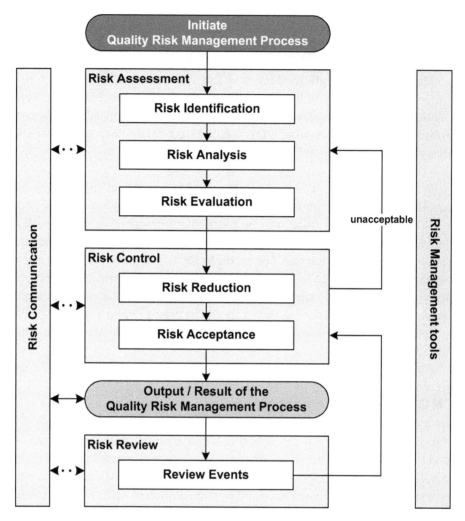

Figure 14.1   Overview of a typical quality risk management process
Source: ICH Harmonised Tripartite Guideline. Quality Risk Management Q9.

RISK ASSESSMENT

Assessing a risk starts with identifying potential hazards, which can be done using information such as historical data, theoretical analysis, informed opinion or concerns of stakeholders.

This is followed by the estimation of risk associated with each of the potential hazards. This focuses on the probability and impact of each hazard and the likelihood of detection.

Finally, the estimated risks are measured against given risk criteria to decide how they need to be managed.

RISK CONTROL

Once the level of risk is known, decisions can be made as to whether they need to be eliminated, reduced or accepted. The purpose is to reduce the risk(s) to an acceptable level and the amount of effort expended should be proportional to the size of the risk. The development of appropriate control strategies, appropriately applied, should be the outcome of the risk management process. For example, a drug that was found during clinical trials to be fatal to some patients would be withdrawn (risk elimination), a drug that was found to cause drowsiness would carry a warning that patients should not drive while taking it (risk reduction), while a drug that caused mild nausea in some patients would carry a notice of that fact in the patient information leaflet (risk acceptance).

RISK COMMUNICATION

This is the sharing of information between the decision makers and other interested parties, including regulators, industry, healthcare workers and the patient.

Training for Risk Assessment

Risk management will generally be a team activity. The people taking part in the activity will need to have training and/or experience in a number of areas:

- skill-based: they will need to know how to work in teams;

- rule-based: they will need to know how to use the various tools and techniques that are available and to decide which ones are appropriate in each circumstance;

- knowledge-based: they will need to know sufficient detail about the process or area under consideration.

Case Study

In this final section, we are going to look at an example of how consideration of the five elements of process management – *man, machine, method, material* and *environment* – can be used to reduce risk to the patient.

We will look at how we can use risk management to set priorities for auditing sites. This was one of the starting points for the regulators in their adoption of risk management; however, it can equally be applied to decisions relating to drawing up a schedule for supplier accreditation.

Consider the scenario of a manufacturer that has just had a regulatory inspection. One of the observations was that there is no system in place for supplier auditing. The company is a large one; it purchases approximately 50 APIs and about ten times as many excipients. It knows that when the regulators return in a year's time, it needs to have put in place an auditing system and to show that it is making good progress. However, it does not have enough resources to audit all its suppliers in one year. So the question it has to address is which sites should be audited first? A task team was set up to work on the problem, with representatives from production, quality assurance, quality control and purchasing.

The first step taken was to define the theoretical risks associated with a supplier of starting materials. Table 14.1 shows the list of risk categories identified by team. The next step was to take each risk category in turn and define what would constitute high, medium or low risk, as shown in Table 14.2

Table 14.1   Identified risk categories for suppliers of starting materials

Risk category	Process element
Route of administration of the drug	Method, Machine
History of previous supply	Man, Material
Supplier's quality system	Man, Method
Type of company	Material, Man
Country of origin	Material, Environment
Products on manufacturer's site	Material, Environment
History of previous audits	Man

Table 14.2   Definitions of levels of risk in suppliers of starting materials

Risk category	Low	Medium	High
Route of administration of the drug	Topical	Oral	Parenteral
History of previous supply	> 3 years	< 3 years	None
Supplier's quality system	GMP	ISO 9001	None
Type of company	Excipient chemical test laboratory	Repacker	Manufacturer
Country of origin	EU/USA	PIC/S member	Non-PIC/S member
Products on manufacturer's site	Single	Multiple	Multiple, high potency
History of previous audits	< 5 years	> 5 years	None

Once this table was complete, each supplier was reviewed against the list and scored against each category in turn. A high risk is weighted more than a medium risk, which is weighted more than a low risk. On the basis of the score for each company, priorities can be derived simply by sorting the list in descending order of risk score. Table 14.3 shows the scoring for two hypothetical suppliers. It can be seen that company A shows a higher overall risk than company B and therefore should be higher on the priority list for being audited.

The outcome of this exercise is thus a list of companies in the order in which the audits should be prioritized. The methodology has clearly taken the risk to the patient into account and has also considered all five elements of the process. The approach is formally documented.

The activities can then be matched to the level of resources available. For example, if there are sufficient resources to carry out 20 audits in the first year, then numbers 1–20 on the list would be the ones to be carried out.

From the point of view of the regulatory inspectors, it may be possible that they challenge the amount of resources applied, but they would find it hard to challenge the logic of the approach that has been applied to the prioritization.

The risk assessment tool used in this case is risk ranking, which can be very useful. It is a tool used to compare and prioritize risks. Risk ranking of complex systems typically requires the evaluation of multiple diverse quantitative and qualitative factors for each risk. The tool involves breaking down a basic risk question into as many components as needed to capture factors involved in

Table 14.3 Risk assessments of hypothetical suppliers of starting materials

Company A: Total risk score = 17

	Low		Medium		High	
Route of administration of the drug	Topical		Oral	1	Parenteral	1
History of previous supply	>3 years	1	<3 years		None	
Supplier's quality system	GMP	1	ISO 9000		None	
Type of company			Repacker		Manufacturer	1
Country of origin	EU/US		PIC/S member	1	Non-PIC/S member	
Products on manufacturer's site	Single		Multiple	1	Multiple, high potency	
History of previous audit	<5 years		>5 years		None	1
	Total Low	2	Total Medium	3	Total High	3
	x 1	2	x 2	6	x 3	9

Company B: Total risk score = 13

	Low		Medium		High	
Route of administration of the drug	Topical	1	Oral		Parenteral	
History of previous supply	>3 years	1	<3 years		None	
Supplier's quality system	GMP		ISO 9000	1	None	
Type of company			Repacker		Manufacturer	1
Country of origin	EU/US		PIC/S member		Non-PIC/S member	1
Products on manufacturer's site	Single		Multiple	1	Multiple, high potency	
History of previous audit	<5 years	1	>5 years		None	
	Total Low	3	Total Medium	2	Total High	2
	x 1	3	x 2	4	x 3	6

the risk. These factors are combined into a single risk score that can then be compared, prioritized and ranked.

Sources of specific risk information for risk ranking might include not only the results of quantitative analysis but also the elicitation of expert opinion in instances where there are data gaps and large uncertainties. In this particular case, the five elements of process management were used as a framework to draw on accumulated knowledge.

Conclusion

In the past decade, there has been recognition by the regulators that a culture change is required both within the agencies and the industry. Companies are required to apply a science- and risk-based approach to pharmaceutical manufacturing. The same approach is being developed by the agencies to the assessment of marketing authorization applications and manufacturing facility inspections.

Risk management is a complement to process excellence and robust process design. When a process is well characterized and controlled in a pragmatic and effective manner, there is little more a manufacturer can do to ensure the consistency of the drug product. Care must be taken to bound risk properly and avoid making decisions in regions of hypothetical possibility. A well-designed and constructed process will minimize operational risk by the use of smart partitioning of controls, minimize patient risk by producing consistent, low variability finished dosages and keep the company from getting caught up on a whirlpool of hypothetical possibilities.

15

Customers

Consumers aren't statistics. Customers are people.
(Stanley Marcus, 1905–2002, American businessman)

Introduction

The concept of customers has changed significantly since we started working in the pharmaceutical industry. We see today's use of customer satisfaction approaches as a surrogate for process management. It is important to understand the changes that have occurred over the past four decades that have had a significant effect on process management approaches. The customer-focused strategies have, in our experience, further diverted the pharmaceuticals industry from a path of process and product excellence by creating an inward focus aimed at meeting interdepartmental service level goals rather than directing energy towards understanding and building robust processes. In other words, the term *customer* has been transformed to become a surrogate measure of process management excellence.

Life used to be simple. It was understood across the organization that the customer was the person who paid monies in order to purchase the pharmaceutical product. Manufacturing operations focused on meeting the production schedule at a reasonable cost. Manufacturing and process management emphasis were internally directed towards product compliance to 'pass' the minimum GMP standard so as not to get into trouble with the local regulatory agency. Process design was a function of the formulator's skill, projects were 'tossed over the wall' and quality was a policeman of the operation. Priority was given to meeting individual departmental goals. Small molecule research was highly productive and new companies could be established with relatively small amounts of cash. There was a good chance of generating a ROI. However, these perspectives were not conducive to process

Table 15.1   Influencing factors of customers

Year	Event	Impact
1962	Kefauver-Harris amendments to the Food, Drug and Cosmetic Act	Thalidomide incident led to efficacy requirements for new drugs
1972	Drug Efficacy Study (DESI)	New drugs introduced between 1938 and 1962 were allowed to remain on the market pending final safety assessment by the National Academy of Sciences. Old line products were discontinued if clinical trials were not conducted by the sponsor
1974–1979	Belmont Report (National Research Act)	Commission on Protection of Human subjects resulting from abuses in Tuskegee experiments, Willowbrook and other patient abusive practices
1975	Helsinki Declaration	International declaration of principles of ethical practice of human experimentation
1970s	Manufacturing quality revolution	Quality is free (Crosby) Quality circles, statistical process control, TQM, adoption of military standard sampling for attributes and variables
1976	Medical device amendments	Faulty medical devices resulted in approximately 10,000 injuries, including 731 deaths
1970s–1980s	Service quality research	Internal marketing and internal customer. SERVQUAL standardized measure of service quality (Frost and Kumar 2001)
1984	Drug Price Competition and Patent Term Restoration Act 1984 (Waxman-Hatch Act)	Expanded the drug industry market to include generic manufacturing
1987	Prescription Drug Marketing Act	Direct towards consumer advertising and related control
1990s–today	Prescription Drug User Fee Act, Food and Drug Administration Amendments Act (FDAAA) of 2007, QbD, PAT et al.	Expanding FDA capability and authority to ensure safe and effective medications. Fostering innovation on behalf of patients

understanding, process excellence and total customer satisfaction. Beginning in the mid-1960s, the pharmaceutical business climate changed drastically in response to global competition, cost containment legislation and a shift from a manufacturing economy to a service economy. Table 15.1 provides a simple summary of several of the more important events that have shaped our current view of customers as surrogate end points for process understanding management.

Two approaches to customer service seemed to prevail. The concept of the internal marketing and the internal customer was conceptualized by marketing research in an effort to foster improvements in employee–customer interactions in the service sector. In the private sector, the emphasis was directed towards broad-view concepts such as 'quality is free' (Crosby 1979), TQM (Juran 1998) and international harmonization such as the International Standards Organization (ISO) and/or refinements of problem-solving techniques (Ishikawa 1986; Kepner and Tregoe 1981). In the public sector in the USA, the Consumer Confidence Index was introduced in 1967 as a consumer opinion survey by the Conference Board Inc., a research organization founded in 1916 (Conference Board Inc. 2011). Consumer confidence was a measure that was factored into business leaders' long-term plans.

Economies in the West were moving from agriculture and manufacturing towards a service-driven economy as foreign competition was increasing rapidly, especially in the automotive industry. During the 1970s and 1980s, it was not uncommon to be greeted by employee indifference while shopping, whether in Europe or the USA. Products were relatively cheap and could be tossed out if defective. It was therefore not surprising that this time period showed some of the lowest levels of consumer confidence since the metric was developed. In the late 1970s, academic research began to focus on the service sector as new and fertile grounds for cutting-edge research. Early conclusions tied the level of external customer satisfaction to the profitability of the company and showed a strong correlation between frontline employee attitudes and external customer satisfaction. Purchasing options were quickly becoming available to the consumer as the import or export ratio began to shift from a producer economy to a consumer economy. If the consumers did not enjoy the shopping experience, they were able to take their business elsewhere in order to receive the service they desired.

In around 1978, the concept of the internal customer and internal marketing was born as a broad-view business strategy. This led to an inward view of service and a change in the orientation towards customers. Interestingly, the original concept was limited to service industries, as pointed out by Frost and Kumar (2001).

By the late 1980s and 1990s, the concept of the internal customer spread into the quality/process management vernacular. As Juran points out, the internal customer is not the dictionary description of a customer and is not intended to be considered as such (1992). We have observed many pharmaceutical companies practising 'internal customer service' with elaborate performance agreements between departments. This is detrimental to fulfilling the process management purpose of the pharmaceutical manufacturer. The single most important consideration is to develop and run a robust process and to control the variation of the overall system. The concept of the 'internal customer' is appealing and few can argue against it from the *frontline* service perspective it originally targeted. However, adopting elaborate internal customer agreements to improve process management design and process control is a fallacy of logic termed wishful thinking.

We do not believe that the application of the concept of internal customers is helpful for pharmaceutical process design and management. In our view, the final purchaser, be it a hospital, a doctor or a patient in the pharmacy, is the one and only customer. Everyone else is a member of a process chain with a specific role in the manufacture of consistently high-quality pharmaceuticals available from the pharmacist when prescribed by the doctor or required for self-medication. Product excellence can only be ensured by the simplicity of process design and the accuracy of the process signals during production. In other words, excellence comes from simplicity.

The fundamental roles associated with pharmaceutical process design and management are to convert excipient materials and pure active drug substances from a raw state to finished produce in accordance with marketing authorization requirements. While customer satisfaction is important, success is the outcome of effective process management.

Challenges Related to Customers

There are five customer-related challenges that obscure process design and management and ultimately hinder the industry goal of product safety, efficacy and availability:

- ends justify the means as the customer;

- drug development process as the customer;

- new and novel technology as the customer;

- sponsor's success as the customer;

- self-diagnosis is not a customer goal.

ENDS JUSTIFY THE MEANS AS THE CUSTOMER

Without going into elaborate detail, pharmaceutical products are developed in the context of preventing past medical and scientific atrocities in which patients were treated unethically without respect to human rights. Legal mandates require study to begin with compound conceptualization, animal model testing, limited human modeling from animal data, human study in three phases and finally approval of the product with post-approval monitoring. Figure 15.1 summarizes the general concept of increasing knowledge and understanding during the evolution of a molecule. The marketing authorization application summarizes the study and the limited known effects of the compound on the patient. The goal of process management is to maintain consistency of the medicine. It is fundamental then that process management should have a deep understanding of the compromises to the health of the patient.

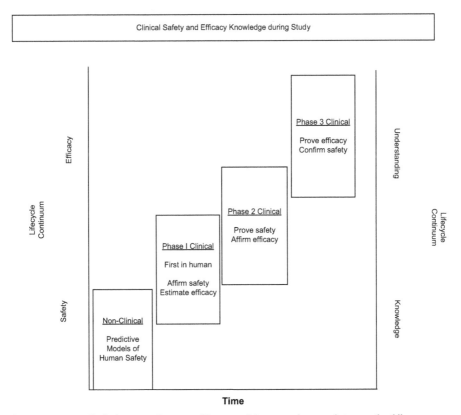

Figure 15.1   Gaining understanding and improving safety and efficacy

As markets have become more global, the historical context of customer needs has changed. For example, the assumption of 75 kg average mass in Europe and the USA will not work in China, where the patient is closer to 50 kg average mass. It is important to understand intended use in the various populations. This concept cannot simply be captured in the context of the 'external customer' since it is too general. Failing to design the process to minimize variation is likely to hinder a broader understanding of safety and efficacy.

DRUG DEVELOPMENT PROCESS AS THE CUSTOMER

Numerous parties consider themselves to be customers. There are internal customers, health authorities, doctors, healthcare maintenance organizations and, last but not least, the patient. In terms of process design and product excellence, there can only be one customer – the patient. All other groups or individuals play differing roles in the product lifecycle chain. Playing a role is different from being a customer. We should not confuse customer service goals with respectful interactions needed to ensure process design is executed. Table 15.2 summarizes end responsibilities from a lifecycle management perspective. If the goal of process consistency becomes obscured in any way, the efficiency of the chain performance will be affected adversely.

Table 15.2   Overview of drug product lifecycle roles

Element	Party	Goal or outcome
Product development	Sponsor, manufacturer	Develop a product with consistent performance characteristics
Non-clinical and clinical trials	Sponsor, CRO	Use product with evolving consistency to establish safety and efficacy in humans
Logistics	Manufacturer, distribution	Procure components and distribute product to supply on demand
Sales and marketing	Manufacturer	Inform medical community of availability and intended use
Diagnosis and approval	Physician, healthcare insurance organizations	Determine appropriate, lowest-cost product for the indication
Availability on demand	Pharmacist	Stock proper medications to meet the random or long-term use requirements for individual patients
Independent assessment of safety and efficacy	Health authorities	Highly trained scientists who evaluate safety and efficacy on behalf of the patient population
Intended use	Patient	The customer

Implied in all of the discussion of pharmaceutical customers – the patient – is the simple unspoken truth that patients seek relief. If the pharmaceutical company concerns itself with elaborate internal metrics and service agreements rather than keeping an eye on the process, the amount of time necessary to gain understanding is jeopardized. The science of pharmaceutical products is sophisticated and getting more so with every new innovation in technology. Considering the design of the process during the early stages of inception is becoming even more essential. The framework in this text can assist by identifying the critical elements of the development so as to reduce the volume of post-approval changes.

NEW AND NOVEL TECHNOLOGY AS THE CUSTOMER

It is important to distinguish how technical hurdles are overcome in order to result in a safe and efficacious pharmaceutical. Few, if any, mechanisms of action are understood with certainty. There is statistical evidence of the outcomes, but we still lack the methods to properly reveal the precise interaction of the drug substance as it enters the bloodstream. There is more that we do not understand than we do understand. Therefore, it is imperative that process design be incorporated to identify with greater certainty the underlying process elements that will prevent the erosion of technological control established in the original marketing application.

Most change in technological controls relates to the adoption of cutting-edge quality or business practices with the promise of great benefits to the user. As we pointed out previously, businesses like to see immediate results to improve profits and will adopt quickly. This belief in a magic bullet – also known as a silver bullet in the USA – has relegated simple proven practices to history and has introduced unproven concepts as a basis of developing 'new' knowledge, which is often locked away in an archive. This book seeks to reinstate the proven techniques as a starting point to evaluate current processes and to establish a strong process design for products that are in the development stages.

SPONSOR'S SUCCESS AS THE CUSTOMER

The only manner in which a drug can legally be introduced to commerce is with an approved marketing application. As a result, the techniques are not fully transferrable to pharmaceutical process design, especially when it comes to altering the critical scientific summaries that make up the marketing authorization application. This consideration must be made as the process is being designed. Care must be given to the technical accuracy of scientific summaries provided in regulatory variations or supplements. Inattention to proper details hampers a company's ability to change and improve, and ultimately could result in delays to timely regulatory approvals necessary to avoid market shortages of drug products.

SELF-DIAGNOSIS IS NOT A CUSTOMER GOAL

Finally, the customer patient is not expert in self-diagnosis and self-prescription. Some would say that drug development should begin with the patient defining his or her wants and desires in a pharmaceutical compound. Beyond generalities of 'unmet' needs, it is often difficult to articulate what exactly a product should look like or which process is necessary to ensure consistent drug performance. Thus, discussion of what the patient customer wishes should be secondary to the practice of process excellence. Understanding the consistency of the process will help to clarify labelling claims so that there is negligible opportunity for the drug product to adversely contribute to issues relating to absolute consistency among all doses over the lifecycle of the product.

Customer Satisfaction through Process Focus

We propose five solutions to the challenges discussed previously. Each solution brings the process design closer to a point of absolute consistency (within methodology uncertainty). Other approaches are also possible. The following points should be viewed as a beginning rather than an end:

- focus on process design and excellence in performance;

- increase process design sensitivity through centred means and narrow distributions;

- verify the most significant controls by DOE;

- evaluate deviation or changes based on compromised state of health;

- set process standards to vulnerable populations.

FOCUS ON PROCESS DESIGN AND EXCELLENCE IN PERFORMANCE

Process design should not focus inwards. Resources should be coordinated and roles understood so that the process focuses outwards towards product consistency and the product performance when prescribed to the patient. When designing a new process or re-engineering an older one, it is important to have the proper representation of key hand-off points to minimize disruptions during the execution of manufacturing operations.

Simply put, if internal customer strategies are employed, these should be modified to a process excellence model, which holds each step accountable for the success of the next one. In other words, one step should master their output to ensure the success of the immediately following step as well as those further down the line. Each employee should have the authority to seek corrective actions when process change is discovered, including temporarily ceasing activity until the errant issue is resolved. Finally, we recommend the inclusion of experienced individuals either as a direct working member or a supporting subteam member to minimize miscommunication. Experience guards against group thinking in which ideas are adopted readily but not necessarily after robust debate.

INCREASE PROCESS DESIGN SENSITIVITY THROUGH CENTRED MEANS AND NARROW DISTRIBUTIONS

Effective problem-solving or process improvement requires a statistically stable process, which is characterized by centred mean values and narrow distributions around the mean. This is the most certain way to reveal actual problems. The resulting solutions should be fairly obvious and quick to implement. All previously mentioned distractions would become moot. The logistical planning and scheduling would better hit the intended inventory replenishment schedules without the need to divert attention to find out who failed to meet their internal customer target time. Manufacturing operates most efficiently and effectively when problem solutions are directed towards customer product fulfilment based on all involved parties agreeing on the facts underlying the solution.

VERIFY THE MOST SIGNIFICANT CONTROLS BY DOE

When setting the controls necessary to ensure consistent process outcomes, a scientific referee technique is necessary to distinguish the most important factor from among several limited choices. DOE is the method of choice. In terms of process management for consistent patient outcomes, historical experience is a good starting point. As development continues, the process design team is often faced with the challenge of identifying the most important among three or more choices. These become the critical controls necessary to verify adequate process sensitivity of measure so that when change occurs unexpectedly, the frontline operator will know that something has changed from the original process design assumptions.

EVALUATE DEVIATION OR CHANGES BASED ON COMPROMISED STATE OF HEALTH

Change is an inevitable fact of business life. When change occurs, it is important for the quality unit to consider the patients' disease state and the associated compromises in bodily function. The decision to deviate or change a process must incorporate consideration of the disease ramifications. For example, when considering the acceptability of a raised – but within limits – microbial count for process water or component ingredients, a patient-focused process consideration should be given to probable changes of stomach pH as the result of other medicines administered. The microbial species in question may be able to bypass the body's natural defence of stomach acid and result in unintended harm to the patient.

SET PROCESS STANDARDS TO VULNERABLE POPULATIONS

As mentioned previously, the most vulnerable sectors of the population must set the standard of control for the drug manufacturing process. We previously discussed the example of deaths among neonates in Brazil. The injectable product met all endotoxin specifications, but the neonate patients were intolerant of standard quantities of endotoxin and died.

Conclusion

Customers are the reason why business exists. However, the legal framework of the pharmaceutical industry does not provide for direct interaction as found in the service industry, for example. To succeed in achieving high levels of customer satisfaction through the delivery of safe and effective medicine, the process development team, as a top priority, must design for minimum variability within each process step and for consistency of process outputs.

There can be no distractions from the many different surrogate 'voices of the customer' in the quest for excellent process design. By focusing on controlling those parts of the process that are associated with pharmaceutical dose production, customer (patient) satisfaction will be accomplished as a natural outcome of effective process management.

16

Process Integrated Accounting

We have the most crude accounting tools. It's tragic because our accounts and our national arithmetic doesn't tell us the things that we need to know.

(Susan George, 1934–, American political activist)

Introduction

This chapter deals with the alignment of managerial accounting within the framework of process design. This approach was developed and implemented on the realization that financial accounting can neither discriminate cost drivers nor capture frontline employee work efforts accurately. The technique is deceptively simple and is intended to be used over a narrow application. By this we mean a single process within a department, such as tablet compression in manufacturing or a chemistry laboratory within R&D.

The currently accepted manner of accounting aggregates disparate business costs, creating a very insensitive measure of operating performance. The cost improvements in one area can be quickly hidden by expenditures in other parts of the business. Under this scenario, it is difficult to show, beyond soft returns, the value of the improvement effort. For example, if a process improvement, such as improved intrateam communications, reduces the cycle time of an activity, it is difficult to show that the improved capability actually allows additional new business considerations without an increase of costs due to hiring. The underlying reason for the mismatch has its roots in the evolution of accounting as applied to manufacturing operations. We call our approach Process Integrated Accounting (PIA).

For the most part, the rules of accounting are well proven but are old in design and too convoluted at the financial reporting level. When many accounting rules were designed, the economy was primarily agrarian or artisan. As the Industrial Revolution continued to take global hold, the cost of machines compared to the cost of labour was initially very high. The relation of these elements has since reversed so that labour and materials are a significant part of cost and machines are relatively low cost. Financial accounting for the most part does not provide the appropriate measures of cost at the frontline of business operations.

The sensitivity of these measures is relative in that 93–95 per cent accuracy is sufficient, since the accuracy used in the PIA approach is of secondary concern. The more relevant task is to create an accounting that captures time and cost from productive work efforts as well as non-productive activities. Quickly exposing the cumulative non-productive time of a work group opens up possibilities for timely continuous improvement efforts. Timely access to information is more important than categorization to the penny or cent. The outcome is to hold organizations accountable for accurately capturing costs for the purpose of demonstrating effective internal fiscal controls. Adopting the style of accounting structure suggested here will significantly enhance the accountability and result in accurate and relevant cost and time data being available on the frontline.

Challenges Related to Accounting

For the purposes of this discussion, accounting is used in the broadest sense of responsibility. The issues discussed point to the need for simple changes to adopt a managerial approach of cost management and capture. The system described is deceptively simple, but has been used successfully in laboratory operations. While the process description of laboratory systems differs from manufacturing systems in absolutes, the principles are universal in their application. The universal applicability of the tool is the focus of our discussion.

There are four issues that need to be overcome in order to align process accounting with process design. The two should work hand in glove, so, as the process is being designed, a financial department member should be identified for inclusion on the team. The challenges facing accounting in the pharmaceutical industry are as follows:

- purchase volume discounts skew costs;

- outdated view of frontline managerial cost and time capture;

- soft cost is not considered as a decision-making tool for managing frontline costs;

- after the fact averages, too many facts and not enough information.

PURCHASE VOLUME DISCOUNTS SKEW COSTS

Walmart has used this strategy very effectively to shift product procurement costs towards smaller retail establishments. In so doing, the manufacturer reduces margins in favor of high-volume purchasers while not altering the fundamental structure of the process, which is the true control of the cost of goods. The same is true for the pharmaceutical industry, where large buying groups or even countries with socialized medicine demand prices that could be lower than or approach cost. Consider for a moment the North American controversy of the low cost of prescriptions in Canada compared to the USA. The same product is offered at a lower price due to heavy discounts to promote sales in Canada. The difference is made up by higher-cost goods being sold to smaller retailers. In this case, the smaller retailer is the patient's healthcare plan in the USA. Economy of scale sounds fine in theory, but cost of manufacture in the pharmaceutical industry does not truly follow the economy of scale argument and low-cost volume buying.

In pharmaceutical production, the lowest cost is achieved from a campaign strategy, in which cleaning, batch reconciliation and release testing are all minimized by reducing or eliminating the problem of cross-contamination. There is a practical limit to the number of batches that a pharmaceutical company is willing to risk if somewhere between the start of the campaign and the end of the campaign an unexpected problem such as contamination arises. There is significant industry buzz relating to continuous processing and the improvements and cost containment of such approaches. It seems to us that many of the points made for this strategy overlook the issue of demand being a function of patient health. For reasons of potential adulteration, equipment must be routinely cleaned. Cleaning cannot be eliminated to further reduce costs. So, if frontline costs are captured as an aggregate quantity, then the true measure of cost is not likely to relate to the realities of the process design.

There is a good reason why polymer resin manufacturers or potato crisp manufacturers have selected a continuous processing approach. It has to do with matching process output to market potential. A weekend sale of potato crisps will bring in greater revenue and reduce the immediate cost profile related to the specific time period of manufacture. The same is not true for prescription pharmaceuticals. Industry companies cannot have sales in the sense of consumer foods like potato crisps. As a matter of fact, some of the largest fines paid in the USA by the industry have been levied specifically for misleading patients or physicians with unbalanced marketing and advertising campaigns. Accounting control must be aligned to the process in order to reveal changes in the cost assumptions of time and materials.

OUTDATED VIEW OF FRONTLINE MANAGERIAL COST AND TIME CAPTURE

As systems have become more automated with in-line automation, programmable logic controllers and sophisticated analytical instrumentation, the opportunity to make an accidental mistake has increased substantially. This has been the case in the management of cost and material use at the frontline. At precise high-volume processing, even the smallest error can lead to unexplainable deviations. In conventional accounting systems, details of the hidden factory, a second level of work not allocated in the system, are merged with the planned costs. Cost information is not fed to the frontline manager in a usable way. When worker time and costs are averaged, it is nearly impossible to identify the opportunities for improvement found in the hidden factory.

Frontline management has been trained to consider accounting as two general accumulation buckets. Firstly, what is the lowest possible cost for a piece of equipment and, secondly, do the workers show up on time? This narrow focus increases the risk to effective process management by firstly procuring material or machines that are not adequate for their purpose and secondly by sending an unintended message to the worker that showing up as a warm body is more important than successfully contributing to consistent product production. It is time to expose the hidden factory.

SOFT COST IS NOT CONSIDERED AS A DECISION TOOL FOR MANAGING FRONTLINE COSTS

The frontline operation is a unique environment in which to operate. Often, new techniques will not necessarily eliminate tangible head count, but the improvement may reduce the risk of overtime hours or even provide additional free resource to pursue other significant challenges without the additional headcount being needed. We define soft cost as the estimated efficiency of the labour necessary to operate the current process based on average labour and benefit costs. Soft cost is a benchmark tool to estimate the net benefit of improving the efficiency if the process is changed. The savings are described in terms of higher personnel utility – for example, accepting a new work contract with the existing staff or reducing the time required to accomplish a standard task. We have found that a relative soft cost evaluation, such as reducing the amount of pre-sample compendia search, can approximate the magnitude of improvement as a confirmation of a new strategy. For example, in the case of the compendial literature searches discussed, the payback of purchasing the on-line compendia, with bookmarks, was three to four months.

The company did not believe in the appropriate use of soft business measures, so receiving approval for purchase of the system required attesting to the fact that the head count previously allocated could be removed from departmental costing estimates. Fortunately, the actual head-count savings also included attrition by retirement without the need for replacement.

AFTER THE FACT AVERAGES, TOO MANY FACTS AND NOT ENOUGH INFORMATION

As we said earlier in this chapter, aggregating and averaging costs is the most certain way to keep the hidden factory hidden. It is difficult to exactly estimate the extent of the hidden factory, but based on the our experience of implementing the PIA system described later in the chapter, the analytical cycle time reduced from an average of 14 days to about 5 days during the four months of the project. This was achievable only when the hidden factory of process issues were exposed at a detail level to allow discrete and effective corrective actions.

When the accounting system in the laboratory was first evaluated, there were twice as many unique categorical divisions as there were chemists and microbiologists. Where averages hide variations and smooth the curve, too many factual bits of data suggest change is present when it is not. The data bits are noise rather than signal. Framing the time-keeping system to distinguish between the two ensures performance at the proper levels of control.

Solutions to Accounting Challenges

We propose one integrated approach to developing accounting systems that complement process design; PIA. The features of the system were developed and implemented in a chemistry and microbiology laboratory setting. We focus on personnel time, as many companies have an excellent cost-tracking system for materials and consumable commodities. The simplicity of the approach and the timeliness of information gathering and reporting are the two major benefits. With respect to simplicity, the process described consists of only seven categories of time in the 'as designed' level of data. In the 'hidden factory' level there are only five categories and these are subsets of the 'as designed' level with respect to the business responsibilities of the particular phase of the process. The key points to consider in designing the system are as follows:

- speed of information availability is the first concern. Information must be available on demand;

- accuracy of information is a secondary concern. Estimates of 90 per cent are accurate enough to start. Continued use of the system incrementally improves accuracy;

- the definitions for placement of employee time are critical. A department must all input time according to the same set of definitional rules. This step ensures the effectiveness of the aggregation feature;

- defined departmental activities should not exceed 7–9 categories;

- hidden factory objects should not exceed 7–9 categories.

This tool works on a quality principle called rational grouping or a type of database structuring of data table content. The steps define database table structure in general terms. The definitions are not to be integrated into the tables, but serve as guidance to the user as to where the information should be placed. Well-designed processes also take advantage of this common-sense approach.

This technique integrates well into financial accounting. For smaller contract manufacturers, the billing accuracy rose to 98 per cent and client invoices could be issued in approximately 30–45 minutes as the laboratory time was directly uploaded to the spreadsheet programme in the cost accounting department. The data entry time for the laboratory went from about 1+ hours per employee per week (35 person staff) to 15 minutes per employee per week (the number of time categories was reduced from 70 to 7).

We will now walk the reader through the general steps of the process. A schematic is provided in Figure 16.1 to demonstrate the database table layout. It should be noted that persons are identified only for the purpose of being able to assess the root cause of a problem rather than finding the person who 'makes a mistake'.

Step 1: Define the users and data to be captured in table form, for example, individual personnel names, project titles or numbers, etc. This allows for the application to contract manufacturers as well as large pharmaceutical companies. The user definition and project titles promote specificity of a given event to a given problem-solving exercise. The use of drop screens is highly recommended to avoid corruption of the database with typographical errors. These items should be limited whenever possible. The tool must not be a time burden.

Step 2: Identify and define accounting measures in three general categories:

  – Administrative (1);

  – Personal Discretionary Time (1);

  – Business Processes (5–7).

Administrative time captures core activities necessary to run the group, such as training, meetings, time-keeping, component ordering and the like. Personal Discretionary time incorporates personal allowances for holiday leave, sick time or leave to tend to issues outside of the workplace. Business processes relate to time specific to the routine effort needed to produce the drug product according to local GMP.

Step 3: Create definitions of what time is to be placed in each bucket for the 'expected' events of a process that runs normally. This is a critical point. Every user must understand where to place his or her time. Hidden factory items are any deviations from the items identified as characteristic of the process. Normal activities would include considerations of the process elements – *man, machine, method, material* and *environment*. For example, Administrative would logically group such times as ordering supplies, writing procedures, providing training in company procedures, company holiday time and the like. Personal Discretionary time would include personal holiday, personal improvement training, volunteer time supported by the company, etc. It is possible to have a 'hidden' factory for administrative, but this is a remote consideration at the beginning.

Business Processes are the general aspects of the department's business and would include, for example, component and excipient testing, in-process testing, release testing, stability testing and the like. Definitions should be made for the expectations of the system as if it were running properly. For example, raw material/component testing would be considered 'operating according to design' if a sufficient sample is always delivered for testing. If the laboratory must request additional samples for the first time test, then the time necessary to do this would be captured in the 'hidden factory' part of the PIA system.

Step 4: For the process steps, create a 'bucket' to capture all the time necessary to resolve the issue that required more than one time to perform the step properly. This table should have only total time, project name and be attributable to a specific person. The definition should include all the time necessary to write reports, investigations, analyse additional samples and the like.

Step 5: Beta test the system on a small scale first to ensure that the design is providing rational information. The simplest way to carry out the beta test is to have one or two employees perform a limited time trial of the new system before launching the programme full scale. The limited trial will provide rapid feedback about user acceptance and system performance.

Figure 16.1 provides a conceptual layout of the data system for capturing process-driven time within a group or department.

Tables 16.1 and 16.2, respectively, provide examples of cost categorization for a laboratory setting and a dry blend, direct-to-hopper tablet compression scenario.

Case Studies

Two examples of real-life results achieved by this technique will provide evidence of the value of the approach.

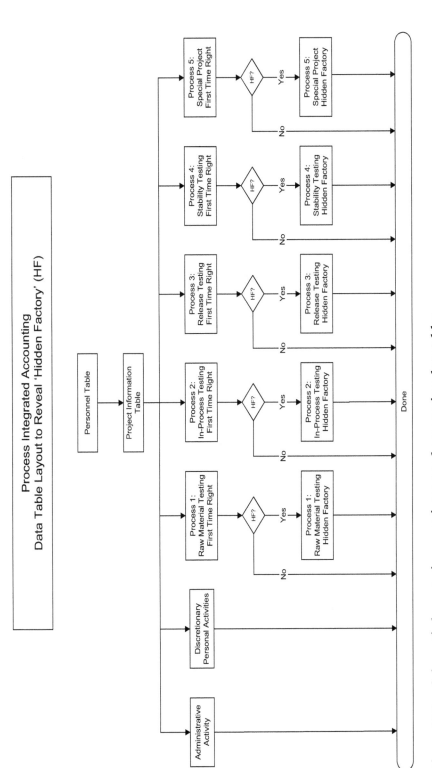

Figure 16.1   Schematic layout of process-integrated accounting data tables

Table 16.1   Suggested definitions of activities for a laboratory operation

Administrative activity	Supply ordering SOP writing Maintenance shutdown Company holiday Timesheets Meetings General training Calibration Sample logging
Personal Discretionary activity	Vacation/holiday Sick time Development training
Process 1: Raw material release test	Sample preparation Direct testing Documentation Clean-up
Process 2: In-process control testing	Sample preparation Direct testing Documentation Clean-up
Process 3: Release-to-market testing	Sample preparation Direct testing Documentation Clean-up
Process 4: Stability testing	Sample preparation Direct testing Documentation Clean-up Summary and conclusions discussion
Process 5: Special projects	Transfer protocol development Client meetings Sample preparation Direct testing Documentation Clean-up Protocol write-up

CASE STUDY 1

One of us was assigned managerial responsibility for a laboratory operation at a pharmaceutical manufacturing site. When the assignment started, the laboratory required 14 days on average to finalize the release paperwork. On average, nine new samples, consisting of raw materials, in-process materials or final product awaiting release, were received daily. While the testing turnaround time was slow, no one could say for certain which aspect of the analytical work was a major contributing factor in causing the delays. Each of

Table 16.2   Suggested definitions of activities for a manufacturing operation

Administrative activity	Supply ordering SOP writing Maintenance shutdown Company holiday Timesheets Meetings General training Calibration Sample logging
Personal Discretionary activity	Vacation/holiday Sick time Development training
Process 1: Material verification	Reconcile pharmacy weighing and lots Document information on batch record Record machine identifications
Process 2: Blender set-up and qualification	Visually check materials for consistency Dispense materials to blender Start process Transfer to totes and deliver to compression
Process 3: Tablet press set-up and operation	Verify incoming paperwork Set up press for punches and dies Check cleanliness Verify information on batch records Run blend to optimize press Run product Record in-process control values Shut down when finished
Process 4: Send to warehouse	Reconcile quantity Initiate movement to warehouse Label containers Stretch-wrap full pallets
Process 5: Equipment clean-up	Disassemble press Transport parts to washroom Transport punches and dies to maintenance shop Vacuum loose dust Clean base machine Clean room Tag room dirty

the 35 team members had a different *opinion* as to the root cause. The logistical challenge could only be tackled by a simplification strategy of matching the process elements to a managerial-style accounting model.

Since its inception, the laboratory time-tracking system had evolved into 70 categories. Very few measures related to the core laboratory process of receiving samples, testing samples, and reviewing and releasing samples that met written specification requirements. There were no measures of job efficiency in this measurement system. Verbally, everyone stated they had too much work, the methods worked inconsistently (even though the method was 'validated') and the only solution was to hire more staff. Few facts were available to identify and quantify the time spent over the 14-day period.

To solve the problem, the laboratory work process was clearly defined and integrated with the accounting system, as described earlier in this chapter. Within two weeks, one time driver emerged – raw material testing. Several underlying factors of the challenges to raw material testing became evident:

- samples arrived in the laboratory with no advance notice;

- reference standards were often out of date and invalid;

- contract laboratory testing often required 'expediting charges' to meet site schedules.

Five chemists were dedicated to testing raw material samples and had often required additional help. Based on an average 14-day receipt-to-release period, approximately 560 man-hours were required to deal with the current receiving rate of samples (8 hrs/day x 5 chemists x 14 days = 560 hours). Three solutions were applied. Firstly, a new programmed query of the company inventory computer system was written to allow the chemists to request on demand the planned delivery dates of all materials for the upcoming four-month period. Secondly, procedures were modified to require a review of on-site reagent standards dating monthly, and reorder new standards based on the four-month purchasing schedule. Finally, contract laboratories were notified about four weeks in advance of a pending sample receipt. The contract laboratory could 'reserve' a spot in the schedule and verify that all reagents and standards were within dating. The test samples could then be shipped overnight for a morning delivery.

About two months after making the system changes using the PIA approach, the average time of completion dropped to five days or a total resource requirement of 200 man-hours for the current number of samples (8 hrs/day x 5 chemists x 5 days = 200 hours) as the result of being able to identify efficiency barriers. The capacity of the five chemists increased by about 360 man-hours over an approximate three-week period (560 hours – 200 hours = 360 hours positive variance) from simply isolating key barriers that existed within the current process.

The time savings realized was a 'soft cost' in that head count was not eliminated, but the improvement clearly was worth the internal cost charges for the minor amount of programming necessary to allow the test group to accomplish more with the same resource. Finally, expediting charges were virtually eliminated.

CASE STUDY 2

In the same laboratory operation, chemists performed in-process release testing of a multi-component vitamin and mineral tablet. The product contained varying quantities of vitamins such as ascorbic acid at hundreds of milligrams per tablet and minerals such as selenium at microgram levels, thus providing a difficult matrix to chemically analyse. The PIA scheme previously applied was used to isolate a key component of slow laboratory turnaround time for the vitamin product; a low percentage of tested right-first-time of in-process samples for release testing of the finished tablets.

The re-test rate for the vitamin was about 40 per cent. At stake was a 'laboratory hold' disruption of the production schedule for packaging the tablet. Not only was time and money wasted at the laboratory, but the manufacturing operation delay started to pile up overhead costs beyond the standard cost model. There were even missed delivery schedules. A meeting with the test chemists quickly revealed process design flaws within the test method and specification for vitamin E.

The first correction was to the sampling plan. The analytical method required a single tablet for testing the level of vitamins and minerals in the tablet, often referred to as the assay. The solution to the problem was to increase the sample quantity to ten tablets to have a better estimation of the average amount of vitamin E present. The assay is always based on an average of multiple units. Measuring a single unit is never a substitute for an assay, no matter how much cost can apparently be saved. In fact, this was a false economy, since additional costs were being incurred for the laboratory investigations.

The second correction related to the specification range. Vitamin E is used as a single-component dietary supplement in doses typically from 400 IUs to 1200 IUs. IU stands for 'International Unit', which is the way in which potency of vitamin E is described. The tablet in question contained only 15 IUs per tablet (on average). The specification range had been previously re-evaluated and set to a range of 12–18 IUs based on a wrongly applied C_{pk} analysis by a well-meaning statistician. The original specification was significantly wider, 10 IUs to 25 IUs, but the 'statistics' suggested the range was too wide and could drift out of statistical control. The irony of this situation was that the level of vitamin E contained in the product was almost a 'trace quantity' when compared with typical dietary supplement dose levels. The specification was restored to the original range.

The final correction taken was to widen the authority of the laboratory manager to approve a method change with proper documented rationale. The SOP allowing this was also written. When assistance was first sought from the Laboratory Technical Services team, the response was 'we are too busy and cannot issue a new document for at least 12 months'. A new SOP was written and approved by site procedures. The laboratory manager now had the authority to issue an amendment to the procedure to allow a composite sample of ten tablets to be used for analysis. The very next lot passed test the first time. No further test failures occurred.

It is difficult to place an accurate value on these improvements; however, the savings – keeping to delivery schedule, eliminating overtime, etc. – were estimated to exceed €225,000 ($302,000).

Conclusion

The changes proposed to establish a process-integrated accounting system are simple and straightforward. The technique overcomes the single biggest shortcoming of current financial and managerial accounting – illogical aggregation of costs associated with the efficient operation of a process. In other words, current accounting models rely on broad averages of costs and time as the basis of decision making. The PIA approach allows the user to develop a discriminating view of the reliability of the process in action.

PIA is not a replacement for broader-view managerial accounting considerations, nor is it intended to replace conventional double-entry ledger income statements or balance sheets that are the hallmark of financial accounting. The key to successful implementation is to align with and apply measures to a well-structured process model. A well-focused integration of time and cost at the frontline operation will expose process hindrances quickly.

If the system expands much further beyond this design, the effort required to capture time for a particular job begins to take away from the time necessary to complete the work assignment. The logic of the design is to ask the following question: was the work done right first time and how long did the effort take? Or did it require more than one attempt to get the job completed? When this happens, the total time of 'done right first time' plus 'two or more times to get it right' is clearly identified from the aggregate labour cost captured in the financial reporting system. The hidden factory, the time spent beyond doing the job right first time, becomes a highly focused process point to which problem-solving can be effectively applied. With daily time entry by each team member, it is possible to identify continuous improvement opportunities to tackle at the beginning of the next week.

Appendix

Regulatory and Critical Analytical Controls Summary
[Drug Product or Drug Substance Names]
Assay, Impurity/Degradant, Uniformity of Dosage by HPLC

Method Valid for Dosages	Method and Validation Summary	
Immediate Release Tablets: 5, 10, 25 mg	Analytical Method 1234.00 Revision 1	Effective: 2-July-2011
Delayed Release Tablets: 50mg		
Hard Gelatin Capsules: 5, 10, 25 mg	Method Validation Val 1234.00	Performed: 15-June-2011

Standard and Solution Concentrations and Preparation

Stock Standard:	25mg/mL	• Standard weight:	≥ 50.x mg
Working Standard (A):	0.25mg/mL	• Impurity/degradant weight:	≥ 10.xx mg
Stock Impurities/Degradants:	0.5mg/mL	• Sonicate each stock solution until dissolved:	5-10 min.
Working Impurity/Degradant (B):	0.05mg/mL	• Vigorously mix working solutions:	10-15 min.
Sample:	0.25mg/mL	• Prepare solutions at room temperature	
		• Protect solutions from sunlight	

Solution Storage and Stability

STORAGE: 25°C ± 5°C		STORAGE: 5°C ± 2°C	
Stock Standard:	3 days	Stock Standard:	5 days
Working Standard:	2 days	Working Standard:	5 days
Impurities / Degradants Stock:	3 days	Impurities / Degradants Stock:	4 days
Impurity / Degradant Working:	2 days	Impurity / Degradant Working:	2 days
Sample:	1 day	Sample:	2 days

Mobile Phase Composition, Grade and Preparation

COMPONENTS		GRADE	
Water:	740ml	HPLC	• Formulation: Volume:Volume
Acetonitrile (ACN):	250ml	HPLC	• Beginning with water in a suitable vessel, add other reagents
Tetrahydrofuran (THF):	10ml	HPLC	• Initial mix time: 10-15 minutes
Perchloric Acid:	1ml	HPLC	• Degassing time: 15-20 minutes. Stir during degassing.
			• Filter before use: 0.22 micron PTFE membrane filter

Stationary Phase Requirements		Instrument Description and Settings	
Column:	Intersil ODS 3V-C18 or equivalent	HPLC System:	Agilent 1100 or equivalent
Packing:	5 µm	Detector:	Perkin-Elmer UV
Length:	15 cm	Elution:	Isocratic
ID:	0.46cm	Temperature:	Ambient
		Flow Rate:	1 mL/min
		Wavelength:	254 nm
		Injection Volume:	10 µL

Sample Analysis

ANALYTICAL SEQUENCE		SAMPLE PREPARATION	
Components:	4	Components:	
System Suitability:	6	Water-	neat
Standards:	3	ACN -	50:50(v/v) in water
Samples:		THF -	5:95 (v/v) in water
Assay	2	Perchloric Acid –	10:90 (v/v) in water
Uniformity	10	System Suitability:	25mL(A) + 10mL(B) in 100mL; QS w/mobile phase; mix well
		Standards:	25mL(A) in 100mL; QS w/mobile phase; mix well
		Samples:	
		Assay:	10 whole dosages in 250mL volumetric; QS w/mobile phase; Sonicate 10 min.; Shake 15 min; Filter 0.22 µm PTFE membrane
		Uniformity:	1 whole dose in 100mL volumetric: QA w/mobile phase; Sonicate 10 min.; Shake 15 min; Filter 0.22 µm PTFE membrane

Specific Instructions

✓ Component run time: 10 minutes
✓ Discontinue analysis if contamination in components is evident
✓ Bracket Assay Samples (2) by Standard
✓ Bracket Uniformity Samples (5) by Standard
✓ Maximum bracket size 5
✓ Class A actinic glassware for samples, standards and impurities

Laboratory Procedural Summary
[Drug Product or Drug Substance Names]
Assay, Impurity/Degradant, Uniformity of Dosage by HPLC

Method Valid for Dosages	*Method and Validation Summary*

The specific details to refresh analyst with newly identified information and knowledge added to the current document. Instructions are to promptly orient the analyst to idiosyncratic issues and nuances of the method. Only points of method related to doses and method identifications appear in this section.

Standard and Solution Concentrations and Preparation

The specific details to accomplish the Regulatory Method requirements are detailed here step by step. Each step is numbered and includes specific instructions as to balance identifications, specific techniques, special qualifications or similar considerations to assure minimization of variability at a the optimal cost effective point. Instructions must be in compliance with cGMP rules and other commitments made to Health Authorities. Specific revision reference be traceable to the specific version. Do not reference formatting changes. For example:
Instruction #7. Compare area counts to validation standards. Remake standard if area >3.0 different (Cc-01)

Solution Storage and Stability

The specific details to accomplish the Regulatory Method requirements are detailed here step by step. Each step is numbered and includes specific instructions as to sample identity and handling, such as wrapping volumetric glassware in foil or storage in a cabinet to avoid direct sunlight. Instructions must be in compliance with cGMP rules and other commitments made to Health Authorities. Only points of method related to solution stability and storage appear in this section.
Initial issue of method is considered to be Cc-00 and should not be referenced. Applicable to all sections.

Mobile Phase Composition, Grade and Preparation

The specific details to accomplish the Regulatory Method requirements are detailed here step by step. Each step is numbered and includes specific instructions as to balance identifications, specific techniques, special qualifications or similar considerations to assure minimization of variability at a the optimal cost effective point. Instructions must be in compliance with cGMP rules and other commitments made to Health Authorities. Only points of method related to mobile phase preparation and use appear in this section.

Stationary Phase Requirements	*Instrument Description and Settings*

The specific details to accomplish the Regulatory Method requirements are detailed here step by step. Each step is numbered and includes specific instructions about column life or performance history to assure the analysis does not experience potentially foreseeable Out of Specification interruptions. Instructions must be in compliance with cGMP rules and other commitments made to Health Authorities. Only points of method related to instrument and column information appear in this section.
Initial issue of method is considered to be Cc-00 and should not be referenced. Applicable to all sections.

Sample Analysis

The specific details to accomplish the Regulatory Method requirements are detailed here step by step. Each step is numbered and includes specific instructions as to balance identifications, specific techniques, special qualifications or similar considerations to assure minimization of variability at a the optimal cost effective point. Instructions must be in compliance with cGMP rules and other commitments made to Health Authorities. Only points of method related to sample handling and preparation appear in this section.
Initial issue of method is considered to be Cc-00 and should not be referenced. Applicable to all sections.

Specific revision reference be traceable to the specific version. Do not reference formatting changes. For example:
Instruction #16. Calculate results using spreadsheet Assay-Impurity-CU Drug X V.5 to calculate results (Cc-01)

Specific Instructions

The specific details of safety and handling that a trained chemist should be aware of prior to beginning the analysis. Instructions may include use of fume hoods, disposal of solvents, general safety such as eyewear or how to handle emergency response to contamination, such as a shower. Only points that are incidental to the practice of science are included in this section.
Specific revision reference be traceable to the specific version. Do not reference formatting changes. For example:
Instruction #2. Use nitrile gloves when handling reagents (Cc-01)

Change History and Approvals
Method 1234.00
Assay, Impurity/Degradant, Uniformity of Dosage by HPLC

Method Valid for Dosages	*Method and Validation Summary*

Each section is summarized for content understanding of the rationale for the change. Each section is fully reconciled.
Rev. 00 – Original method
Rev. 01 – No change

Standard and Solution Concentrations and Preparation

The revision history as it applies to each individual group of the method. Each section is summarized for content understanding of the rationale for the change. Each section is reconciled, even when no change is made.
Rev. 00 – Original method
Rev. 01 – Add verification of area count following preparation. Should not differ by greater than 3% of validation value.

Solution Storage and Stability

The revision history as it applies to each individual group of the method. Each section is summarized for content understanding of the rationale for the change. Each section is reconciled, even when no change is made.
Rev. 00 – Original method
Rev. 01 – No change

Mobile Phase Composition, Grade and Preparation

The revision history as it applies to each individual group of the method. Each section is summarized for content understanding of the rationale for the change. Each section is reconciled, even when no change is made.
Rev. 00 – Original method
Rev. 01 – No change

Stationary Phase Requirements	*Instrument Description and Settings*

The revision history as it applies to each individual group of the method. Each section is summarized for content understanding of the rationale for the change. Each section is reconciled, even when no change is made.
Rev. 00 – Original method
Rev. 01 – Columns now subject of incoming quality assessment for conditioning and theoretical plates. Add requirement to verify integrity of vial septum at the end of analytical run.

Sample Analysis

The revision history as it applies to each individual group of the method. Each section is summarized for content understanding of the rationale for the change. Each section is reconciled, even when no change is made.
Rev. 00 – Original method
Rev. 01 – Update in spreadsheet calculation to automatically round to proper significant figures.

Specific Instructions

The revision history as it applies to each individual group of the method. Each section is summarized for content understanding of the rationale for the change. Each section is reconciled, even when no change is made.
Rev. 00 – Original method
Rev. 01 – No change

List of References

Abboud, L. and Hensley, S. 2003. New Prescription for Drug Makers: Update the Plants. *Wall Street Journal*, 3 September, 1.

Bacon, F. 2000. *Novum Organum*, translated and edited by P. Urbach and J. Gibson. 6th edition. Peru, IL: Open Court Publishing Company. First published 1620.

Begley, S. 2011. Brain Freeze: How the Deluge of Information Paralyzes our Ability to Make Good Decisions. *Newsweek*, 7 March, 32.

Bolton, S. 1990. *Pharmaceutical Statistics.* 2nd edition. New York: Marcel Dekker, Inc.

Conference Board Inc. 2011. [Online]. Available at: http://www.tradingeconomics.com/united-states/consumer-confidence [accessed: 22 February 2012].

Covey, S.R. 2004. *The 7 Habits of Highly Effective People: Powerful Lessons in Personal Change.* 2nd edition. New York: Free Press.

Crosby, P.B. 1979. *Quality is Free: The Art of Making Quality Certain.* New York: McGraw-Hill.

Current Good Manufacturing Practice in Manufacturing, Processing, Packing or Holding of Drugs 2002: General Code of Federal Regulations Title 21 – Food and Drugs, Part 211. Washington, DC: Food and Drug Administration.

Deming, W.E. 2000. *The New Economics for Industry, Government, Education.* 2nd edition. Cambridge, MA: MIT Press. First published 1993.

Dettmer, H.W. 1997. *Goldratt's Theory of Constraints.* Milwaukee, WI: ASQC Quality Press.

Fairfield, H.P. 1917. *The Starrett Book for Machinists' Apprentices.* Athol, MA: L.S. Starrett Company.

Famulare, J. 2007. *Benefits of a Pharmaceutical Quality System.* Paper to the PDA/FDA Joint Conference, Bethseda, MD, 2 November.

FDA 1987a. *Submitting Documentation for the Manufacturing of and Controls for Drug Products.* [Online]. Available at: http://www.fda.gov/downloads/Drugs/GuidanceComplianceRegulatoryInformation/Guidances/UCM070630.pdf [accessed: 22 February 2012].

FDA 1987b. *Submitting Supporting Documentation in Drug Applications for the Manufacture of Drug Substances.* [Online]. Available at: http://www.fda. gov/downloads/Drugs/GuidanceComplianceRegulatoryInformation/ Guidances/UCM070632.pdf [accessed: 22 February 2012].

FDA 1994. *Format and Content for the CMC Section of an Annual Report.* [Online]. Available at: http://www.fda.gov/downloads/Drugs/Guidance ComplianceRegulatoryInformation/Guidances/UCM070565.pdf [accessed: 22 February 2012].

FDA 2004. *Pharmaceutical cGMPs for the 21st Century: A Risk-Based Approach. Final Report – Fall 2004.* [Online]. Available at: http://www.fda.gov/Drugs /DevelopmentApprovalProcess/Manufacturing/QuestionsandAnswerson CurrentGoodManufacturingPracticescGMPforDrugs/ucm137175.htm [accessed: 22 February 2012].

FDA 2007a. Melamine Pet Food Recall of 2007. [Online]. Available at: http:// www.fda.gov/AnimalVeterinary/SafetyHealth/RecallsWithdrawals/ ucm129575.htm [accessed: 22 February 2012].

FDA 2007b. Information on Heparin. [Online]. Available at: http://www.fda. gov/cder/drug/infopage/heparin/default.htm [accessed: 22 February 2012].

FDA 2008. FDA Seizes Contaminated Heparin from a Cincinnati Manufacturer. [Online]. Available at: http://www.fda.gov/NewsEvents/Newsroom/Press Announcements/2008/ucm116977.htm [accessed: 22 February 2012].

FDA 2011. Bovine Spongiform Encephalopathy. Available at: http://www.fda. gov/AnimalVeterinary/GuidanceComplianceEnforcement/Compliance Enforcement/BovineSpongiformEncephalopathy/default.htm [accessed: 22 February 2012].

Frost, F.A. and Kumar, M. 2001. Service Quality between Internal Customers and Internal Suppliers in an International Airline. *International Journal of Quality and Reliability Management,* 18(4), 371.

Garrett, D.O. et al. 2002. An Outbreak of Neonatal Deaths in Brazil Associated with Contaminated Intravenous Fluids. *Journal of Infectious Diseases,* 186(1), 81–6.

Hadingham, E. 2008. Unlocking Mysteries of the Parthenon. *Smithsonian,* [Online] February. Available at: http://www.smithsonianmag.com/history-archaeology/ Unlocking-Mysteries-of-the-Parthenon.html [accessed: 22 February 2012].

Hammer, M. and Champy, J.A. 1993. *Reengineering the Corporation: A Manifesto for Business Revolution.* New York: Harper Business Books.

Haskins, G.R. 2006. *A Practical Guide to Critical Thinking.* [Online]. Available at: http://www.skepdic.com/essays/haskins.pdf [accessed: 22 February 2012].

Herzberg, F., Mausner, B. and Snyderman, B.B. 1959. *The Motivation to Work.* New York: Wiley.

ICH 2005. *ICH Harmonised Tripartite Guideline. Quality Risk Management Q9.* [Online]. Available at: http://www.ich.org/fileadmin/Public_Web_Site/ICH _Products/Guidelines/Quality/Q9/Step4/Q9_Guideline.pdf [accessed: 22 February 2012].

ICH 2008. *ICH Harmonised Tripartite Guideline. Pharmaceutical Quality System Q10.* [Online]. Available at: http://www.ich.org/fileadmin/Public_Web_Site/ ICH_Products/Guidelines/Quality/Q10/Step4/Q10_Guideline.pdf [accessed: 22 February 2012].

ICH 2009. *ICH Harmonised Tripartite Guideline. Pharmaceutical Development Q8 (R2).* [Online]. Available at: http://www.ich.org/fileadmin/Public_Web_Site/ ICH_Products/Guidelines/Quality/Q8_R1/Step4/Q8_R2_Guideline.pdf [accessed: 22 February 2012].

ICH 2011. *Draft Concensus Guideline. Development and Manufacture of Drug Substances (Chemical Entities and Biotechnological/Biological Entities) Q11.* [Online]. Available at: http://www.ich.org/fileadmin/Public_Web_Site/ICH _Products/Guidelines/Quality/Q11/Step_2/Q11_Step_2.pdf [accessed: 22 February 2012].

Imai, M. 1986. *Kaizen: The Key to Japan's Competitive Success.* New York: McGraw-Hill Professional.

Ishikawa, K. 1980. *QC Circle Koryo: General Principles of the QC Circle.* Tokyo: QC Circle Headquarters, Union of Japanese Scientists and Engineers.

Ishikawa, K. 1986. *Guide to Quality Control.* Tokyo: Asian Productivity Organization.

Juran, J.M. 1992. *Juran on Quality by Design. The New Steps for Planning Qulaity into Goods and Services.* New York: Juran Institute Free Press.

Juran, J.M. 1998. *A History of Managing for Quality: The Evolution, Trends, and Future Directions of Managing for Quality.* Milwaukee, WI: ASQC Quality Press.

Kepner, C.H. and Tregoe, B.B. 1981. *The New Rational Manager.* Princeton, NJ: Princeton Research Press.

Lewin, K. 1997. *Resolving Social Conflicts & Field Theory in Social Science.* Washington, DC: American Psychological Society.

Mayo, E. 1949. *The Social Problems of an Industrial Civilization.* Abingdon: Routledge.

McCormick, K.E. 2008. *Manufacturing in the Global Pharmaceuticals Industry: Key Drivers, Company Strategies and Regulations.* 3rd edition. London: Urch Publishing Ltd.

McNally, G 2007. *Lifecycle Approach to Process Validation.* Paper to the Pharma Conference Inc. Conference: GMP by the Sea, Cambridge, MA, 29 August.

McVay, D.W. 2005. Exploring the Language and Practice of Quality: Part 3 Process Thinking or Product Thinking: It's a Matter of Perspective. *RA Focus,* February, 13–17.

Military Standard 105A 1950. Washington, DC: US Department of Defense.

Nasr, M.M. 2006. *Perspective on the Implementation of Quality by Design (QbD).* Paper to the 9th APICCEFIC Conference, Prague, 10 October.

Pautler, P.A. 2003. The Effects of Mergers and Post-Merger Integration: A Review of Business Consulting Literature (draft). Bureau of Economics, Federal Trade Commission, January.

Rentz, E.D. at al. 2008. Outbreak of Acute Renal Failure in Panama in 2006: A Case-control Study. [Online]. Available at: http://www.who.int/bulletin/volumes/86/10/07-049965/en [accessed: 22 February 2012].

Schonberger, R.J. 1986. *World Class Manufacturing: The Lessons of Simplicity Applied.* New York: Free Press.

Siegel, A.F. 2003. *Practical Business Statistics.* 5th edition. New York: McGraw-Hill Irvin.

Sharfstein, J.M. 2010. Johnson and Johnson's Recall of Children's Tylenol and Other Children's Medicines and the Phantom Recall of Motrin (Part 2). [Online]. Available at: http://www.fda.gov/NewsEvents/Testimony/ucm227852.htm [accessed: 22 February 2012].

Shewhart, W.A. 1931. *Economic Control of Quality of Manufactured Product.* New York: D. Van Nostrand Company, Inc.

Smith, A. 1904. *An Inquiry into the Nature and Causes of the Wealth of Nations.* 5th edition. London: Methuen & Co., Ltd. First published 1776.

Story, L. 2007. Lead Paint Prompts Mattel to Recall 967,000 Toys. *New York Times.* 2 August. Available at: http://www.nytimes.com/2007/08/02/business/02toy.html [accessed: 22 February 2012].

United States v. Barr Laboratories Inc. Civil Action No. 92-1744, US District Court for the District of New Jersey: 812F. Supp. 453. 1993.

USP. 2005. *United States Pharmacopoeia 28 / National Formulary 23: Supplement.* Washington, DC: USP.

Wheeler, D.J. and Chambers, D.S. 1992. *Understanding Statistical Process Control.* 2nd edition. Knoxville, TN: SPC Press.

WHO (World Health Organization) 2010. Medicines: Counterfeit Medicines. [Online]. Available at: http://www.who.int/mediacentre/factsheets/fs275/en/index.html [accessed: 22 February 2012].

Index

Note: Page numbers in **bold** refer to figures; those in *italics* refer to tables.

For Product Safety Concerns and Information please contact our EU
representative GPSR@taylorandfrancis.com
Taylor & Francis Verlag GmbH, Kaufingerstraße 24, 80331 München, Germany

www.ingramcontent.com/pod-product-compliance
Ingram Content Group UK Ltd.
Pitfield, Milton Keynes, MK11 3LW, UK
UKHW011454240425
457818UK00021B/810